ROBERT CLARK OF THE PANJAB

HENRY MARTYN CLARK

GYAN

Published by

Gyan Publishing House
5, Ansari Road
Daryaganj, New Delhi-110002
Phone: 011-47034999, 9811692060
E-mail: books@gyanbooks.com

Distribution Network
gyanbooks.com
India, USA, Canada, UK, Australia

ISBN: 978-93-7447-346-7 (PB)

First Published, 1907

2nd Impression 2026

Printed at: Gyan Press, Delhi.

ROBERT CLARK OF THE PANJAB
Author: HENRY MARTYN CLARK

ROBERT CLARK OF THE PANJAB

ROBERT CLARK OF THE PANJAB

Frontispiece.

ROBERT CLARK

OF THE PANJAB

Pioneer and Missionary Statesman

BY

HENRY MARTYN CLARK, M.D. (EDIN.)

> "*One who never turned his back but marched breast forward,*
> *Never doubted clouds would break,*
> *Never dreamed, though right were worsted, wrong would triumph,*
> *Held we fall to rise, are baffled to fight better,*
> *Sleep to wake.*" BROWNING.

NEW YORK CHICAGO TORONTO

FLEMING H. REVELL COMPANY

1907

I DEDICATE THESE MEMOIRS

TO

MY MOTHER

SISTERS AND BROTHERS

PREFACE

THE period covered by the long life of the Rev. Robert Clark in India was prolific in men great in camp and council, and amongst them he takes a place as a maker of history in the Panjab. I have made no attempt in these pages to compass all his manifold activities. I have rather sought to show how he dealt with first principles and their practical application, and have moulded the personal narrative to set forth the pioneer and the statesman.

Several chapters of a descriptive and historical nature have been included, to indicate the conditions under which Mr. Clark did his life work. These need not detain readers familiar with Indian affairs.

Many faithful and brilliant men and women, within as well as without the Missionary ranks, were fellow-labourers with Mr. Clark. If I have not mentioned them, it is only because of the limitations imposed by the character of the present monograph.

I am well aware that in many respects I am not qualified for my present task, and it was only with extreme reluctance, and after long hesitation, that I responded to a call that I could not ignore. As I lay down my pen, no one can be more conscious than I am of the many imperfections in this record of the main aspect of Robert Clark's life.

To explain apparent inconsistencies in the spelling of Indian names, I should perhaps state that I have followed no hard and fast rule. In quoted passages, I have retained the spelling as I found it. Elsewhere in the book, I have indifferently followed the scientific or the customary form. Both are in vogue in India. Cashmere is as common as Kashmir, Cabul as Kabul. In many instances the use of the Hunterian form would be simple pedantry. Thus Lakhnau or Lahor are rarely, if ever, used for Lucknow and Lahore. Few would recognise Cawnpore in Kahnpur or the Deccan in Dakhin.

It only remains to make acknowledgment to the friends who have assisted me with material and advice. To the authorities of the Church Missionary Society I am deeply indebted for permission to make the fullest use of official documents and published records. All these have been of the greatest help, and have been extensively drawn upon. To the Rev. George Tonge, Secretary of the Church of England Zenana Missionary Society, and to Mr. Porter, librarian, Church Mission House, I am greatly obliged for keen interest and valuable aid. To the Rev. Horace William Snape, present incumbent of Harmston, and to Mrs. Snape, my special thanks are due for generous hospitality and the readiest of help in making local inquiries.

I must also gratefully acknowledge much useful

criticism and other aid from my old friend, Mr. C. K. Moore, during the progress of the book.

My obligations to Mr. Cuthbert Lennox are not easy to acknowledge. He inspired the work, his constant encouragement and unfailing active interest have fostered it, and followed it to a conclusion. Much else has there been of help at his hands which, though not specified here, will always be gratefully remembered.

H. MARTYN CLARK, M.D.

EDINBURGH, *January* 1907.

CONTENTS

LIST OF ILLUSTRATIONS

ROBERT CLARK OF THE PANJAB

CHAPTER I.

ANCESTRY AND BOYHOOD.

IN the year 1821 the Reverend Henry Clark, M.A., the father of the subject of this memoir, was preferred to the benefice of the village of Harmston, in the hundreds of Kesteven and the county of Lincoln. His armorial bearings show that he was of gentle birth, of a good South Country stock, his immediate progenitors having migrated northwards from Devonshire. Hamlet Clark, his grandfather, had settled in Leicester. The Poll Book of that city shows that he was of St. Nicholas Street, in the parish of St. Nicholas, and was living in 1768. He married Elizabeth Smith, of the parish of St. Andrews, Holborn, in 1735, and they had a family of three sons and seven daughters. The second son, Henry, by his marriage with Martha Johnson, on 4th April 1783, became the father of the future vicar of Harmston in 1791, and of a daughter, Martha. Shortly after his settlement in Harmston, on 30th May 1828, the Rev. Henry Clark married Mary, daughter of Robert Blackwall.

The ancient family of Blackwall of Blackwall, in the

Peak, was well known in the reign of Henry III. Sir Thomas Blackwall, the head of the family in the days of the Civil War, was a zealous Royalist. He spared neither blood nor treasure in the Royal cause, and so impoverished himself that he died in reduced circumstances after the Restoration, unrequited by Charles II. In 1634 the family pedigree is signed as head by Gervaise Blackwall, "Citizen Skinner" of London. The Rev. Anthony Blackwall, M.A., born in 1674, attained distinction as a critic, lecturer, and educationalist. He was rector of Clapham from 1726 to 1729.

Another member of the family entered the Church, in the person of William, born 1675, third son of Robert Blackwall. At the date of his death, in 1731, he was rector of "Blower," the modern Blore, famous in the Wars of the Roses. His only son, Thomas, followed in his father's steps, and became rector of Mayginton. By his marriage with Sarah Miller he had a daughter and two sons, one son being Robert Blackwall, the father of Mary, who became the wife of the Rev. Henry Clark, as already stated.

Residence in Harmston must be conducive to longevity, for there are yet those living who remember the far-off days when the nineteenth century was young, and can give us the charm of personal touch with Mr. and Mrs. Henry Clark. In the pages immediately following, the writer is able to draw largely upon the authentic recollections of these ancient parishioners.

The new rector was a man of gifts, refinement, and sterling common sense. Strong in purpose and of transparent sincerity, he was full of the kindness and tact that spring from a sympathetic heart, and the welfare of his people commanded his labours by day and his thoughts by night. He is described as a splendid preacher, evangelical in his teaching, and a faithful pastor. Given these qualifications, it is small wonder that he speedily won the reverence and affection of his people, and became a veritable father to them. Indeed, the aged still speak of his prayers and exhortations, and remember the celebrations of the Lord's Supper on Wednesday nights, initiated for the benefit of labourers, shepherds, and neat-herds who were unable to attend on Sundays.

Mrs. Clark proved herself a fit helpmeet, alike in work and home. She was a woman of rare powers, sweet and gentle, abounding in labours and ministrations, and practical withal in everything she did: she even kept a medicine chest for the benefit of the poor —we are speaking of days long gone by. By word or look or by something less tangible, she helped and brightened wherever she went. An aged woman well remembers Mrs. Clark's farewell visit to her dying mother, who had served her faithfully many years. "Good-bye," Mrs. Clark said to her old servant, —"good-bye. I can tell you nothing more than you know, and you will soon know more than I do."

As must ever be the case where religion is vital, the energies of the pastor and people speedily overflowed the bounds of their parish. The cause of Christ in the world lay near to their hearts: Harmston subscribed very liberally to the Bible Society, as well as to Missions abroad, and the interest shown was systematic and general. In this connection, we get a glimpse into Mrs. Clark's character from an anecdote related by an old parishioner. A certain Mrs. Hutchison was only able to give one farthing a week for the missionary cause; yet, fair weather or foul, Mrs. Clark made it a point to call personally for the monthly penny.

ROBERT CLARK, born on the 4th of July 1825, was the third son in a family of five sons and three daughters who in the course of years sprang up around Mr. and Mrs. Clark.

Broad Lincolnshire can show no prettier village than Harmston. Even to-day the deep peace of rural England reigns there unbroken. The health and beauty which surrounded him left their mark on Robert Clark. The home itself was refined and beautiful. The parents showed no partiality, and the children were plainly and carefully brought up in an atmosphere of order and love. Obedience, courtesy, self-denial, punctuality, and neatness came to them almost by instinct. Needless to say, their deepest interests were ceaselessly cared for, and in the peaceful quiet of this ideal home the sterling virtues which form good character and make true men and women were sown upon good ground. While the parents were treated with reverence, they were still the friends and companions of their children; and the children among themselves were the most united of brothers and sisters.

The Rectory had been built on Mr. Clark's arrival by the united efforts of a man from Lincoln, who was responsible for the front, and a certain Conyers of Doddington, still living, who built the back! Two large rooms, the blue and the green, were set apart for the use of the boys and the girls respectively. The cook, a maid, and table-servant, with a woman to char and wash, and a gardener-groom, formed the establishment.

As was then almost invariably the custom among

families of standing, the rector kept his own cows and sheep, and also a pig. The food was abundant, simple, wholesome, and nourishing. Meat was sparingly used, but milk, bread and butter, farm, field and garden produce, all the best of their kind, formed the diet on which the children throve. Breakfast was served at eight, to admit of school at nine. A middle-day lunch was followed by dinner at five. The napery, even in the kitchen, was always snowy white, and the tin and pewter used by the servants in lieu of crockery were ever bright and clean. The butter, as an old servant notes, was made up in "Devon fashion." Wheaten bread was seldom used; a little appeared on the table for the parents and guests, but bread made of rye was the staple on ordinary occasions.

Robert Clark, in common with the other children, enjoyed splendid health. He had but one serious illness, and that in infancy. He was always considered the clever one of the family, but was for all that very fond of games. Then, as now, there were toys, swings and tops, hoops and trap, bat and ball, cricket of course, "kibbles" (marbles), and "ball play." This last is now unheard of. The name is not particularly descriptive, for no ball entered into the play. It appears to have been a sort of assault or tilt at a knot in a suspended rope.

Later on, these amusements were replaced by the sports and relaxations of a country life. Robert was a good shot. There was much friendly intercourse between the Rectory and Harmston Hall, the residence of the Thorolds, lords of the manor. The Brant and the Witham, in the valley at the foot of the lofty Cliff

Ridge on which Harmston is built, were open to him, and in bathing and fishing he spent many a happy day. He is remembered as a cheery lad full of life and fun, kindly in word and deed, remarkable for his great politeness to ladies, his good manners, his love of flowers and animals, his courtesy to his mother and sisters.

Other recollections of the aged village folk are worth noting for the insight they give into the nature of the lad. There was one Jamie Gray of Thorpe, a turner of clothes-pegs, and "Master Robert liked to help him" in his toil. The village shoemaker, then but a journeyman, made a pair of boots for Robert, and "they fitted him fine." Though now eighty-two years of age, he still rejoices in the thrill of mingled pride and pleasure he felt when Master Robert was "that pleased, he told me I was fit to be a shoemaker in Northampton." "Ay," he adds, "good young fellers were they Clark lads."

Robert had a keen sense of humour, but his fun was ever kindly, and sometimes had a purpose in it. A certain farmer had a woefully neglected ass, and one fine day Robert spent some hours in washing, grooming, and adorning the animal. Saddling her, he rode down to the farm to call on the owner. The farmer was loud in his admiration of the beautiful beast, and repeatedly congratulated Robert on his new mount. We can imagine his feelings when he was eventually introduced to his own donkey and left to his reflections.

Robert first attended a school conducted by a Mr. Hall in the neighbouring village of Waddington. The sisters went to a boarding-school in Lincoln, and thereafter to one in London. Later, the brothers were sent, possibly to Boston, but certainly to the Grammar School at Lincoln. The distance from Harmston to Lincoln was six miles, and the lads boarded in the city. The girls were taken home on Fridays by Jacob Gell, the man-servant; the boys followed on the Saturday in time for the five-o'clock dinner, and these weekly re-unions did much to foster the influence of the family life.

The Harmston school feasts were famous throughout the district, and missionary meetings were important occasions at the Rectory. Such gatherings, whether in the vicinity or the parish, commanded the heartiest support and service of Mr. and Mrs. Clark, and it need scarce be said they strove to enlist the interest of their children. On one occasion as they were driving home from a Church Missionary Society's meeting in Lincoln, Robert, still a boy, was seated behind his parents. Overhearing Mr. Clark say to his wife, "We would give all our boys for the cause if they were willing," he interjected, "You will not be called upon to make the sacrifice in my case, for that will never be me. I won't be a parson, much less a missionary." When the time to choose a profession arrived, Robert Clark elected to enter upon a commercial life.

CHAPTER II.

YEARS OF PREPARATION.

ROBERT CLARK'S parents may have felt disappointment at their son's choice, but, with the practical common sense which guided them throughout life, they set to work to give effect to his decision. He had resolved to enter commercial life, and they would see that he did so fully equipped. They judged it expedient that he should be sent to Germany to learn the language and acquire a sound commercial training. Their eldest son, Henry, had also chosen commerce for his future career. Mr. Clark selected a suitable school, and, although Continental travelling was then beset with many difficulties which do not exist nowadays, Mr. and Mrs. Clark went themselves to Germany, and, having fully satisfied themselves, settled the brothers at Boningheim, near Heilbronn, in Wurtemburg.

The school was Protestant and evangelical in character. The pupils were drawn from Germany, Switzerland, and France, many pastors' sons among their number. With one such, afterwards the well-known Pastor Appia of Paris, Robert formed a lifelong friendship.

There were no visits home during the days of training in Germany. This was due in part to the difficulties in travelling, but mainly to the fact that the parents wished their sons to be in no way unsettled, so that they might profit to the full by the land to which they had gone. At the conclusion of his training in Germany, Robert returned home to Harmston, and some months went by while his parents were considering how they could give him the best start in commercial life.

In 1842 we find him entered in the house of Messrs. Jones & Hodgson, merchants, of Exchange Buildings, Liverpool, and living with the vicar of one of the city churches, Mr. Carpenter, father of the present Bishop of Ripon. He devoted his whole energies to the requirements of his new life, and at the end of three years his future was bright with the promise of a prosperous career. But the years had been fruitful in other ways than that of business. At some unknown point he had faced the one tremendous question of life: God had become to him a God for all days and every day, and the Divine Will the law for all things and everything. Whether the great change came suddenly as in a lightning flash, or gradually as when in the dawn light displaces darkness, we cannot tell. In after life Mr. Clark never spoke of these secrets of his soul. The ministrations of his parents, helpful companionships, and the forces steadily at work in his happy, godly home, had all had their share in shaping his inner life; and in the whirl of the great city and the turmoil of business life these sacred influences were conserved and deepened in the home of which he was a member. In particular, he was greatly influenced by Mrs. Carpenter, a saintly woman, full of zeal and fervour, who had a deep love for Missions. In all probability, some apparently chance spark fired a mine that had been carefully laid during many years. The how, and when, and where of Robert Clark's definite surrender to God we know not, but it was made about this time.

Robert reviewed his life and prospects in the new light which had come to him, and began seriously to think that the Christian ministry rather than a commercial life was the sphere in which he could best serve God. He paid a visit to his home, to talk the matter over with his parents; but the serious nature of the change involved pressed so heavily upon him that he said nothing of what was in his heart on this occasion.

Eventually, he wrote from Liverpool, on 20th November 1844, to tell his parents what was passing in his mind, and proposed to come home to discuss the matter. His father replied, on the 22nd of that month:—

"I have written to Mr. W. Jones [Robert's principal], and I expect that he will speak to you, and that *you* will know his sentiments before *I* shall have his answer. I thought it best to tell him *all* about it. Your visit to Harmston is quite a secondary and minor consideration. We shall be glad to see you here any time, and we should prefer talking this matter over—but we *can* transact the business by letter. We will not be hasty in the matter, for it requires serious and long deliberation. Tell us *all* your mind and feelings and reasons, and we will always exercise our best judgment for your welfare. With respect to expenses and money, *that* shall not be an impediment in the way: we do not wish for and we cannot afford needless expenditure of time or cash, and we do not like being 'given to change.' Still, the Christian ministry is so high and superior an employment, that we cannot even now say No—if, after due thought and prayer, there should seem to be a way out for you, into the Church. We hardly expect you here next week, but if you *should* come, you can borrow money off Mr. Carpenter, if need be. We were not fully aware of the extent of your trouble in your face, and in your mind ; and we feel much for you. Always be open to us and make us your friends—tell Henry I will write to him in a day or two. Mr. La Tour has a List of Books for your reading. . . . If your future destination is to be changed, we must make that our main study, and we will turn it well over in our minds. God bless you, dear Robert, and believe me,

Ever your affectionate father, H. CLARK."

On the same date his mother wrote :—"My dear Robert, I have felt very thankful since we received your letter yesterday. I hope the Lord has put it into your heart to choose (tho' late) the most noble service—but you must count the cost. It is no light matter to be servant to the King of Kings and Lord of Lords. Read carefully and prayerfully Hebrews xi. 25, 26. You are in the way of earning money where you are—now *that* must be given up. You seem aware that we did what we believed to be *best* for you when we *took* you to Germany and then placed you with Mr. Jones. We did not consider our own trouble or expense, but your good. If you had made up your mind at once to enter the Church it would have been less expense and less trouble. But I see the *Hand* of God in it. You were heedless and thoughtless about your own soul, and therefore a very unfit person to be a teacher for the souls of others. *Now* it seems to me the Lord has seen in mercy to open your heart to attend to the concerns of your own soul, and therefore I hope *He* will fit and prepare you to attend to and teach the souls of dying sinners. It is no light matter. 'If any man lack wisdom, let him *ask*' (James i. 5, 6). We have kept praying for you ever since you were born, particularly in that sad sickness. I remember it seemed to comfort you when I walked up and down that nursery floor carrying you in my arms—and praying for you, that sooner or later He would take you to Himself, [that] living or dying you might be the Lord's child to serve and glorify Him, either in this world or the next, just according to *His Will*. You are now a man and quite unconscious of what then passed. May the Lord be with you, and bless you in *every step*, and make you a blessing in every place where He may please to place you, is the prayer of your own dear mother, MARY CLARK."

The whole matter was considered with characteristic thoroughness. In the end, the parents were convinced of the reality of the call which had come to their son. The Liverpool life ended with the approval of those with whom he had been connected, and Robert left, the richer by business training and the formation of lasting friendships.

From Liverpool, Robert returned to Harmston. It was arranged that he should go to the University of Cambridge. His earlier education had been moulded for commercial life. During the further years in Liverpool the non-commercial branches of knowledge had lain fallow. A good deal of preparatory study had therefore to be done before he joined the University, and to this he addressed himself with steadfast heart and sound common sense. The preliminary reading was done in part at home and in part with a tutor at Yaxholm. He writes from the latter place to his brother Henry on the 12th April 1845 :—

"I am getting on here pretty well, I hope, on the whole. We have plenty to do—I have one great advantage in having nothing else to do but read,—although I should not be sorry to have somebody to take a walk with now and then. I am now giving the best part of my time to mathematics, but of course not to the exclusion of classics. We have come to this conclusion for these reasons—That it will be easier for me, as I am situated, to take a mathematical rather than a classical degree; because no person *can* go out in classical honours without knowing a good deal of mathematics, *i.e.* sufficient to take a Jun. Opt. degree; whereas, for the other, there is hardly anything but mathematics, and as it is too late for me to do well in both we have chosen the latter as the easier to get on in—more especially since Mr. J—— himself is much better able to get me on in that than in classics. For my own choice I think I would have preferred classics, but since the other seems to be the best, I must try to get on in it as I can."

We have a glimpse of him in those preparatory days from the memory of one still living. She says: "My days at old Harmston were *very* red letter ones, all were so kind and friendly. Robert Clark was my ideal in early days—so utterly unselfish. He was in the way to be a rich merchant when his mind changed, and he was whole-hearted for spiritual work. When I first knew him he was reading hard for college, but in the two hours' leisure which he allowed himself, his first question was, 'Now, girls, what can I do for you? Shall I read aloud, or shall we go for a walk?' I well remember one walk. We were half way along the top of a *very* long field, when we discovered a bull among the cows; he had already caught sight of us, and was coming full tilt up the field. Robert said, 'Run for your lives, girls,' took off his straw hat and held it in his teeth while he came backwards after us, facing the bull. We had just got over the stile into safety when he vaulted over it, as the bull came up."

In due course the preliminary work came to an end, and in October of 1847 Mr. Clark entered Trinity College, Cambridge.

All through college life home and friends were cherished. We may quote from a letter to his brother Henry. "I write to wish you many happy returns of your birthday, but more especially to congratulate you on coming of age. What your presents on the occasion are to be, I cannot inform you (not being myself in the secret), further than that I believe that Hamlet's and mine is to be a gold chain, which I hope you will like. I suppose it is not bought yet, but that it, with your other presents, will be presented to you on Mama's birthday, as Hamlet's were to him, and that your birthday will then be more especially kept when we are all together at home.

"Are you still in your Orange Lodge, or have you left it, and how do you get on with the Debating Society? How does F. Grove get on with his Musical Society? What instrument does he perform upon? Has F. given you my Hind's Arithmetic—if he has not, I hope you will manage to get it from him in some way—it is quite too bad of him. I don't care half so much about the book itself as about his humbug—if you *do* write to him, tell him I told you that I have repeatedly wanted it. He is a capital book-keeper, in every sense of the word. How's Massie Something & Co. getting on? What is Brown doing? has he set up yet? Please remember me to them all.

Robert threw himself whole-heartedly into undergraduate life; his best energies were devoted to the work in hand; but though he was a diligent student he found time for the purpose of life which had brought him to the University. The end was not lost sight of in the absorbing claims of the means. Soon he became a teacher in Jesus Lane Sunday School. He consorted with men like-minded with himself. His rooms in Trinity were a centre of hearty spiritual life. He became a leader in a Bible Class for undergraduates. His labours widened and his influence deepened as the University curriculum went on.

During student-days he was a steady reader, and, as all good readers are, with pencil in hand and note-book within reach. The journals of that period contain comments, reflections, and jottings for future work, of which the following may serve as a sample:—

> Justified—
>
> Freely by Grace, Rom. iii. 24.
> Meritoriously by Christ, Rom. v. 19.
> Testamentally by Faith, Rom. v. 1.
> Evidentially by good works, James ii. 18.
>
> We must not ask "What thinkest Thou?"—but "How readest Thou?"

As a student Mr. Clark neither sought nor expected academical honours. His rule was—

> "Work cheerfully, not tearfully,
> Though wearily you plod;
> Work carefully, work prayerfully,
> And leave the rest to God."

In that spirit he conscientiously, to the best that lay in him, did the day's labour, "ye nexte thynge."

Undergraduate days came to an end with success and high distinction in 1850. In that year he took his B.A. degree, and his name stood as that of 28th Wrangler in the honours lists.

CHAPTER III.

CALLED TO BE A MISSIONARY.

HIS degree obtained, Robert Clark stood once more at the parting of the ways, face to face with a momentous question on which depended far-reaching issues. The young graduate had now to decide the sphere of his future service. He was consecrated to live for God in the work of the Christian ministry, but where could he spend life to the greatest advantage for Christ?

A college tutorship in his own University—a position alike honourable and lucrative—awaited him. It would have been the first step in a prosperous academic career, and one rich in opportunities for good work amongst some of the brightest minds that, in coming days, were to mould their generation. The curacy of All Saints', Derby, was also offered him, and this opened up the prospect of the direct work of a beneficed clergyman in all its multifarious prospects and possibilities. But the overwhelming need of the heathen world was insistent in its claims upon his heart.

We have noted the deep interest in Missions which obtained in Harmston, and in the home and heart of its vicar. Robert Clark was reared in a missionary atmosphere, but the first deep personal interest came to him while in Liverpool, through Mrs. Carpenter, and the flame then lighted by that missionary-hearted woman burned brightly during his college days. Besides, Cambridge was astir on the subject of Foreign Missions. A remarkable movement was going on. This had for its centre the saintly Nicholson, Fellow and Tutor of Emmanuel, Honorary Secretary of the Church Missionary Society at Cambridge University, and a man abundant in enterprise and labours. Undergraduates interested in the evangelisation of the non-Christian world rallied round him. His teaching, example, and sympathy fostered and furthered the love of the cause, and this resulted in the noble array of missionaries which went from Cambridge to fight the battles of the Cross. The names of many of them are to-day household words in missionary history. Bishops Speechley, Royston, and Moule; Brocklesby-Davis, the brothers Fenn, Clement Cobb, and John Barton, were among the band. Mr. Nicholson's activities were shared, among others, by Ragland of Madras, and Gell, for several decades Bishop of the same diocese. Robert Clark was one of the inner circle, and formed lifelong friendships with many of the future missionary veterans. With some of them he was to be intimately associated in work at a later day.

In this crisis of his life, Robert Clark consulted with no one. After a time of silent dispassionate thought, he made his decision. Mrs. Carpenter had planted, Mr. Nicholson had watered, and now he heard the clear call of God to the work abroad. No claims, to his mind, were as urgent as those of the Mission Field: the work of his life should be there, if God so willed.

He notes in his journal:—

"I am now twenty-five, and it is high time I was

doing something. I have given this place, Cambridge, a good trial, and I am thoroughly dissatisfied with it. My positive reasons are simply that there is a difficulty in getting men to go. I have no reason against going, therefore I ought to go. I have not a shadow of regret at leaving home; if a branch is cut from a tree, the other branches will spread and fill up the gap. 'The Lord hath need of thee' is a sufficient answer. I am free, and can go cheerfully. I am full of thanks to Him who gives me the good will and the strength to carry out my purpose."

Mr. Clark told his parents of his wishes on April 12th, 1850, and left the final decision in their hands. The news was as if a sword had pierced their hearts. Heathen lands in those days were very far away, the facilities for travel and communication, which have now caused such a shrinkage of the globe, did not then exist. After the first shock, they rose true-heartedly to the measure of their privilege and duty. They gave their assent, and communicated the news to their children, while Robert put himself in communication with the Church Missionary Society,—but the story is best told in their own words.

On April the 26th, 1850, Mrs. Clark wrote to Henry at Liverpool:—"Now I have something of consequence to tell you, and first I must beg you to pray most earnestly to our God to give us all Wisdom from above that we may be guided so as to do the thing that pleaseth Him. You will wonder what I am alluding to. Well, I will tell you. On the 12th, Robert went to Cambridge, and when he was gone, on the study table your dear Father found a letter marked 'Private' outside. Copy: 'I may as well tell you at once why

I want two or three days to consider as to the Derby curacy. I have been thinking for some time about the relative want of clergymen *abroad* and at home, and when I stopped up at Cambridge the week before yesterday, I came to the determination to ask you to let me go abroad, and that for several reasons too long to mention here. Now, Mr. Ragland of Madras is in want of a curate. Will you let me go out to him, under the auspices of the Church Missionary Society, or elsewhere, should it seem desirable? If you will let me, I shall send you my *reasons* and *future plans* in my next letter; but if you make objections, I will accept the All Saints' curacy at once. I shall be guided entirely by you. I have never mentioned this to anybody as yet, and if you wish me to stay in England I should like to say nothing at all about it; and even if I do go abroad, I don't want to make any bother or talk about it, but merely to go there, as I should to any other curacy.' This news came upon us with a blow such as I can hardly describe. It seemed as if I were at that time following him to the grave. We have always wished to love our children with the same love—just alike to all—and when we first went to Liverpool to seek for a place for you, they asked us whether we wished you to go to China or elsewhere? We rejected the idea with abhorrence, how could we part with you in that way? But that was for a worldly purpose, and I feel as if I could not give my consent to part with a child into those distant parts, for *any* worldly motive. This, however, seems a different case, and I hope that God will make us willing to part with him in the day of *His* power, if it be His will to make use of Robert. The thing is quite decided in Robert's mind, and acquiesced in by us, his parents. Therefore we need not *trouble* him about reasons to the contrary. He does not wish it to be made matter of public talk, but would rather, he says, go to his Mission Station quietly, as he would go to any curacy in England. It is not *now* known to anyone (I mean on April 26), except to your Father, Mother, and Aunt Elizabeth, Mr. Tucker, and Mr. Venn; and, to save Robert the trouble, we inform you, for he is very much engaged with this and college matters. You may answer this letter to him if you like.

"May 1.—We have been waiting for wise reasons to send this. You must keep praying with us that we may all be guided rightly, and that *all* things may work together for good. Pray for your Father and for your own dear Mother."

On the same day the Rev. Henry Clark wrote:—

"The matter spoken of in Mama's note is not yet public, but the whisper *may* escape from the Church Mission House, where Robert has been (though Mr. Tucker, etc., are requested to keep silence); and I cannot bear the thought that it should reach the ears of my children through any other medium than a letter from home. There can be no doubt of the Society's willingness to accept your brother's services, but as no arrangements are or can be made for the present, may I beg you to mention it to *no one*, not even to John, to whom I will write in a day or two. Hamlet and Elizabeth will be informed by to-day's post. You will hear more particularly. I can only add that Robert's resolution is fixed and that we approve, both Mama and I, though at a great cost of feeling. Robert heard the Lord Bishop's sermon, breakfasted with the clergy on the Tuesday at the Church Missionary anniversary, and was at the meeting, on the platform. He returns to college this evening, after visiting Harrow."

On the 9th of May, Mr. Clark again writes to his son Henry :—"I have no fresh news about Robert; it is now thought that he cannot leave England before the summer of 1851, and therefore we are about to inquire after a curacy for him, and would like London or a large town, and I agree with you it is a noble undertaking. Hamlet admires your brother's devotedness, but prefers the Colonies to any heathen lands, and the Propagation of the Gospel Society to the Church Missionary, and *above all* he likes his own Pastoral Aid Society, and says that his own countrymen at home are worse *than the heathens*, and stand in need of the Gospel to guide them right. Robert's mind is decided, and I do not think that he will flinch from his good purpose—if he has health; he only regrets that he cannot immediately go forth to his missionary work."

Robert's resolve commended itself to the other members of his family, and he was strengthened by their satisfaction. He writes to his brother Henry on the 9th of May, from Trinity College :—". . . It gives me no little satisfaction, I assure you, to find that all our family, at least the grown-up portion of it (with perhaps the single exception of Hamlet), are unanimous in their approval of my going abroad. In fact, most of them seem to consider it a subject of congratulation than otherwise. I little thought, when I settled down in Jones's office in Liverpool a few years ago, that I would so soon leave it for Cambridge, and then go abroad as a missionary. But, however, we are led on step by step, often without knowing where we are going to or what may be the consequence of any single step we may take; but if we are sure that the step is a right one, we need not have any apprehensions about the consequences. I have not yet heard from John; what is his opinion about it? I do not know when or where I am going. Indeed, it is not impossible that I may take a curacy in England for a year. However, if we should probably not meet all together many times more, I think we ought to make the attempt to do so this year."

The days that followed the offer of service to the Church Missionary Society were busy ones for Robert Clark. There were interviews with the Secretaries of the Society and the appointed members of the Committee, and with the medical advisers, and meetings and discussions to attend on the subject of his offer. Mrs. Clark wrote: "In every step Robert has consulted his father." It was not till the 30th of May that Mr. Clark was able to tell his son Henry: "Robert is accepted by the Church Missionary Society. Place and time not settled. If India, not this year. The Committee wish him ordained on their title at Christmas. I prefer his taking orders on an English title and curacy, if only for a short period. . . . Some will praise and some will blame your brother, *we* shall feel the parting stroke. It is easy to give £1 or £10, but not to offer a child. It is separating a limb from the body, a parting for life. Robert has gone through pretty close cross-questioning, and has done it, as you say, nobly. He has gained some friends. . . ."

The title for ordination offered by the Society would have given what are known as Colonial orders, which, while sufficient for work abroad, do not permit of the exercise of the ministerial office in the Homeland, without special sanction. Mr. Clark preferred "English orders" for his son. These carry no limitation at home or abroad, and so it was ultimately arranged. He was ordained Deacon, in 1850, by Dr. Wordsworth, Bishop of Lincoln, in that Cathedral on a title to the curacy of Harmston, and the year which he spent as his father's curate was one of much happiness as well as profit.

Harmston Church to-day is one of the most handsome and well kept in the county. The nave and aisles have been rebuilt since the days under review. The venerable Saxon spire remains unchanged. In 1850 it was flat-roofed and high-pewed. The blue-lined pew of the Hall magnates was on one side; the Rectory pew, amongst the earliest of Robert's memories, was on the other. Now he ministered in the church of his baptism and confirmation, and amongst his own people. The position was obviously beset with many difficulties, but tact and grace made him first acceptable, then beloved, during his short yet fruitful service in his native village.

Former parishioners remember the faithfulness of Robert Clark's ministry, and the kindliness and sympathy which characterised it. An aged man has not forgotten his courage in reproving a group of men under particularly difficult circumstances. "Master Robert," he says, "was ever one to speak straight if he saw anything as shouldn't be. He went straight up to them and spoke straight too, and they didn't forget it either."

Another grey-haired man, then a chubby scholar, recalls one Sunday afternoon when, instead of being in the Sunday school, he, with several friends like-minded, was indulging in youthful pranks in the church porch. Mr. Clark surprised them, and "Boys," said he, among other things, pointing each word with his finger, "always remember, 'Thou God seest me.'" A small incident, perhaps, but not forgotten to this day, such is the power of a word!

"Remember Master Robert? Ay do I," exclaimed a man in his eighties. "Why, he married me to her, come fifty year." "Her," still buxom and hearty, was busy about her home, despite the weight of years, and both agreed that he was "good."

In another way Robert left a permanent mark of his year of service: he set to work, collected funds, and built the schools of which the village is still justly proud.

During the year, the preparations for the new life occupied the household. While some things were purchased, many were made at home. For one thing, "Home made is heart made;" for another, outfitters did not exist then to the extent they now do. An old sewing maidservant, still living, describes the making of the bed and table linen, the towels, the fine linen shirts, pleated as was the fashion of the day, with loose wrists and narrow neck-bands, the collars, the ties, and the other articles of personal use. Her memory has retained with curious tenacity the three pairs of shoes, the two changes of nightcaps and of slippers, and the six pairs of knitted white woollen gloves which formed part of the outfit.

In 1851, Robert Clark was ordained Priest by Dr. Wordsworth in Lincoln Cathedral, and was now ready for work abroad. The Church Missionary Society first proposed to send him to Africa, afterwards it was decided that he should join his Cambridge friend Ragland at Tinnevelly, at Ragland's request. Ultimately, however, his destination was changed from the extreme south to the far north of India. The Panjab had been newly conquered, and while the smoke and dust of hard-fought battles still hung over the land the call came to carry the Gospel to its warrior races. Robert Clark, the Rev. Thomas Henry Fitzpatrick, M.A., T.C.D., late curate of Bishop Ryder's Church, Birmingham, together with Mrs. Fitzpatrick, were appointed the first missionaries to that great land.

The Valedictory Meeting for the out-going missionaries was held in London on the 20th June 1851, at the National School Rooms in Liverpool Road.

Instructions were delivered to the missionaries by the Honorary Secretary, the Rev. Henry Venn, and after acknowledgment by each, the band generally was addressed by the Rev. W. W. Champneys, rector of St. Mary's, Whitechapel. The Panjab party were addressed more especially by Pfander, that great missionary to the Moslem world. The Rev. W. Jowett commended the party in prayer, and so the meeting closed.

The bustle of departure was now in the air. Mr. and Mrs. Fitzpatrick sailed on 1st July. Before doing so, they visited Robert Clark's home, and took part in very interesting farewell meetings in Lincoln and Harmston.

The last day came, and the mother's grief was sore. It is told as an unprecedented thing that for a whole week she did not go down to the village.

Robert Clark's departure from home evoked a great demonstration, still vivid in some memories. They recall how Jacob Gell took the huge packing-case for India to Lincoln in a big cart. The day before Robert left Harmston there was a special farewell service in church; next day was observed as a general holiday; the whole village went along the Ramper Road to

Lincoln, to speed "Master Robert" on the first stage of his long journey; nobody stayed at home. Amidst cheering and tears, great wavings of handkerchiefs and hats, and the fervent prayers and good wishes of young and old, the consecrated missionary fared forth. Most of the family accompanied Mr. Clark to London, where a few final days were spent, and on 29th August he sailed from Portsmouth for Calcutta in the East Indiaman *Trafalgar*.

It was Robert's Clark's guiding principle to do with all his heart the work that lay immediately to hand. He did not wait to reach India to be the missionary; the long voyage was utilised for study and preparation and in ministrations, and he had pleasant intercourse, which ripened into fruitful friendship, with several fellow-passengers who afterwards became men of mark in the world of Anglo-India. The course of the voyage was followed by his old parishioners with the greatest interest. They had a paper given to them which told of the various ports of call, and they remember "a beautiful letter" which was sent to them and was read in church. After Madeira, and St. Helena, and the tropical belt of the ocean were passed, there came the usual long rough tumble round the Cape of Good Hope, and then the ship arrived safely in the Hugli, and Robert Clark landed in Calcutta on 4th January 1852. He took his way up country by such conveyances as were then possible. Boats, dhoolies, bullock-carts, and an ocasional mail-cart, in time brought him eighteen hundred miles to his station, Amritsar, which was reached in April. We have a glimpse of him in his own words:—

"I was just twenty-five when I was ordained, and twenty-six when I came to India, and was known everywhere for my rosy English cheeks and juvenile appearance for a cleric. I thank God who gave me my wish and led me to stick to it; it is that which tells at last more than anything else: choosing very carefully one's line with much thought and prayer, and then sticking to it, and going on year by year, with one settled object before one's eyes.

"The race is not to the swift, nor the battle to the strong, nor yet bread to the wise, nor yet riches to men of understanding, nor yet favour to men of skill; but, as Solomon says, 'I prayed, and understanding was given me. I called upon God, and the spirit of Wisdom came to me, a pure influence flowing from the glory of the Almighty, the brightness of everlasting life, the unspotted mind of the power of God and the image of His goodness. Oh send her out of the holy heavens and from the throne of Thy glory, that being present she may labour with me that I may know what is pleasing to Thee: nevertheless I perceive that I could not otherwise obtain her except God gave her to me.'"

From the hand of a master missionary we have yet another picture of him in those days. In January 1852, on his way up country, he was the guest of the veteran Weitbrecht at Burdwan, who notes:—"I have been busy to-day in loading two bullock-carts with my little tent, books, etc., and was going to proceed to the westward when the arrival of a dear brother missionary, Mr. Clark, rendered it desirable for me to put off my departure till to-morrow. We were delighted with Mr. Clark. He appears to possess all the qualifications for becoming an eminent missionary. He is now on his way to the Panjab. It is very cheering to see such promising labourers arrive in this vast country."

CHAPTER IV.

THE STORY OF THE PANJAB.

IN order to realise the problem Mr. Clark had to solve, as a pioneer missionary to the Panjab, it is essential that the reader should know something of the condition of that country as it was at the time of his arrival; and for this reason it is necessary here to enter with some little detail into facts which, while sufficiently familiar to those conversant with Indian affairs, are naturally unknown to others whose studies have not lain in that domain.

The Panjab (pronounced Pŭn-jăb) derives its name from the great rivers, five in number, which water its plains. It is compounded from the Persian words *pănj*, five, and *ăb*, water. The rivers are the Satlaj, Beas, Ravi, Chenab, and Jhelum; a sixth, the Indus, which flows through the land, and receives the others as its tributaries, is not included in the classic five.

The "Land of the Five Rivers" forms the North-Western Frontier of India. Thrust wedge-wise between the Peninsula on the one hand and Central Asia on the other, it has been the great bridge which has served for the passing of many nations between these two regions. The development of the Panjab and the character of its people are in so special a manner the outcome of the position which has made it one of the greatest of the highways in the migrations of mankind, that it is material to an understanding of the subject to grasp some facts of Panjab history.

From time immemorial, successive tides of conquest have rolled over India from the direction of Khorassan. The invaders have entered through the gateways formed by the passes which pierce the girdling mountain wall of the Panjab, and have swept over her doabs, or intrafluvial tracts, to the riches of Hindustan. In the Panjab it has ever been "an axe age, a spear age," and a confusion of races, since the twilight of time. As a result, the land is a palimpsest. Hardy men are the Panjabis, and the bordering Afghans and Beluchis; for the centuries of battle and storm have fashioned warrior races amongst the most stalwart on earth.

At the head of the long line of invaders, the Aryan Fathers come first in the dim dawn of history. The steady stream of Persian invasions culminates in the dominion of monarchs such as Ahasuerus of the Book of Esther, "who ruled from India even unto Ethiopia." The conquest of Persia in turn led Alexander eastwards in the steps of the dynasty he had overthrown. By a Panjab river, the Macedonian defeated Porus; by another, he raised his lost "memorials" and celebrated his games ere he turned homewards, lamenting that there were no more worlds to conquer. The ebb and flow of the tide of war continued throughout the reigns of the Seleucidæ, and during the days of the Græco-Bactrian kingdom of Ariana, until that too was swept away, this time by the irruptions of the Tartar hordes.

The commencement of the Christian era saw the breaking of a new tide into the Panjab. The Middle

Scythian Horde, known as the Getæ—the Massagetæ of Herodotus—expelled by the victorious Huns from its possessions on the confines of China, swept through the mountain passes to find a new home by the waters of the Panjab. A long struggle followed, first with the Hindu kings, and later with the Sassanian monarchs, who fiercely assailed the invaders. Eventually the Getæ, reinforced by successive Scythian waves, overcame all resistance. This Scythian stock is of more than historic interest. It is the main element in the Panjab population of to-day, and the Getæ survive in the Jats (Jŭtts) who form the bulk of the Panjabi peasantry.

To the Scythian there succeeded foes of another mould. In the fulness of time, the lowering cloud of Islam passed from Arabia to burst eastwards and westwards in a storm of ruin and desolation. Muhummudanism first touched India in Sindh. These early expeditions, however, were mainly the raids of marauders. The great campaigns and lasting conquests came, as ever, through the old-time warways of the Panjab.

The Moslem fury desolated the land in the twelve several invasions of the Afghan (Uffghän—the *gh* guttural) sovereign, Mahmoud of Ghazni. A vast Hindu confederacy under Pal, King of Lahore, was routed in battle at Peshawar (Peshäwŭr). Thereafter this irresistible scourge ravaged unchecked. Hindu India reached its most abject depths in November 1024 A.D. In that year, Mahmoud sacked the holy city of Somnath. The treasure he acquired there was immense, but he prized more highly the title he then won of Mahmoud, "the Breaker of Idols."

The Quran (or Koran, as it is popularly called in the West) went hand in hand with the sword of Muhummud. Islam was to be no passing phase or mere court creed: the conquered must witness to the unity of God and the truth of His prophet. The Moslem rulers therefore, with consummate foresight, propagated the faith amongst the villagers. Dynasties might come and go, Islam should abide for ever, because it had gripped the men of the soil.

Eventually Khusro Malik of Lahore appears as the first indigenous Moslem ruler of the Panjab. Mahmoud's Indian empire slipped away from his dynasty, in its decay. The Panjab, the final possession of his line, eventually passed to another Afghan conqueror, Muhummud of Ghaur. Qutubuddin Eibek, the victorious general of the Ghaurian monarch, proclaimed himself king on his master's death, and so founded the far-famed Muhummudan Empire of Delhi.

The Mongols, under the terrible Jenghis Khan, are next found devastating the land. The ravages of Genghis, or Jenghis Khan, mark the beginning of a period of a hundred and fifty years of misery, during which the Panjab was the arena of the struggles for supremacy between the Mongols and the Pathan (pronounced Pŭtt-hän) kings of Delhi. The final acts of the Mongol drama were played out towards the close of the fourteenth century, under that veritable destroying angel Timour Lang, to wit Timour the Lame, known as Tamerlane in the West. His horrible cruelties are unparalleled alike in magnitude and ferocity, even among the records of this stricken land. The nearest approach to them is to be found in the sanguinary massacre during the invasion of Nadir Shah, the Persian, when that excitable savage caused human blood to flow until, in Delhi, the stream reached to the girths of the horses in the streets.

Tamerlane quitted the Panjab in 1399. Thenceforth, until 1525, there is nothing but a record of misrule and devastation, "of noise of battle and garments rolled in blood." In 1525, yet another wave of conquest swept towards India. In that year, the young King of Ferghana, in Central Asia, by name Zehiruddin, crushed by the pressure of hostile neighbours, formed an ambitious decision. As he himself tells, he "put his foot on the stirrup of resolution, and his hand on the rein of confidence in God, and mounting the horse of purpose set forth to the conquest of Hindustan." He is known in history as the Emperor Baber, founder of the great Moghul dynasty of India.

It was in the dark days before the coming of Baber that the Sikhs (pronounced Sĭckhs), with whom the Panjab was to be identified, had their rise. The sect was, in its inception, purely religious. Indeed, the genius of the Orient is religious, and the rise and fall of various religious systems is a remarkable phenomenon in the lands of the East. Religions as well as many religious reformers have had their birth in India, and two of the greatest of these, Goraknath and Nanak Chand, were natives of the Panjab. Sikhism had its origin in the teaching of the latter. This great man, the son of one Kalu, a Hindu of the Khatri caste, was born in A.D. 1469 at Talwandi, a village on the banks of the Ravi, in the district of Lahore. The idolatry of Hinduism and its gods many, and the fanaticism and superstitions of Islam, were to him alike abhorrent. He preached, as others before him had done, the unity of

God and the brotherhood of man. The destruction of caste naturally followed. He taught full religious toleration towards all. All religions he regarded as but so many avenues leading to the one great centre, God. On this basis, supplemented by certain moral precepts, he promulgated an eclectic religion, which should embrace all men, and reconcile all creeds. Those who accepted the *Sikhshya*, or teaching that he gave, became his Sikhs or disciples. He himself was the Guru or teacher, the "dispeller of darkness." The teaching was excellent in some respects: its weakness lay in this, it conferred no moral power on men to enable them to follow it. The purest system of mere ethics must eventually fail as a regenerating power in the battle with the sins and sorrows of the mass of mankind.

The new religion was no exception to the rule. The initial force of Nanak's teaching speedily spent itself, and the inevitable followed. His successors made innovations designed to adapt the new creed more closely to the passions, prejudices, and circumstances of a crude people.

Angad succeeded Nanak as Guru, Amar Dass followed, and he was succeeded in turn by Ram Dass, the fourth Guru. In 1581 Ram Dass built a temple in the midst of a holy tank which he had excavated: *Ambrita Saras*, "The Lake of the Water of Immortality," was the name given to the tank. A great city sprang up in due course round the shrine, and was called Ram-Dasspur after the Guru. That name is now seldom heard: holy lake and city alike are known as Amritsar, the Mecca of the Sikh people.

Two events in the history of the fifth Guru, Arjan

Mal, mark an era in the story of Sikhism. He compiled the "Original Sikh Scripture," the *Adi Granth*, from his own writings and those of his predecessors in the Guruship, and during his pontificate the first persecutions befell the Sikhs.

All the Gurus had been quiet, peaceable men—mystics—and their followers were inoffensive devotees. But the sect had increased, and the jealousy and fanaticism of the ruling Moslem power were aroused. In 1606, the hierophant Arjan was cruelly put to death, and his followers proscribed and persecuted.

The character of Sikhism thereafter rapidly changed. Har Govind, the sixth Guru, fanned the flame of opposition to the Moslem, and this steadily grew. Har Rae and Har Krishn followed in succession in the Guruship. In 1675, the ninth Guru, Tegh Bahadur, was executed at Delhi by the Emperor Aurangzeb. His son, Govind Singh, the tenth and last Guru, completely revolutionised Sikhism, by welding the body of peaceful devotees into a national and political confederation on the basis of a great military brotherhood. Fanatical hate of the Muhummudans was its ruling principle, which Moslem cruelty only inflamed to an almost incredible height. Every Sikh in future underwent an initiatory rite, whereby he became a Singh, or lion, and other rites and customs of the faith, even in things most trivial, were designed to foster the martial spirit, and abhorrence of Islam.

Govind Singh wrote a new Sikh Scripture, known as the *Daswin Badshahi di Granth*, or the "Book of the Tenth Kingdom," to distinguish it from that of the earlier Gurus. He proved himself an able general, fertile in resources; and, having marshalled his disciples, he entered into a death-struggle with Aurangzeb. Despite heroic efforts, the tide of battle set steadily against the Guru. He met with crushing disasters. His sons were brutally killed, his followers were routed, and he fled, a broken man, to die a lunatic far from the Panjab in the Deccan.

The Sikhs were defeated, dispersed, hunted down and destroyed like wild beasts; yet they rallied again and again, glorying in death, and despising all that malignant cruelty could do. In 1742 they were notably strengthened by the accession of the peasantry, the Jats, who made common cause with them against the oppression of the Muhummudan rulers. The great Durrani monarch, Ahmed Shah Abdali, then sat on the throne of Cabul. The Panjab kept him fully occupied. The Mahratthas of Sivaji rolled up from the south-west, to meet with irretrievable defeat on the plains of Panipat. The Sikhs were in continual turmoil. Ahmed Shah traversed the Panjab in repeated and ever victorious campaigns against them. His vengeance was terrible. Holy Amrita Saras, as it was now called, was filled up; the temple and sacred city were polluted with slaughtered cows; and the mosques, desecrated by the Sikhs with the blood of swine, were cleansed in turn by the blood of kine and that of troops of the defeated followers of the Gurus. Ahmed Shah chastised the Sikhs with such an iron hand that they seemed to be for ever annihilated. Yet, time and again, though scattered as the chaff of the threshing floor, no sooner did the Durrani return to Afghanistan, than they again took the field, sturdy and unsubdued, remorseless in their hate to the Moslem.

The scattered units rallied round the flag of various

chiefs, who became the heads of the twelve great Misls, or principal military confederacies that knit together the followers of Govind Singh. To ensure unity of action, the Sikh organisation was further developed by the institution of a strong central council called the Gurmata, or "Wisdom of the Guru," that directed the Misls in the war with Islam.

In 1764, Ahmed Shah, aptly named the "Terror of the Sikhs," finally abandoned the Panjab, and the Misls promptly parcelled out the country amongst themselves. The Sikhs became lords of the land. The story of the Panjab is now identified with that of Sikh rule, which showed developments unique in history.

A certain Chart Singh set up as a petty chieftain near Lahore on the strength of a little mud fort which he had wrested from a Moslem governor. His father began life with a slender patrimony—a horse under him and a sword buckled on his thigh. His grandfather had been a Jat farmer in humble circumstances. Chart Singh was followed by his son, Maha Singh, a man prompt, fearless, and energetic, who enlarged his power in every direction. Eventually, Maha Singh became the recognised head of one of the most important confederacies of the Sikhs. He died in 1792, and was succeeded by his only son, the famous Maharajah Ranjit Singh, signifying "The Lion Victorious in the Field,"—and never was name more appropriate.

Ranjit was only a boy of twelve when he succeeded his father. His prospects seemed hopeless, alike as regarded his house, divided against itself, and the opposition of cunning foes innumerable. In personal appearance he was ill favoured, sorely marred by smallpox; and he was illiterate, yet of extraordinary talents. He rapidly rose, surpassed all competitors, crushed every opposition, and by sheer force of genius became lord paramount of the Panjab. More than this, his sway extended over Afghanistan, Trans-Indus to the Khyber, over lovely Cashmere; to the snowy ranges of the Himalhyas, and beyond, to Ladakh and Little Thibet. The river Satlaj formed the boundary between this magnificent kingdom and the empire of the British.

The fortunes of the two powers had been curiously similar. In 1756–57, Ahmed Shah had to all appearance annihilated the Sikhs. On 18th June 1756 the British Fort of Calcutta was carried by storm, and the tragedy of the Black Hole enacted by Suraj-ud-Dowlah. It was the darkest hour of earlier British history in Hindustan, and the darkest hour for the Sikhs. Eighty years later, the Briton and the Sikh were lords of India from Cape Comorin to Peshawar. In November 1838, "the Lion of the Panjab" and Lord Auckland, Governor-General of India, met each other on a veritable "Field of the Cloth of Gold" at Ferozepore. Treaties of friendship between the two powers were concluded; but Ranjit Singh was even then near his end, and his death let loose the forces of anarchy.

The history of the Panjab now becomes a record of revolting butchery. The strong hand of Ranjit was gone. Corruption and incompetence ran riot. Seldom, even in the history of the most barbarous states, has there been such a series of swift-following murders as, between 1840 and 1845, bereft the Sikh kingdom of Maharajahs, rulers, and councillors. The pressing element of danger came to be the magnificent Sikh army which Ranjit Singh's genius had created, and his sedulous care had brought to perfection. All that Western science and art could do had been lavishly done for a great warrior people. The last of Ranjit Singh's line, a child, Dhalip Singh, now sat on the throne of his father, and his mother ruled in his name. The real power lay with the army, which had the Government and people alike at its mercy. The turbulence of the soldiery daily became more difficult to restrain, and it was evident that the army would assuredly desolate the land unless an outlet could be found for its destructive energy. The queen mother and her counsellors, in this dire strait, in the teeth of every obligation, resolved on the desperate expedient of letting loose the recalcitrant soldiers to harry the British territory. The reasons for this decision are not germane to this narrative.

The thunderbolt was launched. The Sikhs crossed the Satlaj. The British were rudely roused from profound peace to meet the most stalwart foes they have ever encountered in the East. But the Sikh Wars with their stricken fields are matters of history. In 1849 the Panjab was annexed to the British dominions, and the land entered on yet another phase of its chequered career.

CHAPTER V.

THE PANJAB: ITS PEOPLES AND RELIGIONS.

FROM what has been said in the previous chapter, it will have been seen that, through long centuries, war and oppression were the portion of the land of the Panjab. The advent of nations and the waxing and waning of successive dynasties were merely changes in the factors, not the facts, of the cruel burden of oppression. Of all the tyrannies under which the Panjab had suffered, the politico-religious rule of the Sikhs had been the most grinding and desolating, and at the time of the British annexation the misruled and wasted country was reduced to the lowest ebb.

The load of taxation was crushing: the land tax alone ostensibly amounted to one half of the gross produce. The legal taxation was but a moiety of the burden the unfortunate people had to bear, for in effect there was no law save "the good old rule, the simple plan,"—and frequently the overlords ruthlessly took all a villager had of crops or cattle. Offices and taxes were farmed or assigned to rapacious favourites. The pitiless holders harried and plundered the people: they had to recoup themselves, as well as to meet the enormous bribes which were essential if the favour of the Court was to be retained. Taxes were collected from defaulting villages by the effective expedient of turning loose upon them regiments of soldiers, which proceeded to "eat up" the countryside. Forced labour was a national institution. Every kind of injustice and spoliation were openly perpetrated by the Maharajah and his subordinates, through governors, judges, and magistrates, downwards to the lowest ranks of the officials. All of them were children of the horse-leech, insatiable in their greed. To quote the native idiom, "they drank the blood of the people *dabke*," that is, in brimming bumpers, and the corruption was universal amongst the people as amongst the officials: every man oppressed whomsoever he could.

Public order was as non-existent as law. As the Panjabi saying pithily puts it, the case was one of *hanne hanne raj*—every saddle was a throne. Might alone was right. Bloody feuds and fatal fights were the order of the day. In the large cities there were as many camps as there might be factions. Thus, for instance, the various quarters of the walled city of Amritsar, the religious metropolis, were strongly fortified against each other. Offensive and defensive coalitions amongst the rival camps were common. Goods were taxed in transit from one part of the city to another, as if they had crossed the frontiers of rival kingdoms. Villages raided each other. Irrigation wells were protected by towers in which the husbandman took refuge. The harvests were reaped with the sword girt on the thigh, and watches were set, as in time of war. Personal difficulties were settled by arbitration, or by pole-axe, bludgeon, gun, or sabre. Traders were harassed every few miles by inquisitorial examinations and rapacious mulcts. Torture, mutilation, and shocking forms of punishment were frequent.

Satti, or widow burning, infanticide, child stealing, Thuggee, traffic in women and girls, and things unnameable and untellable, flourished luxuriantly. The roads were mere tracks, and were infested by footpads, and beset with many dangers.

A "holy man," in conversation with the writer, once mourned over the good old days (the Golden Age he called them) when he "could plunder twelve men of a morning before it was time to drink buttermilk," that is, about 8 a.m. Bands of dacoits preyed on the highways and habitations.

It need scarcely be said that arts and manufactures languished in such a condition of affairs. The productiveness of this, one of the most fertile lands of the East, was greatly reduced. Water is of prime importance in this hot country, but the irrigation works of the Moghul emperors had been abandoned to decay. As a result, large tracts of ground lay sterile; villages and homesteads ceased to exist; and the drain on life was incessant. Wild animals, of which the Panjab has an ample variety, from lions and tigers to the smaller beasts mischievous alike to life and crops, increased in the depopulated land.

The disintegration of the country and the forces of disorder were greatly intensified by the fanaticism in which they in large part had their origin. The faith of Muhummud had been forced at the point of the sword. Sikhism, as a cult, promulgates no propaganda by force. Hinduism, from which it sprang, inculcates many evils, but it does not outrage the convictions of men by brute force as does Islam. As a religion it is free from violence and the persecuting spirit. It seeks no converts, and interferes with no man's faith. The religious strifes of Hinduism have all been engaged in to preserve her rights from violation, and not to enlarge their domain or to seek accessions from the outside. But the Sikh now repaid with interest the galling cruelty and intolerance which the ferocious spirit of Islamism had meted out to him in the days of its power. The exercise of the religion of Muhummud was grudgingly permitted. The public call to prayer required by Islam was abolished, and by regulations of rigorous severity the Moslem was taught that his star had set, and that it behoved him to walk warily. The mutual hate between Sikh and Moslem was deep and unquenchable. It has outlasted generations of British rule. The writer has seen a Sikh roused to fury, and restrained with difficulty from violence, because in the failing light a passer-by mistook him for a Muhummudan, and addressed him in all humility and good faith by an honourable Moslem title.

The physical features of the Panjab range from the mighty masses of the Himalhyas, through breezy uplands and broad plains, to the arid wastes of the Great Desert. Climatic conditions, therefore, show a wide variation. The intense heat of the long hot weather alternates with the frosts and cold of the severe winter. The thermometer marks all degrees, from the burning plains to the eternal snows on the everlasting hills.

The races of mankind which dwell in the "Land of the Five Rivers" are as varied as its climate and physical conditions. Every type of development and civilisation, from the rudest to the most polished, is to be found within its borders. The races are so heterogeneous, and so widely divergent in the scale of social progress that it is difficult to realise that the Panjab is their common home. There are primitive tribes of hunters and fishers with whom it is still the dawn of civilisation. Nomads of many kinds are abundantly represented. The Cathæi of Arrian, "of manly form, open countenances, and independent gait," still roam the Panjab plains and deserts, with their immense herds of buffaloes and camels. There are pastoral and semi-pastoral peoples, sturdy hill men, and sinewy desert dwellers, men of the rivers, men of the cities, and the agricultural masses of the village population, Aboriginal, Aryan, Turanian, Mongol, and what not, with a fine blend from the neighbouring nations, Indian and Central Asian, having for the most part no possibility of fusing, as in other lands, into one great united people. Differences of language, custom, and religion, and all-pervading caste have kept the types apart, so that time has but blurred, not blended, the original lines.

The Panjab, with its nations, peoples, and kindreds, is of necessity a polyglot land. Persian, largely understood, was the polite tongue, the language of the Court and diplomacy. Hindustani or Urdu then formed a *lingua franca* understood somewhat in the larger cities. But amidst the multifarious languages and dialects of the land, Panjabi, one of the later prakrits of Sanskrit, stood out and still stands out as the mother tongue of the country—homely, rugged, strong, and vigorous as the people themselves.

Physically the Panjabis are a well-grown, handsome people. They are hardy, powerful, athletic, sinewy in limb and tall in stature, and their mental powers are of a like high order. Morally they are the product of centuries of ignorance, superstition, and darkness. Religion with them is not a matter of the heart, but of outward observance. A man is good or bad, not according to his relation to morality, to say nothing of things spiritual, but as he observes the rites of his faith. Thus a Hindu may commit every iniquity and be a good Hindu still; but let him drink a drop of water from the hands of one of a forbidden caste, and at once he commits a sin terrible in its penalty here and hereafter. Similarly, indulgence in evil will not brand a Moslem with disgrace; but let him eat the forbidden thing and he is an outcast avoided by his fellows. Pig's flesh degrades as villainy and rascality cannot do. This moral obliquity permeates the whole people, and the result is ruin. The ceremonial requirements of the various religions, in fact, have left the inner life of their followers without any restraining influence or power, so that they have fallen a prey to their own worst corruptions.

At the date at which our narrative has arrived, the people as a whole were illiterate and coarse, rude in manner, crude in life and method.

The belief in magic, witchcraft, and the black arts generally, has struck its roots deep in the East. Signs and omens control all life, and it is impossible to understand Eastern lands unless these things are steadily borne in mind. Much that appears on the surface to be the outcome of mere vacillation or simple folly, is in reality a matter that goes far deeper. Superstition, protean in shape, diverse in manner, but ever forceful and rigid, dominates the people. The poison warps opinion and judgment, and directs public policy as well as private affairs; it pervades every rank of society, from the despot on the throne to the rabble in their rags. "It affects every act of life, and claims equally the soldier on the battlefield or the criminal at the tree of execution."

At the time of which we write, superstition held the Panjab in complete thrall. Astrologers, interpreters of dreams, soothsayers, necromancers, magicians, and all the fraternity of forecasters and of the occult flourished mightily. The belief in witchcraft was profound. Omens, lucky and unlucky days, were a study which concerned everyone and every act of life. They were rigidly noted and scrupulously observed. A journey would be unhesitatingly postponed if a man tripped as he left his house, or met a dog shaking the head and ears. To sneeze on entering or quitting a room or house, to meet a corpse or a Brahmin, or to hear the howl of a female jackal during the night, were things of evil portent. A town would not be entered, however pressing the business might be, in the face of such warnings as a partridge call on the right, or a flight of cranes from the left to right, or a braying jackass, or a meeting with a bareheaded person. Examples might be multiplied to any extent.

An evil omen might be neutralised by a good one. In the conduct of affairs, good and bad omens would be summed up, and a balance struck on the preponderating side. The vendors of charms to ensure good fortune, to bring ill luck to enemies, to compass every conceivable purpose, did a thriving trade. Divination by the casting of lots, and various other methods, was commonly applied to everyday life.

The Maharajah Ranjit Singh constantly resorted to such practices when some great matter was afoot. In full conclave of his court, the Maharajah's wish and the reverse were written on two slips of paper;

these were placed on a volume of the Granth, the sacred Sikh Scripture; a little boy was brought in, and whichever slip the boy chose determined the policy to be pursued. The Maharajah and his Council were content, for had not Heaven spoken? On such small pivots do the weightiest affairs turn in Eastern lands.

The darkness and shadow of death which had so long covered the Panjab produced results still more terrible which cannot be ignored. Hinduism is in some of its aspects a thing most impure. Sensuality and the degradation of womanhood follow Islam as night follows day. The people in general were dissolute in proportion to their opportunities, and not infrequently they were shameless in their evil. The Sikhs, debarred from the use of tobacco by the command of Guru Govind Singh, debauched themselves with spirituous liquors and intoxicating drugs. Indeed, the consumption of these articles was an act of religion. The writer has often seen, in the famous Golden Temple of Amritsar as well as in lesser shrines of the Sikhs, the maddening Indian hemp being prepared and drunk. In the Golden Temple, as elsewhere in holy places, there is a station for the free distribution of the drink to all who ask for it. The reason is that Indian hemp preparations are supposed to be greatly conducive to spiritual meditation, and as such are peculiarly the adjuncts of "holy" life.

The profoundly sad fact in the degradation of these peoples is that it is the direct outcome of the systems which profess to reveal the Deity to them; and it must be kept in mind that they are amongst the most religious of peoples of the religious East. False creeds pervert the deepest instincts, to the ruin of heart and soul; moral corruption is the result of the principles which the faiths inculcate; and it is pathetic to realise that at the root of every abomination and evil practised in the name of religion in the Panjab there lies Truth. Rightly apprehended, that Truth would have raised this gifted and valiant people to the meed of greatness that their qualities richly merit.

The religions of the Panjab must be briefly summarised, because the relation of this country to the great religions of India is most noteworthy. The Panjab was the first home of the Aryan Fathers on their entrance into the great Peninsula. The Vedic hymns were chanted, and the sacrifices, with their elaborate ritual, were first offered on Panjab soil; and, as a matter of fact, the Land of the Five Rivers is still the most Aryan part of India. From this stronghold, mighty Hinduism—the great system that still holds the majority of Panjabis—went forth in her career of conquest as the religion of India. As wave after wave of varying beliefs swept the land in the wake of various conquerors, they broke against the wall of Hinduism, and with one exception all these beliefs were absorbed by it. There was room in that wonderful system for every god and every philosophy. The vanquishers were in turn vanquished, and owned the sway of the Brahman; and the stern, uncompromising creed of Muhummud itself, while not absorbed, has in India been deeply permeated and modified by all-embracing Hinduism.

The Panjab has a large share of the holy places of Hinduism. Sites, shrines, holy mountains, and sacred waters are to be found in abundance, and by their sanctity they draw pilgrims from the countless sects and schools of thought that constitute the Hindu faith.

Buddhism, the mighty rival of Hinduism, is to-day non-existent in India. The pure morality and the hopeless, godless creed of Gautama could not in the long run hold a people whose history shows they must have a god. From Buddhism, which had supplanted earlier Brahmanism, the pendulum swung back to the gods many of the latter-day Hindu pantheon. At one time Buddhism flourished luxuriantly in the Panjab, part of the holy lands of the Buddhist world. The first great synod of Buddhism was held at Jalandhar, a city in the Panjab, a synod that sent forth the first missionaries to win the world for Buddha; and the country is still covered with the ruins of famous sites and shrines that witness to the power and glory of this religion when at its zenith.

A degraded form of Buddhism called Lamaism is all of that religion remaining to-day in the land of its birth and glory. Lamaism obtains in the Himalhyan valleys of Lahoul and Spiti. They are on the Indian slope of the range, and form part of the government of the Panjab; but their affinities, social, ethnic, and religious, are with Thibet.

The religion of Sakhya Muni died hard in India. Jainism arose as the product of a compromise between expiring Buddhism and rejuvenated Hinduism in its conquering strength. Flourishing Jain colonies are still dotted over the Panjab, though the religion has no general hold.

When, with the marching years, the faith of Muhummud entered into the affairs of men, the Panjab played its part. It was the citadel from which Islam dominated the Peninsula, and it yet remains the most Moslem portion of India. Northwards of the river

Ravi, the followers of the Quran numerically displace those of Brahma, and from the Indus onwards the land is practically Moslem. The conditions begin to approximate to those of Central Asia rather than to Hindustan. Muhummudanism in all its ramifications and warring divisions—for there is no more fond delusion than the vaunted unity of Islam — is in abundant evidence in the Panjab.

Sikhism completes the enumeration of the principal religions of the land. Whether they be of vast antiquity, or, by comparison with faiths hoary with the centuries, mere outcomes of yesterday, world-old Animism underlies them all.

It was to such a land and to such peoples that Robert Clark was sent, as the Ambassador of the Prince of Peace.

To the Hindu his message was of one God, to the Moslem of one Mediator between God and man. To the Sikh he had to tell of the one Guru, the True Light which lighteneth every man. To those seeking wearily for the *Sat Sangat*, or the true union and communion with God, he had to preach the fulness of the gift and fellowship of God the Holy Spirit. To one and all of the sin-sick children of Adam, by whatever name they might be called, he had to proclaim the brotherhood of Man in the Fatherhood of God, full salvation without money or price, through the tender mercy of God in His love, by Jesus Christ, His Son.

Joyful as the sound of the message is in the countries where it is the precious inheritance of men from their earliest days, its full blessedness perhaps only those can realise who have experience in heathen lands of a dying, despairing people, without God, and without hope.

CHAPTER VI.

FOUNDING THE PANJAB MISSION.

IN the days of the Sikh dominion, Ludhiana formed the outpost on the British side of the frontier. It was one of the two important cities on the long line of demarcation formed by the winding course of the Satlaj where the two empires met. At the time of the Sikh Wars, Ludhiana was an established station of the American Presbyterian Board of Foreign Missions, having been occupied in 1836.

The fast closed territories of the Maharajah could not but claim the interests of all who had the extension of the Redeemer's kingdom at heart, and the missionaries at Ludhiana had that unevangelised region beyond ever before them. It commanded their study and prayer—and they were men of prayer. The great week of world-wide intercessory prayer originated with these "men of Ludhiana." But they did more than pray: they prepared themselves, in every way possible to them, for the work their faith anticipated when the set time of favour should dawn, and the Panjab be gladdened with God's message of love. As we have seen, the long-watched-for day came in 1849 with the triumph of the British arms.

Two of the Ludhiana missionaries, the Rev. Messrs. Newton and Forman, with their assistant, Mr. Goloknath, made a tour of exploration in the country. As they journeyed, they found much encouragement. On all hands there was an eager and expectant people, the most manly and least bigoted of any in India. As a result, the Presbyterians definitely occupied the country as a field of missionary labour.

Meanwhile the call to a larger conquest of the Panjab had come to the Church Missionary Society from the Christian men who had been victors alike in her tortuous diplomacy and her bloody fields.

The sentiment which cannot abide Missions, and cries "Away with them," was not, however, lacking; nor were there wanting those candid friends who, in Missions as in aught else, are ever ready with the counsels of prudence and considerations of fitting time and proper opportunity. It was urged that fanatics abounded, both Sikh and Moslem; that the armies of the Maharajah were barely subdued; that the British hold was insecure; that any tampering with the religions of the people would inflame them to fatal frenzy; and that the work of missionaries would form a rallying cry for another national war. It was indeed, in the view of these faint-hearted people, tempting Providence to let the missionaries enter at this juncture. But the fortunes of the Panjab were providentially in the guiding hands of staunch men, unmoved by such considerations of policy or counsels of timidity, and these served their earthly sovereign the more faithfully that they were true servants of God. "Having learned to fear Him, they knew no other fear." In the sphere of Christian duty, confident in the God who had given them the victory, they never paused to ask, "Is it safe?" at the expense of "Is it right?" Missionaries were allowed from the first to enter the Panjab without let or hindrance, and the Missions commanded the interest and support of Christian men in every way that was consistent with their official position and duty.

The great army camps had collected substantial sums for the proposed new enterprise, and subscriptions came in from many other sources. The Panjab Mission was intended to be a thank-offering to Almighty God for victory granted over a terrible foe. The worth and valour of the vanquished had won the respect of the victors. They longed to share with their quondam enemies, now their fellow-subjects, the blessings of the service, gifts, and calling of Jesus Christ.

The call to the Church Missionary Society from the Christian soldiers and statesmen of the Panjab was endorsed by an invitation from the missionaries of the Presbyterian Church who had entered the land. The field was too vast for them to occupy. Their nets brake, and, like the apostles of old, these fishers of men called those of the other boat to their aid. A munificent donation was offered by an unknown friend, on the condition that missionaries for the Panjab should reach India by 1st March 1852. With large-hearted catholicity, the Rev. John Newton communicated the offer to the Church Missionary Society, and in doing so urged it to occupy the field without delay.

In an earlier chapter, we have narrated the sequence of events prior to the arrival of Mr. Clark in Amritsar, where he was warmly welcomed by his colleagues, Mr. and Mrs. Fitzpatrick, who had already arrived, and by such friends of Mission work as Henry and John Lawrence, then stationed in the Panjab.

The sacred city at that time had no houses built

for the needs of Europeans, and Mr. Clark found his first home in a little summer-house in the Ram Bagh, a pleasure garden of the Maharajah Ranjit Singh. The situation was on the great thoroughfare of the city, close to the main gate.

The Panjab hot weather, with its scorching winds and terrible heats, was at hand. To pass it in such a house was to run the gauntlet of a veritable ordeal by fire. Since better could not be, however, Mr. Clark set to work to make the best of it, and in that little house first impressions were received, and first plans were formed, fateful in the religious history of the Panjab. A land, languages, peoples, religions, all equally unknown, surrounded him far and wide. Every act, every word, was pregnant with the germ that should, for good or ill, be the tree of the future.

The temptation which besets the young missionary who has regard only to the tremendous urgency of the work on every hand, is to set to work to do it at all hazards. But body and mind are unprepared; the workman is as untempered clay which can bind no wall, and the result to work and worker alike is apt to be disastrous. The secret in such a service is to remember that the work has to be done, and done in very truth, and so to avoid injudicious efforts, which, however magnificent, are "not war."

Mr. Clark brought sanctified common sense to bear on the multiplicity of the problems which pressed on every side. He put first things first, and took one thing at a time. His foremost duty was to live, for so only could he declare the works of the Lord; and while care-free as regarded the duration of life, he, as a solemn duty, was most careful of health. To preserve it in vigour, he studied the conditions of life in the land to which he had come. Food, clothing, sleep, exercise, recreation, were all ordered in accordance with the new requirements. Health and usefulness in India are greatly made or marred by the servants, and Mr. Clark was careful to choose none but such as would be true helpers to him personally. It was of equal importance that they should not be inimical to the work he had come to do, for it is possible for the servants of a missionary to neutralise his efforts in many subtle ways.

Mr. Clark devoted himself assiduously in these early days to the study of the vernacular, and he did not neglect the even more paramount study of the people. The secret of success in one aspect of missionary work lies in changing eyes with the people of the country; in other words, in seeing a matter as they see it, and think of it as they think. A knowledge of the religions of the people is, of course, necessary; but more important still is it to know the traditions, customs, and prejudices which make up their daily life. The more thoroughly these are known, the more feasible it is to present new truths in the form in which they can most easily be assimilated. Mr. Clark regarded nothing that could help the cause, in however slight a degree, as too trivial for his notice. Wellington declared that he won his battles by attending to the footgear of his soldiers; in the old story, for want of a horse-shoe nail a kingdom was lost; and the secret of power in mundane matters, imperial or missionary, is thoroughness in little things.

The work of preparation was one of infinite difficulty in those far-off days. Grammars, dictionaries, teachers, manuals of all kind, the ripe fruit of experience and labour, now plentifully available, did not then exist to soften the ruggedness of the way. But patient continuance in well-doing can attain much; and while, in one sense, the work waited, Mr. Clark felt that "the husbandman that laboureth must first be partaker of the fruits."

The relation between Mr. Clark and his colleagues was one of mutual trust and co-operation. The fullest confidence was sedulously cultivated. In Mr. and Mrs. Fitzpatrick he found the kindest of friends as well as loyal colleagues. In the trials of that first terrible hot weather Mr. Clark often mentions the great patience and kindness of Mrs. Fitzpatrick. She was ever heartening in discouragements, and constantly ready to smooth the roughness of the difficulties which beset a young worker in a strange land. The principles laid down and measures adopted in the opening years at Amritsar were so thoroughly the outcome of mutual counsel and agreement between the colleagues, that it is not possible or desirable to differentiate between them: each was pledged to the other.

A cordial welcome from the Presbyterian brethren already in the field awaited the new missionaries. Presbyterian and Episcopalian were one in the work of their common Lord. A fundamental law of the Church Missionary Society ordains that friendly intercourse shall be maintained with all Protestant agencies engaged in the preaching of the Gospel. In the Panjab, in addition, close ties of personal friendship united the missionaries of the two Churches, and the rules of missionary comity were made a working basis from the start. These in brief mean that a mission of one Church will not intrude into a field occupied by the agencies of another. The foundation of the work of the Church Missionary Society with respect to the operations of other Churches were thus laid in the blessed spirit of union and brotherly love.

The choice of suitable headquarters for the Mission was, of course, a matter of great importance. Eventually, after much consideration and consultation with friends, Amritsar was chosen, and that with sound wisdom. In those days it was a walled city, girdled with ramparts, pierced with fortified gates, and a malodorous moat surrounded the whole as a farther outwork. It was the largest city of the Panjab, with a resident population of about one hundred and sixty thousand. It possessed also rare qualifications to make it a strong missionary centre, being the Holy City of the Sikh people, the seat of authority and of worship. The new religion proclaimed from Amritsar would command prestige all over the land; within its walls the doctrine of Christ would be brought into immediate contact with the scholarship and whatsoever was best in the religions in possession; and work done there would reach far — a conversion or baptism of any leading man would thrill through the surrounding country. Religious festivals periodically brought the people in hundreds of thousands to the Holy City, and as a consequence Christian truth delivered in Amritsar would permeate the land to its remotest border. The central situation of the city, too, was convenient. It commanded roads and routes on the great lines of travel; it admitted of work among Europeans; and it was within easy reach of friends and supporters. It possessed, in short, all the advantages which accrue in the East to a city that dominates the highways.

Amritsar was further the great commercial city of the land. Her bazaars were thronged by men of all the countries under this part of the northern heavens. Traders from the depths of India here supplied the wants of the whole Panjab. Sindh, Beluchistan, Persia, found their marts within her walls. The wealth of Cashmere, the fruits of Afghanistan, the silks and brocades of Samarkand, Bokhara, and Central Asia, the produce of Yarkand and Western Thibet poured into the many-peopled, multi-tongued city. The Gospel preached in Amritsar would, as a consequence, penetrate into regions inaccessible to the missionary, and would be carried to their homes by those who had heard it in the far city of their sojourn. The first inquirer into the Christian faith in this great city was a Persian merchant temporarily resident in it, who on leaving took the Scriptures with him to his own land.

Amritsar was also the key to the wealth and genius of the Panjab, as well as to neighbouring lands. There was in it a large Moslem population, but the ferocious intolerance of Islam was here checked by the preponderating non-Moslem element. The Gospel could be freely and effectually preached alike to Muhummudan, Hindu, and Sikh, and this made it a place peculiarly favourable to missionary effort.

The colleagues felt it to be a duty of the utmost importance to engage the efforts of the Christian residents on behalf of the work of God, and they were remarkably favoured in finding at Amritsar and Lahore a body of such men full of zeal and interest. A large public meeting at Lahore on the 9th February 1852 resulted in the formation of a local Church

Mission Association officered by various gentlemen of the Province, under the Presidency of Sir Henry Lawrence, and having the missionaries as secretaries.

An incident at the first meeting of the Association deserves to be recorded. The Rev. W. Jay, Chaplain of Lahore, in stating the feeling of the gathering, said: "We all hail the commencement of the Panjab Mission of the Church of England with lively joy and satisfaction; we are yet not unmindful of the earnestness and the Christian zeal of our American brethren, who have gone before us in endeavouring to evangelise the heathen around us. I propose, therefore, that some communication be made to these, on the part of this meeting, to assure them how much we value their exertions; how 'very highly we esteem them in love for their work's sake'; and how earnestly we hope that they may each year receive still higher and higher encouragements in the field of usefulness which they have chosen, and how much and sincerely we wish them good speed in the Lord." The proposition was received with loud plaudits, and the gentlemen assembled rose unanimously to do honour to the Rev. C. W. Forman, the representative of the American Mission, who was present at the meeting.

The Association busied itself with the collection of funds, and, such was the liberality of the Europeans, these mounted up to thousands of rupees. The friends, however, did not rest content with monetary contributions. They co-operated to relieve the missionaries of much secular work in connection with necessary buildings and the like, work which would have taxed their time and energy, and in the end would not have been so efficiently performed.

The spiritual needs of their own countrymen were not forgotten by the Amritsar missionaries. The colleagues ministered voluntarily, from the beginning, to the residents and garrison of the station. Regular Lord's Day services and a weekly Bible Class were helpful alike to the residents and the missionaries.

The principles which regulated personal life and relation with other Communions have been detailed. We have seen that instead of getting out of touch with their fellow-countrymen, as missionaries are apt to do, it was the aim of Robert Clark and his companions to maintain a happy intercourse with them, and gratefully to enlist their fellow-Christians in the service of the Lord.

In relation to the work amongst non-Christians, the colleagues adopted the sound principle that it could be most effectively done by natives of the land. As the homely Panjabi saying has it, "The hound of the land best hunts its game." It was therefore of the most pressing importance to build up a native agency without delay.

Three Indian fellow-labourers had joined the missionaries. One was a convert from Islam, baptized as the result of reading one of Dr. Pfander's books on the Moslem controversy; the other, by name Daud Singh, is remarkable as the first Sikh baptized into the faith of Christ. He was a devotee whose wanderings had brought him to Cawnpore, where he heard the Gospel, and was instructed and baptized in the Mission of the Society for the Propagation of the Gospel by Mr. Perkins. Though greatly valued in Cawnpore, he was cheerfully given for the work in his own land. Yet another Daud Singh, a later convert from Sikhism, also from Hindustan, completed the staff. He had fought against the British in the Sikh Wars as a soldier of the Maharajah, received an honourable discharge from the British Army, which he joined on the annexation of the Panjab, and, while in Benares, was baptized in September 1850. He was first interested by reading the Scriptures in Panjabi.

It is to be noted that all three were married. This was sound policy, in every way. The workers had all the advantages and comforts of home; the work was spared many pitfalls and snares at a time when any indiscretion would have gone far to wreck the Mission. In a land of intense jealousy and seclusion of women, married Indian workers could command an entrance and influence not possible for the bachelor. India is pre-eminently the land of home; round it all things centre, and marriage is emphatically honourable in all. The early marriages customary amongst Hindus need only be mentioned: Muhummud's teaching on the subject is, "He who is married hath perfected his religion." A truly Christian home is the most effective of sermons that can be preached in India: it is a "living epistle," known, read, and understood of all.

While preparing to make full proof of his ministry, Mr. Clark was also watching the signs of the times. He noted that there was a widespread desire for education. Despite the troublous times, the Vernacular schools in the Lahore division numbered 1384, where 11,500 boys were instructed in Arabic, Persian, Sanskrit, Hindi, and like subjects. The city of Amritsar had fifteen schools, where Moslem girls were taught the Quran. The East India Company had authorised an annual grant of five thousand rupees for the endowment of a college at Amritsar. Education had been prized in the past, but the thirst was now for education in the knowledge of their new masters.

In April 1852, Mr. Clark opened a school in the heart of the city, and the roll on the opening day showed an attendance of fifty youths. Half were Sikhs, the rest were Moslems and Hindus; and they comprised Panjabis, Afghans, Hindustanis, and Cashmeris. The popularity of the institution now grew apace. Hindi, Persian, and Urdu were taught, and, with sagacious foresight, English was given a place on the curriculum from the start.

Education in English is now so much the everyday of life in India, that it needs a little effort to realise what an important forward step was taken when, at the point to which we have come, it was included by the Amritsar missionaries in the ordinary school course. The storm which had burst when Dr. Duff first taught English in Calcutta was no long-past memory. Mr. Clark believed that our mother tongue held the ideals which would bring new life to the East, but the real purpose for which the school existed was to teach the Bible. What a wondrous hour was that in which these keen-witted young men and lads gathered round their master to taste for the first time of the living water from the wells of salvation! Christian teachers did not exist, they had to be created. Daily, before school began, there was a class in Scripture study for the masters, and it was eagerly attended. Thus, to haft the Gospel axe laid at the root of the trees of Hinduism and Islam, the helves were hewn from their branches. From the school, by means of the teachers and scholars, a trickle of Christianity began ere long to moisten the arid wastes of the city.

The evangelistic work of the Mission succeeded to the educational. The 20th day of October 1852 is memorable in the Christian annals of the Panjab. On that day the first public preaching of the message of Christ was made in the bazaars of Amritsar, Mr. Clark having made such headway that he was able to speak with precision and fluency in the vernacular.

The colleagues, however, had not deferred all efforts until they were versed in the language; always and everywhere they were missionaries; their mere presence in the city was a sermon in itself. They did whatever they prudently could as soon as it was possible. For instance, Mr. Clark early began to teach his own personal servants at home; and portions of the Scriptures, and tracts prepared by the missionaries at Ludhiana in the days of waiting, were sown broadcast—seed on the waters to be found in God's time to God's harvest. With far-seeing wisdom, also, Mr. Clark gave the aristocracy and gentry, as well as the theocracy and teachers of the various religions of the country, their proper place. Visits paid and received formed a large part of the work of the day, and at all of them the truth of God which he had come to proclaim was the central topic of interest. A constant stream of leading men were thus taught and interested; and this intercourse led to friendships of no small account in the further development of the work.

It was obviously necessary that the Mission should possess its own buildings, and in 1852 the colleagues secured a very large tract of ground outside the city wall. It was a desolate and unprotected site. Old men have told the writer that it was an unsafe place for wayfarers, even in broad day. The price, however, was small, and the situation was admirably suited for the purposes of the Mission. The land far exceeded any present want, but the purchasers had an eye to the future. Houses were built, and gardens were planted, with the characteristic thoroughness which forgot nothing. By the beginning of 1853 the Mission was suitably housed, and Mr. Clark planted the now well-known banyan tree (*Ficus Indica*) of which we shall hear again in the course of our history.

A church had been erected by the residents. In it the missionaries ministered, and it was at their disposal, when it should be needed, for converts.

In launching the Amritsar Mission, Mr. Clark and his colleagues did not forget the wider field of the Panjab. Most of the cold weather was spent by one or other of them in tents, and they systematically made tours in all directions to spy out the land, and to ascertain the disposition of a people to whom the Gospel was now first proclaimed. Preaching and book distribution were steadily carried on among thronging masses of eager people. Such crowds were not seen except at the great religious fairs. All took hold of one truth at least: the missionary and the books declared that Jesus Christ the Son of God is the only Saviour of them that believe.

These most important journeyings were extended in ever widening circles from the centre at Amritsar. Mr. Clark was able to report:—"In this manner almost every one of the important cities of the Panjab between the Satlaj and Peshawar have, at one time or other, been visited. The magnitude of the work has thus been presented to view. It has become evident that the whole of the Panjab is open to missionary efforts, and presents a sphere of labour second to perhaps none other in any part of the world in importance, and in the opportunities which it presents. The character of the people, their geographical position, and their readiness at this present time to hear the Word of God, together with the zeal and liberality of those Christian friends who, by the providence of God, have been sent here since the occupation of the country, have all united to give an importance to missionary work in this country which it is difficult to express in any adequate terms."

CHAPTER VII.

EARLY CONVERTS.

THE combination of favouring circumstances which attended the founding of the work in the Panjab was perhaps unique in the history of missionary enterprise. The political downfall of Sikhism operated powerfully to promote its dissolution as a religious system. The British conquerors and their religion were regarded with just respect by the sturdy warriors of the Panjab, and amongst the energetic and manly-minded peoples of this great and glorious land there was an extraordinary eagerness apparent on all hands to hear the new doctrine. The vicissitudes of centuries of conflict in the matter of religions had accustomed them to balance the claims of divergent faiths and warring creeds. The religious history of the land showed, too, that when once their hearts were won, her brave and intelligent sons were capable of the deepest sacrifices, and knew no half measures. When their souls were touched they did and dared all for the cause they loved.

The British rulers were happily men of high principles, and their spirit and example inspired all the officers of the Government. The progress of the land was marvellous. In a few years the work of an age was done in the Panjab, and perfect peace and good order reigned over a prosperous people. The state of European society was good: Christians, as we have seen, were neither ashamed of their God nor backward of heart or hand in His service.

Mr. Clark realised these advantages to the full in the further development of the Amritsar work on the lines of its inauguration. We have seen the problems which surrounded first beginnings; he was speedily called upon to face those attendant on a later stage, when success began to crown his efforts. There was to be no prolonged period of waiting in Amritsar; he was not called on to endure the long-drawn toil and heart-sickness of hope deferred appointed to many a faithful worker as he strives, while the heavens are as brass, to drive the Gospel plough through an earth like iron. In Amritsar sowing and reaping went on together. Scarcely indeed had the colleagues begun to plant when fruit for the gathering was ripe to their hands.

There was a peculiar fitness in the personality of the first convert baptized in the Panjab, and in the Holy City of Sikhism. He was a Sikh priest, by name Kaiser Singh, over forty years of age, who had first heard the Gospel at a public preaching on the 23rd February 1853. On the 3rd of July of that year he was baptized, taking the name of Shamaun, *i.e.* Simeon. The courage and faith of this first convert cannot be realised by Western standards, for it is impossible to understand by them how unutterably vile baptism would make him in the estimation of his co-religionists. He was at the time incumbent of a Sikh temple in a neighbouring village. Baptism involved his separation from an attached people. It meant an abandonment of the emoluments and high honours of priesthood, and the loss of a position of perfect ease and happiness; above all, it meant loss of caste, and a literal becoming as the "off-scourings of all things." Thenceforth, mere contact with him would be defilement, his very shadow a pollution, his existence an insult and an outrage to the deepest feelings of his countrymen. The primary essential of social being in India is corporate life; in the family, brotherhood, or caste; and it is impossible to exaggerate the all-mastering force of this dependence on others. The writer has personal knowledge of many instances where strong men did not dare to follow their Christian convictions, in the face of the question, "With whom shall I smoke or eat or drink, if I become a Christian?"

At the time of our narrative such considerations exercised even more tremendous force. There was as yet for the convert neither Church nor Christian community: Kaiser Singh went out from everything to nothing—losing all that had made life good and sweet to him in the past. He had learned the fundamental truths of Christianity and felt their inwardness; as the crucial period for his profession of faith drew near, the struggle grew in severity; but, finally, after three days of cruel mental conflict, he, with clear, enlightened judgment, requested baptism, content to bear the reproach of Christ—a solitary man against the whole Panjab world of that day.

The principles which guided Mr. Clark in his relation with seekers after Truth were wise and just. The first essential was that the inquirer should clearly understand what he was called upon to accept and what to reject. To that end, Mr. Clark carefully taught fundamental truths. It is the same still, in matters spiritual, as it was with the man born blind whose eyes the Saviour opened. To absolute darkness there succeeds a stage in which the inquirer sees but a dim and distorted image of Christianity; just as the man in the miracle saw men as trees walking. Mr. Clark therefore recognised that certain truths best serve at certain stages of spiritual development, and what is more, he adapted his teaching to the circumstances of the man. When the time came for the all-important decision to be made, he was earnest that it should not be the result of outside urgence: the command of God, the claim of duty were clearly explained, and the result was left to the workings of the enlightened and awakened conscience.

Mr. Clark was heedful, also, that every man should carefully count the cost of the step he was about to take in following Christ. There could be no compromise between Christ and Caste, or any other evil thing. Loss of caste was, however, then so irrevocable in its nature and tremendous in its consequence that it was not to be lightly incurred. Nothing could be more lamentable than the condition of a man who by becoming an outcaste had lost all things temporal, and yet had fallen short of the things eternal. Mr. Clark, therefore, laid down a principle which was considerate and just. The neophyte could do as his conscience directed him in the matter of caste during the period of his instruction in truth and preparation for baptism. As a general rule, breaking of caste was not required until the administration of that sacrament. Thus a man was not cut off from his people until he himself heard and obeyed the clear call of God to come out from among them and be separate.

The Eastern mind can dissociate truth from practical life with fatal facility. Men of varying creeds and all shades of life will agree most sincerely in accepting a truth propounded to them, though it may be subversive of their faiths, or be pure Christian doctrine. The acceptance is merely abstract however and without prejudice to life or creed, be it remembered. But Mr. Clark was careful to emphasise on the inquirer the duty of living up to the measure of truth received, and lines of cleavage at once began to appear of necessity in the course of the man's daily life amongst his fellows.

The further development of the truth received by the individual inquirer was steadily borne in mind. Mr. Clark early recognised the extreme importance of securing the development of Christianity on the lines of the home. The leaven working in the unit was to leaven the family. The convert was encouraged to learn in the best of ways, by himself becoming a teacher of others, and especially of the women of his household — a plan of action which showed a fine appreciation of the conditions of Eastern life. The sound wisdom and solid advantages of the course are now generally recognised, and indeed only in this way can Christianity become native to the soil.

The actual details of the first baptism were matters for most careful thought. A great point was to be made or lost, according as it was administered so as to disarm the heathen or have the reverse effect. The colleagues stood on the threshold of the unknown. It did not take much prescience to see that to baptize a Sikh priest in the heart of the very Mecca of Sikhism was in all probability to court conflict and stir up wrath. Prudence seemed to demand measures that would minimise the shock to the heathen, and that the baptism should take place in a spot which was safe for the convert. The colleagues, however, were not led astray by any such specious considerations; with rare courage and sagacity they held their solemn service in the city itself, at their house in the vicinity of the Golden Temple; and in so doing they won the confidence of men.

The East is a nettle that requires to be firmly gripped, and there, emphatically, the timorous man in whatever estate, sows trouble for himself. One who temporises, more particularly, in matters of religion, forfeits alike dignity, confidence, and respect. The man who would win and mould men of the East must be of different mettle. He must show all gentleness, courtesy, and a scrupulous regard for the rights of others; but at the same time he must be fully conscious of his duty, and pursue his own way straightforwardly with unhesitating step. These principles were fully recognised by Mr. Clark. It was a rule with him to begin everything as he meant to go on with it, and to do all with transparent sincerity.

Other great purposes were served by the manner of the baptism. To understand these, we must first try to realise something of what India was, nay still is. A darkness inconceivable to the Western mind broods over the people. Some extraordinary rumour or another is generally abroad, and the more monstrous it is, the more implicit is the credence it commands. Many of the reports that dominate the people never come to the ears of Europeans. Now and again there is a glimpse into the seething underworld of ignorance and superstition from which much trouble springs; for these rumours are a fruitful source of unrest, alienation, hatred, and crime. Let a few instances suffice.

When Lord Auckland lay ill at Simla, the Hill people fled in terror to the jungles to save their lives,—Was not their blood wanted to restore the Governor-General to health? A newly formed corps of Bhils deserted *en masse*. They had heard that Government wanted to parade them in line, the better to exterminate them at one blow. The devastating greased-cartridge delusion of Mutiny days need only be mentioned. In the writer's experience, time and again great scares have been abroad. One of them was that the people were being kidnapped to manufacture special drugs or charms by means of which British prowess was maintained. Sometimes the blood or internal organs of the victim were said to be the substance sought for. Or it might be the need was more complicated, and then the wretched creature was suspended head downwards over a cauldron of milk simmering on a slow fire, and the body fat and nerve tissues dripped into the milk to form the precious ointment, *momiai*, necessary to the British conquerors. At another time the rumour was that Government introduced Plague, and sedulously enforced inoculation, because a million souls were neeeded as a retinue by the deceased Queen Victoria in the other world. Or, it might be, the Plague was maintained to check the population, or to avenge an insult to the Queen's statue in Bombay. But all rumours agreed in alleging that Government had introduced and fostered the epidemic. The writer overheard a Moslem villager assuring another that the whistle of the railway engine was caused by the abhorred pig's fat. Even iron screamed out at the unholy application! If such things can be all-powerful forces in the India of to-day, the reader can imagine what they were in the land at the period of our narrative.

The new religion was, as a matter of course, the subject of much speculation. Nothing was known about baptism, and therefore every sort of rumour, repulsive, foul, or merely silly, had full scope. It was asserted that swine's blood, or that of the cow, was the medium employed, according as the neophyte was a Moslem or a Hindu. On another occasion, a Sikh chieftain was present at a baptism in the Amritsar Church. He was so carried away, that, oblivious of time or place, he walked up and looked into the font. He staggered back in astonishment, and with bewildered mien said to Mr. Clark, who was officiating, "Why, it is water after all!" These beliefs die hard. In the eighties of last century it was the writer's privilege to conduct a fruitful work in the village from which the first convert, Kaiser Singh, had come, and some six converts were to be baptized. The church was crowded with non-Christian friends. At the moment of baptism, the village waterman brought in water from the village well, and the intense interest of the spectators was as conspicuous as was their relief, as they realised there was to be no cow's blood.

There is a marked lack of privacy in the East, even

for Europeans. Among the people it scarcely exists. A man's affairs are common property. Seclusion in the conduct of affairs suggests wrong-doing, *a priori*. Mr. Clark always therefore encouraged publicity. The baptism before the people dispelled many false notions. It was seen that the candidate was neither drugged nor bewitched; that he was not called on to revile his ancestry or insult his old faith; that he was under no compulsion; that he freely made a choice of and confessed the new faith; that the element used was plain, pure water; and that no terrible distortion or disfigurement followed the rite, as they had been led to expect. Verily Amritsar had much food for thought and talk on that memorable July morning, when the first sod was turned on the path of the Panjab to God!

Other baptisms followed apace. The school yielded fruit. A month later, a high-caste Brahman pupil of nineteen, much advanced in knowledge, was baptized. In yet another month, two more of Mr. Clark's pupils, a Sikh aged twenty-one, and a Hindu aged nineteen, entered the fold of Christ. The Sikh youth had been one of the first pupils to join the school. At the close of the year, the colleagues were gladdened by a yet more remarkable baptism. The convert was a gentleman of honourable Moghul descent, the son of a teacher of the former kings of Delhi. His name is still revered by the Moslems of that city. This young man could recite the Quran by heart at fifteen, and now, though but thirty, he was a distinguished Moslem Doctor of Divinity. He came to Amritsar to teach the language to Mr. Fitzpatrick, and the reading of the Word of God in the Scripture class for teachers first opened his mind.

Mr. Fitzpatrick notes concerning him :—"He continued all last winter in deep distress, searching the Bible, but more with the design of finding answers to his doubts and our teaching, than for Divine guidance. And when he found that was impossible, he remained in doubt upon the doctrine of the Trinity; but, having learned to submit to God's Word as inspired, he resolved upon becoming a Christian." This baptism was, like the others, *coram populi*, in the city.

The event caused a great stir amongst the Moslems of Amritsar. Several young men of fair abilities systematically studied the Scriptures in the hope of being able to prove them false, from internal evidence. The house of the young convert, Maulvi Aziz Ullah Beg, was much frequented by Moslems of all ranks. They also largely attended his public preaching in the bazars, though generally unable to answer a word to his clear and convincing reasoning.

New factors now entered into the work of Robert Clark: the converts had to be shepherded. Mr. Clark looked on this work as one which it was impossible to overrate in importance. The infant Church was tenderly watched over and nourished. Systematic Scripture instruction, the "sincere milk of the Word," was the first requisite, and he laboured diligently to supply it. In addition he cultivated a close personal touch with each convert. The strength and weakness, the special gifts, special circumstances of each individual, were his study, alike in the interests of that soul and of Christ's work in the Panjab.

With the success which had come to the work, there came also the inevitable persecution. To the private trials which Christians in India have to bear there succeeded public opposition which overflowed into violence. Scholars were reproached for attending the school; personal abuse was heaped on the missionaries and their fellow-workers; and things came to a head when the junior catechist, while preaching alone, was set upon by a rude mob of Kashmiri Moslems. He was severely beaten, and would have been killed had not a hasty report of what was going on brought other Christians to the rescue. Matters required judicious handling. The just mean had to be hit between gladly bearing stripes and abuse for Christ's sake, as part of the persecution which is the Christian's glory, and the wreck of the work by unchecked lawlessness. Nothing in India perhaps calls for a finer discrimination on the part of the missionary than the appeal to Cæsar in such circumstances. It is the right of every subject of the British Crown to go peacefully about his lawful avocations without let or hindrance; on the other hand, Mr. Clark felt it would be a loss if Christianity were to seem to stand because of the secular arm. While his principle was that, where God had given it to men to work under the blessings of a good government, there was a lawful use of the rights which protect all subjects equally as such apart from religious profession: he judged each specific case on its own merits. The treatment Christians were to receive in the future depended on the action taken in respect of this assault; and, be it remembered, in matters of this kind nothing is insignificant in India. By a series of small advances, the way is paved for grave assaults or serious wrongs. A little rudeness or neglect, or some trivial breach of the punctilious courtesy of the land, is first essayed. If this is checked, there is an abject apology, and the attempt ends. Or, it may be, a child is instigated to some slight act of mischief. If this is resented, there are prompt disclaimers and humble excuses.

Should these tentative excursions into forbidden land pass unchallenged, graver forays follow in their wake. It was Mr. Clark's dictum in reference to such matters, "Never allow the smallest thing that ought not to be to pass unnoticed. You need not resent it, but make it clear that you have marked it. Nothing is really of little account in India." The case just mentioned was therefore brought before the magistrate; not in a spirit of revenge, but to prevent a recurrence of such acts. The punishment of the leader was not sought, and he was consequently discharged after being severely reproved. In the course of the inquiry, high testimonials in favour of the Christians were given by non-Christian Government officials. The magnanimity of the Christians was recognised by the people, and the incident was satisfactorily closed. Such disorders, and worse to follow, were in this way nipped in the bud.

The evangelising tours over the country were continued, and calls came to the colleagues to commence work in other places. The European residents of Sialkot, the third city of the Panjab, for instance, offered a hundred and fifty rupees a month for work in their midst.

Striking news also came from the North. Fifty Sikhs and Hindus of the city of Rawal Pindi had diligently studied a Christian tract which had come into their hands, and, convinced of the falsity of their faiths, had separated themselves into a band for further search after truth.

At the close of 1853, the missionary horizon was

truly full of promise for Mr. Clark. Preliminary work was done, the foundations of the Amritsar Mission had been well and truly laid, and the fair building had begun to take shape. In the Panjab, as in every land and clime, the Gospel had proved itself the power of God unto salvation. Evangelistic and educational work had alike borne fruit. The white fields of Sikhism, Hinduism, and Muhummudanism had all yielded their sheaves, an earnest of plenteous reaping for the harvest home of God. Near and far was the glad sound of the wind beginning to play on the dry bones of the valley.

But circumstances of which we now have to tell, were to take Mr. Clark far from the promise of Amritsar.

CHAPTER VIII.

A NEW FIELD: AFGHANISTAN.

THE scene of our story now shifts from the home of Sikhism, in the plains of the Central Panjab, to the far north-western confines of the Indian Empire. A call to commence Mission work in the great frontier city of Peshawar had come, and for this fresh effort, in a new land and amongst strange nations, Robert Clark was chosen.

The Indus divided the former field of work from the proposed new sphere. Its southern banks marked the limits of the Land of the Five Rivers; beyond lay Afghanistan. Our interest centres in that portion of the country which, bordering the river, lies contiguous to the Panjab. The tide of conquest under the Sikhs had reft the Durrani kings of Cabul of their sovereignty over this part of Afghanistan, from the Indus to the Khyber Hills, but that tide had wrought no change in the people. The country was still the land of the Afghan, and the language, customs, and religion of Afghanistan continued to hold unbroken sway.

The new country differed from the Panjab in being a purely Moslem land. The Hindu element was small, though the sprinkling of settlers may have increased somewhat after the conquest by the Sikhs. The votaries of Hinduism were found principally in the city of Peshawar and in the larger towns, and scarcely existed amongst the rural population. In the countryside they were restricted, according to the size of the village, to one or two shopkeepers, squalid in aspect and of mean position. The necessity for their presence had always secured for them a limited toleration. They supplied such small-wares as Afghan life required. Above all, the Afghans were unable to keep accounts without the aid of "the unbelieving idolater," and so, despite the law of Islam, they permitted him to live in their midst. The position was precarious as regarded tenure and fraught with danger to life. It was a case of the war of the wit of one against the rapacious violence of the many. The Hindu, as is the custom of his kind, was the sponge that absorbed the wealth of the Afghan. He was wily enough to secure a certain measure of protection by placing himself under a leading man, content to be looted by one if he could recoup himself from the mass. But when financial affairs became complicated, the Afghan adjusted matters by a method which was simplicity itself. The unbeliever was slain, and his ledgers were burned. Another Hindu was then captured or inveigled to fill the vacant place, and account-keeping began afresh.

The site of Peshawar possesses so many marked natural advantages that it is easy to understand how a big and influential city has grown up there. It stands at the head of a large, densely populated, well-watered valley, almost encircled by a wall of girdling mountains. It lies at the junction of the hills and the plains, to both of which it is the key. It is on the great highway between the countries of India and the lands of Central Asia; it commands the famous passes (of which the Khyber is the best known) that here pierce the barrier of mountains and debouch on the plains, and it therefore enjoys a special importance in religion, commerce, and the strategy of war.

The climate of the land Trans-Indus differs materially from that of the Panjab. The heat, though as fierce, is of shorter duration, the cold is more bitter. The Peshawar Valley was, in the days to which we now refer, notorious for its unhealthiness. Peshawar itself was a veritable "white man's grave." The climatic conditions, however, were not inimical to work. Mr. Clark, in his estimate of the new land, notes:—"The climate favours active exertion. The hot and rainy seasons do not continue more than four months and a half. In the cold season we can travel about in tents for at least five months—many stay out eight—and that cold season is far superior to any period of the year in England."

The change of masters from the Durrani to the Sikh had, as we have noted, left the city untouched. It continued to be one of the greatest cities of Afghanistan, Central Asian rather than Indian in its affinities; it remained as of old the centre of life for the Afghan in his manifold tribes, within or beyond the Border; and its population was then estimated at 90,000.

We cannot in these memoirs compass any detailed account of the Afghan peoples, although their origin, peculiar customs, and racial and social characteristics are replete with interest. Yet a cursory glance at some aspects of the subject is necessary if we are to understand something of the task that awaited Robert Clark in his new cure of souls.

The people is quite different from that on the Indian side of the Indus. The Afghans are a hardy, handsome, sinewy race of men, athletic and well-built. Their complexion ranges from the deep brown of the dwellers in the hot lowlands to the delicate milk-white skin and rosy cheeks of the men of the highlands. Proud of heart and martial in bearing, their bold eyes flash and their whole carriage is instinct with valorous independence. Their mental endowments are of the highest order. Alike in mind and body their qualities are those of a race capable of immense possibilities.

That makes the present degradation of this fine people all the more lamentable. As we have seen, the Afghans are Moslems, and their character is the pitiable outcome of noble, highly gifted natures ruined by the subtle and deadly venom of Islam. It has been truly observed of this baleful system, that "it is the abomination that maketh desolate; its favour and its hatred are alike deadly." The present ruler of the Panjab, Sir Denzil Ibbetson, has pithily remarked that "it is curious how markedly for evil is the influence which conversion to even the most impure form of Muhummudanism has upon the character of the Panjab villager." If that be true of the impure forms of the faith, the purer it is the more disastrous will be its effects. In Afghanistan the form is of the purest; the consequent ruin is complete. The Afghan's nature is strong and enduring as the granite of his own native hills, and the evils he does are the "mighty sins" of a strong man.

The descendants of the old-time peaceful Buddhists are to-day the most turbulent, fanatical, and bigoted of men. They wallow in wickedness, yet, be it understood, are rigidly religious withal. It was once the writer's fortune to fare through the defiles of the Khyber Pass. To ensure his personal safety he had an escort of Afridis of the Khyber Hills, and these beguiled the way by recounting deeds of daring, their own exploits and those of their peoples. They told of iniquity upon iniquity, and horror upon horror; gruesome tales of robbery, murder, and wrong. As they fought their battles over again their eyes glistened, and their cheeks flushed with the joy of strong men in gallant deeds. When the writer took them soundly to task, they listened patiently, with absolute good-humour, even with interest. At the conclusion, one magnificent reprobate replied with profound astonishment, "Man, man, verily thou art one of the foolish! What do I that the Prophet of God, on whom be peace, himself did not do?" What a proof this is that Islam can rise no higher than its fountain-head, Muhummud!

At the time of our narrative, the Afghans of the Trans-Indus districts were what Afghans still are beyond the British border. Their ideas concerning the property of others were something less than elementary. A brother Afghan was lawful spoil, if not of their immediate kin. The stranger, in their terse phrase, was "a bird of gold" to be plucked to the last feather. They were a nation of caterans, resolute and resourceful reavers of the chattels of others. Robbery was an honourable calling; for it they were created, in it they were born. The babe was subjected to a suggestive ceremony. The mother passed the infant to and fro through a hole made in the wall of the homestead, crooning the while, "Ghal Sha! Ghal Sha!"—Be a thief! Be a thief!

Brave to a fault, the Afghan was careless of his own life, and recked still less of the lives of others. The slaying of a man was accounted a matter of no moment. In the course of conversation with the writer, an Afghan of sound worth casually remarked, "If we have to slay a sheep, we think twice of it: a sheep is something, but a man, Sahib—what is a man that he should be taken account of?" Murders were the commonplace of everyday life. The vendetta was the most solemn article of honour. The tale of unexacted blood was a sacred trust bequeathed from generation to generation; a legacy of undying hate given by a father to his sons with his last breath. The land was, indeed, polluted with blood. The moral sense against murder had apparently ceased to exist.

The situation sometimes had its humours. The shrine of a defunct saint proved very lucrative to the village in which he was buried. A constant stream of pilgrims brought to it wealth and honour. Envy and cupidity roused a neighbouring village to found a rival shrine, but there was a difficulty—they had no dead saint. An influential deputation, however, waited on a noted living one, and humbly begged him to accept sepulture in their village on the day he should depart to Paradise. They promised that, if they were so honoured, his funeral should be of the finest, and his shrine of the grandest. The gratified saint acceded to the desire of the suppliants. Then the deputation craved a further boon, that he should consent to depart at once to the realms of the blest. "We cannot wait," they urged; "we will kill you now. We will not hurt you very much—we really must take you back with us." Despite the prayers and protests of the holy man, kill him they did. It is but fair to add that they scrupulously kept their word as regarded both the funeral and the shrine. Murder, bloodshed, and their concomitants apart, there are other evils in the land which will not bear description.

Amongst much that is repellent and abhorrent, however, there are to be found virtues which charm the observer and win his respect. The Afghans are a generous race, prompt of hand and hot of heart, as strong and steadfast in love as they are in hate.

They have a pride of race, also, and a stately dignity that never fails. They come of a long line of conquerors and rulers of men; and they themselves have never been in bondage to any man. The veriest tatterdemalion will show himself stout of heart and unabashed of mien before the most august presences, in the most brilliant assemblages. He bears himself as among equals, for is he not a Pathan?

Mr. Clark once observed that almost every word written by Macaulay concerning the Scottish Highlanders as they were a century and a half ago would apply to many tribes of the Afghans as they now are. "If," he continued, "anyone wishes to know about the Afghans of Peshawar and its neighbourhood, he should read Sir Walter Scott and Aytoun—

"'I charge thee, boy, if e'er thou meet
With one of Assynt's name,
Be it upon the mountain side,
Or yet within the glen,
Stand he in martial gear alone,
Or backed by armèd men,
Face him as thou would'st face the man
Who wronged thy sire's renown;
Remember of what blood thou art,
And strike the caitiff down.'

But the Afghans have not yet had a Sir Walter Scott to tell of all their prowess, and humour, and treacheries, and jealousies, and hospitality. They are a grand nation, or will be so (as the Scots are now), as soon as they have their John Knoxes, and Maitlands, and Wisharts, and Erskines, and Hamiltons, and Chalmers."

Among the Afghans are found many well read in the languages, literature, and philosophies of the Moslem East, for the land is the meeting-place of many tongues. In Peshawar itself, a dialect of Hindi is commonly used, and Persian is employed far and wide. Special importance is attached to Arabic, the sacred tongue, "the language of heaven and the angels." A brawny Afghan, who would unhesitatingly charge a cannon, was reduced to abject terror by an Arabic phrase in the mouth of a malevolent mullah.

The mother tongue of the people is called Pukhtu, or Pushtu. The name is derived from Pukhtun, or Pushtun, by which the Afghans designate themselves. The word is more generally known to the outside world in its Indianised form of "Pathan." The language of the Pukhtun is an Aryan tongue whose affinities are with the Zend and Pahlavi rather than the Sanskritic branches of the family. The sound of Pukhtu is barbarous in the extreme, harsh and rough as the people themselves. The Moghul emperor Akbar is reported to have sent envoys into many lands to learn their varied languages, in order that on their return they might recite in them to their royal master. The delegate to Afghanistan filled a drum with pebbles, and, rattling them hard, said, "Refuge of the world, this is the Afghan tongue." But though the tongue is uncouth it possesses an extensive literature—religious, poetical, and philosophical. Afghan poetry, too, is of especial beauty, and contains rare gems, even according to Western ideals.

The circumstances which made evangelisation possible amongst this ferocious and fanatical people were pregnant with meaning for Robert Clark. He was a keen student of the ways of God among nations—what men call History. But in fact the sequence of events in these northern lands was unequivocal: gross of heart and dead to things celestial must he have been who could not read, writ large in the happenings of the time, the plain purposes of God.

We have traced the march of events that welded the distracted Panjab into a kingdom under one head in the sovereignty of Maharajah Ranjit Singh. When the work was done, the united whole passed unsought into the hands of the British, and then the eternal purpose stood revealed. The Panjab had lain unknown to Europeans, fast sealed to the messengers of God; yet even while men looked, the land was opened, prepared, made ready for the Gospel and the blessings that follow in its train. Still more clear, however, was the finger of God in the ordering of affairs on the Peshawar frontier. The people there were tenacious of their own faith, frantically intolerant of any other. Had the Afghan domination remained unbroken, bigotry would have barred the door to the Evangel of God as effectually as it does in the Afghanistan of to-day. The mountains of Afghan power had to be cast down, and the rough places of the pride of the Pukhtuns made smooth, that the way of the Lord might be prepared. And the instrument of their humiliation was the self-same Ranjit Singh.

We are not concerned with the Sikh conquest of this

portion of the Durrani domains, as history; but it throws such light on the peoples amongst whom Robert Clark was to be the first "Torchbearer of the Faith," that it ought not to be wholly passed over.

Having consolidated his power in the Panjab, the Maharajah Ranjit Singh turned his attention to his Afghan neighbours. The lands of the Durrani dynasty were harried in a preliminary foray. Thereafter the Maharajah himself led the armies destined to invade Afghanistan. The progress of the Sikh force, however, was barred by the Indus, and the troops lay inactive for five weeks on the Panjab side of the river. The difficulty was theological. It was forbidden for a Hindu to go beyond the boundaries of his own land, the penalty of disobedience being the loss of caste, and the flood of the Indus was as prohibitive as the "black water" of the ocean.

History repeated itself; for the exploit of Julius Cæsar's standard-bearer on the shores of Albion was paralleled on the Indus. A gallant old Sikh chieftain eventually forced the situation by plunging into the river, with a ringing "Follow! All lands belong equally to God!" With such an example before them, the Sikhs could not hold back; in a trice their armies broke up, to form up again on the soil of Afghanistan. The regular Afghan army awaited them, and, in addition, the whole countryside was in a blaze, for the mullahs had assiduously preached a religious war. From the villages of the plains, from the circling mountains, from the broken Khattak Hills, a steady stream of men poured out in a frenzy of fanaticism and hate to destroy the infidel invaders. Sikh and Afghan met at Naushera, in the centre of the valley of Peshawar. The Durrani forces retired without striking a blow: the commander of the army, Muhummud Azim, was more solicitous for the safety of his harem and treasure than for the honour of his land. The rough country folk, undisciplined, rudely armed, were alone left to confront the disciplined valour of the flower of the Sikh armies, under the redoubtable Maharajah himself. They faced the position with splendid courage. Shouting the Moslem formula of faith, they hurled themselves again and again on the Sikh masses, and repeatedly carried all before them in a whirlwind of destruction and death, only in turn to be beaten back by the dogged bravery and unfailing nerve of the Sikh, who faced them with his battle-cry of "Victory to the Guru!" Doughty deeds were performed on both sides. Ranjit Singh's great general, Phula Singh, was slain as he led in the thickest of the fight. A Pathan ripped up the huge war elephant on which Phula Singh rode, content to perish by the fall of the beast, if so be the Sikh were slain—a story, by the way, which recalls an incident in the wars of the Maccabees.

There was no thought of retreat or surrender. It was war to the death. The curses of the mullahs and the blows of the women drove any recreants back to the fight. When their scanty ammunition was exhausted, the Afghans fought on gallantly, with cold steel, sticks, and stones, even with hands and teeth. Many a Sikh warrior was found stiff and stark on that fatal field, tight clasped in the death-grip of his foe, with the Afghan's teeth still clenched in his throat.

The battle raged the livelong day, with a ferocity that taxed the generalship of the Maharajah and the mettle of his veterans to the uttermost. Ranjit's one eye in after days used to sparkle with unwonted fire as he told the tale of Naushera. Darkness at last separated the combatants, and during the night some four hundred men—all that remained alive of the Afghans—cut their way through the heart of the Sikh forces, and made good their retreat to the hills. The rising sun found Ranjit Singh victor of the field, and the country was at once annexed to his dominions.

What the valour of the Maharajah had won was preserved by the genius of his famous general, Hari Singh Nalwa, and the cruelty and determination of General Avitable, a Frenchman in the service of the Maharajah, appointed first governor of Peshawar. The power of the Afghans was broken, and their pride was humbled. Naushera remained a bitter memory. "Is it a time to laugh when the bones of your fathers are whitening Naushera?" was a formula which for many years promptly checked undue levity in Afghan homes.

When the British annexed the Panjab, they were reluctantly compelled to include the Trans-Indus Sikh dominions. The treachery of Dost Muhummud, King of Cabul, in the final Sikh war, frustrated the earnest desire of the British to restore Peshawar to Afghanistan. The meaning of this fact scarce needs emphasis. God's counsel was established despite the plans and wills of men.

Robert Clark rejoiced in the opening prospects of work in a purely Moslem land, and he coveted the strenuous Afghan race for God. He saw in Peshawar the key to the Frontier and the regions beyond. The abutments of the mountainous masses of Central Asia on the plains at Peshawar formed the first scarp to be scaled in the conquest of the Central Asian highlands, and in like manner was it in the war with Islam in the heart of Asia. Robert Clark considered Peshawar of supreme importance. The leavening of this portion of Afghanistan was a preliminary to the advance on the mass beyond. Here are his own words:—"We were obliged, against our will, to occupy Peshawar; and, however much we may have desired it, we have been obliged ever since to keep it, although at a great expense of money and life. The will of the Lord was that the Gospel should enter Afghanistan, and be there preached in one of the strongholds of Mohammedanism; and, if I mistake not, His will also is that from Peshawar it shall go forth into the midst of Mohammedan countries, and that, from Turkey on the West and the boundaries of India on the East, Mohammedan countries shall be evangelised. A Mission, therefore, established here, would be for the benefit, not of India, nor of the Panjab, but of Afghanistan: it would be beyond all Indian Missions, to act on the countries in advance, being fixed at the farthest point from India, and the nearest point to other countries to which missionaries can at present go. The intercourse with the countries beyond is very great. Large numbers of natives are constantly coming from them to Peshawar: from Peshawar large numbers of natives go to them. Missionaries are, indeed, as yet excluded, but not so their influence; and there is every reason to suppose that Christian books, in the language of the country, would find ready access, and probably free circulation amongst the people."

We must now tell how Mr. Clark came to be the first missionary to cross the Indus to the Afghans.

CHAPTER IX.

AT PESHAWAR AND AMRITSAR.

THERE is a singular fitness in the fact that the work of evangelisation amongst such a warrior race as the Pathans has been the outcome of the prayerful zeal of British officers. The armies of Britain first entered Afghanistan in the course of the disastrous Afghan War of 1839. In that year, Captain Richard Raban, in common with several brother-officers of the Cabul garrison, initiated a movement to enable the Church Missionary Society to establish a Mission in the cities of Candahar and Cabul.

A sum of money was collected by these faithful men, but the scheme progressed no further. The British authorities would have none of it. So uncompromising and radical was the official hostility to the proposed venture, that a number of New Testaments despatched to the country were ordered to be sent back to India. But God has His own ways of working His will. The returning convoy was looted by the Pathans. The books never recrossed the Afghan frontier, but remain scattered seed to be yet found in God's harvest, for even the ordinary printed page commands respect in the East, and is rarely destroyed by a Moslem. Much more will he treat with reverence "the Holy Gospel of Jesus the Son of Mary," whom he also calls the

"Spirit" and "the Word of God." In the annihilation of the British army and the horrors and humiliation of 1842, the matter dropped from men's minds. The proposals of Captain Raban were, in fact, in advance of his day: the set time was not yet. Those noble men obtained not the promises, but they saw them afar off, and to the eye of their faith clear visions were granted of the glorious things that shall be in the ripeness of God's time.

With the advent of the British into the Panjab in 1849, Peshawar became a garrison town of the first importance. At the time of which we write, the population of the cantonments amounted to thirteen thousand. Trans-Indus, as in the Panjab, the army of occupation was blessed with godly officers. The gross darkness that enshrouded the Pathans in a mantle of death lay heavy on their hearts. They were keenly alive also to the privilege and duty of the Christian's calling in the parting command of their Lord. None the less, it seemed beyond the wit of man to compass a mission to the peoples amongst whom they sojourned, for the propagation of Christianity amongst Afghans seemed beset with difficulties and dangers so tremendous that the official opposition to any effort of that kind was insuperable.

Colonel Mackeson was then Chief Commissioner of the Frontier from the Indus to the Khyber Hills. He was a good man and a great soldier, with a splendid record as one of the most distinguished officers in India. Though personally friendly to Missions, in his public capacity he was firmly resolved that while he ruled no missionary should penetrate north-west of the Indus. In the year 1852, an officer in Peshawar advocated the cause of the newly-established Mission at Amritsar. His plea for funds met with a generous response on the Frontier, and amongst the subscribers was the Chief Commissioner. The liberal donation, however, was combined with a note to the promoter of the appeal in which Colonel Mackeson said, "I take this opportunity of officially informing you that, for political reasons, I shall oppose the passage of missionaries across the Indus." Those who longed to see the Pathans brought within sound of the Gospel carefully considered this declaration of policy, and the upshot was that, some months later, seven officers solemnly dedicated themselves to the founding of a mission amongst Afghans. The position was undoubtedly delicate, and no immediate action was possible; but they prayed insistently, and watched and waited.

A few weeks later, one afternoon, a Pathan sought an interview with Colonel Mackeson as he sat in the verandah of his house. On being ushered into the Commissioner's presence, the man presented a petition for consideration. Scarce had the Colonel begun to read the paper when the Afghan plunged his dagger into the Commissioner's heart. Thus, in the flower of his age, by an assassin's stroke, perished gallant Mackeson. Lord Dalhousie, then Governor-General of India, voiced the general sorrow when he wrote in his official order that the loss "would have dimmed a victory."

Mackeson was succeeded, hot-foot, by the heroic Herbert Edwardes, wise in council, strong in war; a great soldier on the battlefields of India, yet greater in the more strenuous conflicts of life. Though Colonel Edwardes's views on the subject of missions were unknown to the band of prayerful officers, they were prompt to act. They called on the new Commissioner, but in the presence of the stranger they were a little uncertain how to proceed. A cheery "What can I do for you?" speedily put Edwardes in possession of their errand, and he unhesitatingly allowed the Mission. Mr. Clark has noted the interesting fact that Edwardes's reply for the first time officially formulated in India a policy alike just and reasonable as regards the preaching of Christianity in that country. "I see no difficulty in the matter of founding a Mission," said this great ruler of men. "We protect the Hindu and the Muhummudan in the enjoyment of their religion. It is the primary duty of a Christian to preach the Gospel of Christ." That interview marked an epoch. In a moment, official opposition had vanished into the air, and the way to the longed-for goal lay clear before the comrades in prayer. They had already been in correspondence with Mr. Clark, and it was now decided to ask him to address a public meeting at Peshawar on the whole question of a mission to the Afghans. In response to that invitation, the first ambassador of a Kingdom that knows no limitations on earth save that of the human race itself, crossed the Indus. He left Amritsar on the 2nd of November, marched up through the length of the land, evangelising as he went. When he reached the great frontier city in mid December, he himself saw the blood of the murdered Mackeson still uneffaced from the verandah pillars of the Residency.

Much preliminary work had to be done in furtherance of the object that had brought Mr. Clark to Peshawar, and a just estimate of the situation had to be formed. After recruiting from the fatigues of the daily strenuous evangelistic work, and of the long journey accomplished by such primitive methods as were then available, he, as was ever his wont, set systematically to work. His time was fully occupied in interviewing friends, in interchange of views, and in ascertaining necessary facts and figures. The actual campaign opened on Sunday, 16th December 1853, when Mr. Clark preached at the services in the station church. The collection that day on behalf of the proposed Afghan Mission amounted to eighteen hundred rupees.

The public meeting, held three days later, is unparalleled in the history of Missions, at all events in India. The chair was taken by Colonel, or as he afterwards became, Sir Herbert Edwardes. As Chief Commissioner of the Frontier, he dwelt, in a memorable address, on the public aspects of the proposed Mission. Mr. Clark speaks of his words as "almost inspired." They are instinct to-day with the thrill of living truth.

"That man," said Edwardes, "must have a very narrow mind who thinks that this immense India has been given to our little England for no other purpose than that of our aggrandisement—for the sake of remitting money to our homes, and providing writerships and cadetships for poor relations. Such might be the case, if God did not guide the world's affairs; for England, like any other land, if left to its own selfishness and its own strength, would seize all it could. But the conquests and wars of the world all happen as the world's Creator wills them; and empires come into existence for purposes of His, however blindly intent we may be upon our own. And what may we suppose His purposes to be? Are they of the earth, earthy? Have they no higher object than the spread of vernacular education, the reduction of taxes, the erection of bridges, the digging of canals, the increase of commerce, the introduction of electric telegraphs, and the laying down of grand lines of railroad? Do they look no farther than these temporal triumphs of civilisation, and see nothing better in the distance than the physical improvement of a decaying world? We cannot think so meanly of Him with whom one day is as a thousand years, and a thousand years as one day. All His plans and purposes must look through time into eternity; and we may rest assured that the East has been given to our country for a Mission, neither to the minds or bodies, but to the souls of men.

"And how is this to be done? By State armies and State persecutions? By demolishing Hindu temples, as Mahmud of Ghuznee did? or by defiling mosques with Mohammedan blood, as Ranjit Singh did? It is obvious that we could not, if we would, follow such barbarous examples.

"The British Indian Government has wisely maintained a strict neutrality in religious matters. The duty of evangelising India lies at the door of private Christians. The appeal is to private consciences, private efforts, private zeal, and private example. Every Englishman and every Englishwoman in India —everyone now in this room—is answerable to do what he can towards fulfilling it.

"This day we are met to do so—to provide the best means we can for spreading the Gospel in the countries around us.

"They happen to be Mohammedan countries of peculiar bigotry. Sad instances of fanaticism have occurred under our own eyes; and it might be feared, perhaps, in human judgment, that greater opposition might meet us here than elsewhere. But I do not anticipate it. The Gospel of Peace will bear its own fruit, and justify its name. . . .

"For these reasons, I say plainly that I have no fear that the establishment of a Christian Mission at Peshawar will tend to disturb the peace. It is of course incumbent upon us to be prudent, to lay stress upon the selection of discreet men for missionaries, to begin quietly with schools, and to wait the proper time for preaching. But having done that, I should fear nothing. In this crowded city we may hear the Brahman in his temple sound his 'sunkh' and gong; the Muezzin on his lofty minaret fill the air with the 'Auzan'; and the Civil Government which protects them both, will take upon itself the duty of protecting the Christian missionary who goes forth to preach the Gospel. Above all, we may be quite sure that we are much safer if we do our duty than if we neglect it; and that He who has brought us here with His own right arm will shield and bless us, if in simple reliance upon Him we try to do His will."

This noble speech was followed by one from Mr. Clark. He told of what had already been done in the Panjab, and as he limned the possibilities near hand and farther afield that were opening up before the people of God, the hearts of the hearers burned within them. They realised the workings and purpose of the Divine Providence for these unevangelised lands; they saw that the opportune moment had come for the proclamation of the Gospel message amongst those needy souls, and a deep thankfulness filled their hearts. The great forward step in the religious history of the Pathan race was taken with ardent enthusiasm: the Church Missionary Society was formally invited to make a bold extension of its Panjab Mission by undertaking work Trans-Indus at Peshawar. Over fourteen thousand rupees were collected at the meeting for the new departure, and the sum total speedily passed thirty thousand rupees. There were the indifferent, of course, as ever, the doubters, and the sneerers. One young officer, of whom more anon, was absolutely confident that the Mission had not the slightest chance amongst the Afghans without the support of his troopers. In pure mockery he subscribed "one rupee to buy a Deane & Adams revolver to protect the first missionary." But, jeer and flout as men might, God had set an open door before the lovers of the Gospel that none could shut.

The document of invitation drawn up at the meeting was sent on its way, *viâ* the Cape of Good Hope, to the Church Missionary Society in London, and Robert Clark, having achieved the purpose of his visit to Peshawar, returned in due course to his station in the Central Panjab.

The Amritsar Mission throve apace. The keen spirit of inquiry already existing among Panjabis was whetted when, in this year, the Maharajah Dhalip Singh was baptized by the Rev. W. Jay. That event will yet be remembered to the honour of the Land of the Five Rivers. With the exception of the somewhat mythical Presbyter y-clept Prester John, and a Romanist Ziogoon or Shogun of Japan, the ex-sovereign ruler of the Panjab remains the first of his rank in Asia to accept the faith of Christ.

There had been twenty-three baptisms in Amritsar since the commencement of the Mission, and the success of the work brought Mr. Clark, in 1854, face to face with a problem fraught with vital consequences. The indigenous Christian community that now existed marked a further stage in the development of Christianity in the Panjab, and the important question that had to be solved was, What principles should obtain in the choice of a pastor for the infant Church? Mr. Clark early realised with deep insight that the ultimate result of Christian work stood or fell according as Christianity assimilated to itself the environment of its new home or remained fettered in the trammels of Western form and fashion. The prosperity of the Church required the establishment of an indigenous pastorate at the earliest possible moment. The goal he had in mind for the Panjabi ministry was not a weak copy of men and things Western, but a great free type, instinct for the service of God with what was best in the life of the Panjab, supplemented by all that was helpful from the treasures of the West.

The wisdom of this sound policy is so manifestly advantageous, that the principle on which it is based is to-day a mere truism. All missionary organisations are in one fashion or another strenuously endeavouring to translate the idea into action. The fact was not so apparent when Robert Clark advocated it in 1854. There was then much to give legitimate colour to the theory that the European with his superior experience and advantages, mental and spiritual, should for a time at least fill the office of pastor. To that doctrine Mr. Clark gave a very limited assent, only admitting its force in cases of absolute necessity or in the earlier stages of work; but he held strongly that the presence of the foreign missionary was merely an incident in the evangelisation of the land, and that the stranger would not abide for ever. Of course, much had to be done that only he could do. It was his to place the leaven in contact with the mass of the meal; to guide and strengthen the Church he had planted; to be the primary factor in winning those who were in turn to conquer the bulk of their fellow-countrymen for God. But when the Church of the country was able to bear its own witness to her Lord, the foreigner's mission was accomplished, and he would pass on to other fields.

The pastor was ready to hand in the person of Daud Singh, the first Sikh baptized, to whom reference has been made in an earlier chapter. The qualifications of the first pastor testify to the foresight of Mr. Clark and his colleague, Mr. Fitzpatrick. They looked at the matter from the one true point of view, that is, the Eastern. Daud Singh knew no English, to say nothing of more recondite Latin, Greek, or Hebrew. He was lamentably deficient in the merest rudiments of education, as that term is understood in the Occident. But for all that he was equipped and gifted with attainments of a far higher character for work amongst Panjabis. Robert Clark was well content that his young David should go out to combat the Goliath of Heathenism armed with his sling and the stones of the brooks of the land; the armour of the West would have been but an incumbrance as things then stood.

We have seen elsewhere in these pages that men's lives in the Orient are regulated by matters that are of absolutely no moment in the West. For example, superstition concentrates the look of the Oriental first on the personal appearance of the man with whom he has to do. Daud Singh was a Panjabi of the Panjabis, a tall, handsome Sikh, shrewd of eye, with a graceful carriage and a kindly dignity of mien. His tongue smacked broadly of the beloved homely Doric of the land. A flowing beard was not the least of his qualifications; in fact, the possession of an adequate beard is a matter of moment in the Orient, particularly amongst Sikhs, who reckon the cutting of a hair to be the greatest of sins. The reader may recall the classic instance where the lack of beard bade fair to wreck the embassy of Lord Exmouth to the Dey of Algiers. The wrath of the Corsair king was vehement at the insult done him in sending a beardless ambassador to his Court. "Had my King known you set such store by a beard he would have sent your Deyship a goat," retorted the intrepid Admiral.

Daud Singh was also of birth and breeding, and to a large stock of mother wit he added a good education according to Panjabi standards. He had deep experience of life: pre-eminently a man, he was fitted to deal with his virile countrymen. An ex-devotee, he was well versed in the holy books, maxims, and philosophies of the Sikhs; he was of simple faith and transparent sincerity, and he was untiring and eloquent in fervid preaching of the Gospel. Such was Daud Singh: pleasant and seemly, with all about him in keeping with the message he had to deliver. Not only the first Sikh baptized, but also the first Panjabi called to the Christian ministry, he was ordained by the Bishop of Calcutta at Allahabad on the 29th of October 1854.

REV. DAUD SINGH.

CHAPTER X.

PIONEER WORK IN CASHMERE AND THIBET.

THE narrative of 1854 again takes Robert Clark to the banks of the Indus, though not to the point at which it borders Afghanistan. The scene is now far beyond the snowy barriers of the Himalhyas, in the lands where the mighty river first begins to gather up its waters for the long course to the Arabian Sea.

The summer of 1854 found Robert Clark engaged in an exploration of Cashmere, Ladakh, Iskardo, and the contiguous portions of the Himalhyas, and of Western and Little Thibet. The expedition was the outcome of a proposal by Colonel Martin, an officer who had just retired from his command at Peshawar. The subject received much consideration from Mr. Clark. He tells us:—"When the time arrived at which it was necessary to make the decision, a special season was set apart for prayer in our Amritsar Mission, and the different members met together for consultation respecting it. The result was that the members of our Mission unanimously concurred in the opinion that the journey was of very great importance and ought to be undertaken." The expedition was commenced on 20th April, and its object, to quote Mr. Clark, "was to preach the Gospel in the countries beyond. . . ." A secondary object was "to see to what extent there is missionary work to be done in those countries, and how far, and in what circumstances and conditions that work may be commenced, and carried on with the greatest human probability of success."

Three Indian Christians went with Mr. Clark—Sulaiman (Solomon), Shamaun (Simeon), and Yakub (Jacob). Sulaiman was a worker from Cawnpore, Shamaun we have already met as Kaiser Singh, and Yakub was a later Brahman convert, baptized in Amritsar. Thus early did the Amritsar converts follow their leader in perilous ways for the cause of God.

Mr. Clark had the solace of Colonel Martin's company. The Colonel's long experience in India, combined with his passionate devotion to the missionary cause, made him a much valued guide and friend in the journeyings through the wild lands of High Asia. A great interest attaches to the travels, because Mr. Clark was among the first Europeans, at all events in modern times, to traverse these countries, then practically unknown to the West. They were virgin soil for evangelisation; in no period of the world's history had the Gospel been preached in them.

Mr. Clark took his way northward through Sialkot, evangelising as he went. The British border was crossed at Aknur. The route then lay through the territories of Rajouri and Pūnch to the kingdom of Cashmere, and the "Happy Valley" was entered on 20th May. Gulab Singh, sovereign ruler of Cashmere, accorded a hearty reception to Mr. Clark, and showed him many tokens of his goodwill. Mr. Clark did not ask for any leave to evangelise. He deemed it best to feel his way quietly, and then begin to preach. The course was a sound one. No existing obligation made it incumbent to seek permission; to do so, therefore, was to concede a right that did not exist, and thus to establish a wrong precedent; while refusal of the request would have meant a false position, and the creation of a situation of extreme delicacy.

It was a principle with Robert Clark to lay the message he had brought to a land before the great men of it at the earliest opportunity. This course gave rulers and nobles their rightful position amongst their people. It was good policy; but, policy apart, Mr. Clark, while preaching the news of the Kingdom to the poor, was not forgetful of the needs of the rich. His interviews with Maharajah Gulab Singh will concern us later.

Mr. Clark's frank sincerity and statesmanship won Gulab Singh's confidence. He turned a deaf ear to those who sought to rouse his antagonism against the work Mr. Clark had in hand. He had heard the message, he had seen the man, and both were alike good. "Let be," caustically observed the Maharajah; "my people are so vile, no man can make them worse. I am curious to see whether the gentleman's preaching can do them any good."

On his way through the Happy Valley to "The Roof of the World," as men call Thibet, Mr. Clark gave great heed to beautiful Cashmere. There, as throughout his long wanderings, he was indefatigable, together with his comrades, in evangelising by word and by the distribution of books. Two inquirers came to him in Srinagar, the capital of the kingdom. With characteristic insight he was quick to mark others touched and "eminently qualified to teach and exert much influence over" their countrymen. The land lay before him full of endless opportunities, and, turn where he would, he found great encouragement. He remarks: "Many most pleasing opportunities have been given for conversations. Frequently on the carpet in the native house, or under the magnificent plane tree, with the most delightful prospects of wood and valley and snow-peaked mountains and streams of water on every side, we have sat cross-legged on the ground, and talked and listened, and gone away with every cause for the greatest joy."

In due course the sterile ways that led into Western Thibet were entered upon. The marches had been trying, the ways dangerous. There had been savage torrents to ford, rope bridges to cross, and the miseries of what Mr. Clark calls "the very worst road I was ever on." Ponies fell down precipices, or went through the planking of mouldering bridges. "In other places," remarks Mr. Clark, "we had to pass over great slanting beds of snow, one of which seemed to me the most dangerous place in the journey. It was inclined at an angle of about 54°, and terminated in the river, which it overhung, the river having cut it away, leaving a perpendicular wall about five feet high just over the torrent. The road was cut across this bed of snow, and was a little path about six inches broad, of course very slippery: the sloping snow, quite hard, was above and below, and the least slip would therefore have been the commencement of a slide which would probably have terminated in the foaming river below."

This was all, however, a mere preliminary, and not to be spoken of with what awaited the travellers. The really serious part of the way was to come, with the scaling of the grand backbone of the mountains, and the perils of the journey beyond.

The lofty Himalhyan passes of Seojila, Namikar, and Photola were successively surmounted; only one life was lost in these dangerous and arduous journeyings; and Mr. Clark now entered Khachan-pa, or Snowland, as the old Chinese travellers call Ladakh and the Lhassan kingdom of Thibet. As he passed from land to land, Mr. Clark delivered the message of God, and he had ready entrance and welcome among Hindu and Moslem residents, and amidst the Buddhists, who form the vast mass of the peoples of these regions; for he was tactful in manner, sympathetic of heart, and the law of kindness was in his tongue.

Throughout this tour, his preaching was formulated on a carefully considered plan. His object was to proclaim the Gospel, so that it should have free course in many lands amongst people widely divergent in race and religion, and it is instructive to note the principles which guided him. They are best explained in his own words. "We have endeavoured to avoid as much as possible all mention of the existing religions; and have only stated our opinion when expressly called upon to do so. We have also abstained from argument and controversy as much as possible. Our simple object has been to make plain statements of the Gospel, and to set before the people the fundamental doctrines of our religion in such a manner as would be most likely to inform their understandings, and then to call upon them to use every effort to investigate the truth, and to attain to everlasting life according to the revealed will of God. The uncertainty of life and the certainty of death, the contrast between heaven and hell, between realities and vanities, between eternity and time, constitute the stimulating arguments which make this all-important duty imperative on all men. As messengers of God, it would seem that our simple duty is to deliver our message faithfully, and even authoritatively, as a direct communication and command of God to them, and then to leave all results and consequences, of whatever kind, in the hands of Him whose work it is we are endeavouring to perform. We do not, therefore, state at once why it is so, or how it is so, but simply that it is so. Its truth rests upon the truth of the Word of God. If the latter be true, then is the former true also, however difficult or incomprehensible it may seem to men. When this is stated, the proofs, the credentials of its truth, the reasons why we know the Bible to be the Word of God, must then be forthcoming when we are called upon to declare them."

The lands traversed, their peoples and the things pertaining to them, and even their fauna and flora, were subjected to close and systematic study. Nothing in the natural features and capabilities of a country or the condition of its people seems to have been overlooked, and all things were passed under review from the point of possible missionary effort. As the result, Mr. Clark judged the time to be ripe for missions in Ladakh, and he refers thus to the matter in a communication to the Church Missionary Society:—

"I will tell you what my thoughts are about it, reserving to myself a right to alter my opinion whenever just reasons should appear for doing so. We will begin with the principle that the Gospel must be preached here. The only question, therefore, that remains is, how, and when, is it to be preached? We may again simplify these two questions by removing the latter which I have stated; for the experience of all will prove that there is no time like the present for doing anything that has to be done. It can be done, and therefore it should be done, now. Humanly speaking, there is not any outward obstacle of any kind apparent to prevent the Word of God being preached in any part of the country—I mean in Western and Middle Thibet; for I believe there are obstacles down towards Lhassa. The question, 'When is it to be preached?' may therefore be at once answered by the ready reply, 'Now!'

"There is now in Thibet a most important, and, as it would seem, an effectual opening for the Gospel to be preached wherever the Church of Christ, or the emissaries of that Church, are willing to do it. The only question, therefore, that remains, is, How? How is it to be begun and carried out? The missionary to Thibet must be, it seems, exclusively for Thibet. It would be desirable, if not necessary, for him to live almost permanently in the country, or at any rate to remain in it until he is turned out. The latter is not, however, at all a probable event; yet we must still remember that here are no English laws, and a native rule is always different from an English one. I do not mention this, however, to place a difficulty in the way—far from it. I do not think it is a difficulty; nor do I see the slightest reason in the world why English Missions should be confined to countries under English government. We are commanded to preach everywhere: we can do so here, and therefore must. We have nothing to do with results and consequences, but we must obey commands.

"I do not see any reason—but I speak with very

imperfect knowledge — why missionaries to Thibet should be men of very great talent. I should say that the people are, for the most part, ignorant. There is neither Mahommedanism nor Hinduism to grapple with; and Buddhism has here, perhaps, no more hold on the inhabitants than a superstitious fear and dread of what they have been accustomed to reverence; the same, probably, as that which existed in the South Sea Islands, or on the West Coast of Africa. Pious, simple, plain, straightforward missionaries would probably suit this people, while brilliant talents would find much more scope in India, or Persia, or China. The missionaries, however, here must be men capable of enduring hardness, and some fatigue and cold; for most of the country is more than ten thousand or twelve thousand feet high, and the winter is no doubt sufficiently severe.

"A missionary here will, of course, under the present state of affairs, have no English society, except for a few weeks in the summer, when English officers are passing through. The necessaries of life, however, are cheap and plentiful; and we can get mutton, vegetables, China tea from Yarkund, woollen cloths, firewood, bread, eggs, fowls, butter, milk, and fruit, especially apricots, etc., very good, and for very little money. The climate, too, is dry, and seemingly as healthy as any climate could possibly be, and the people seem strong and healthy. They seem to be a very simple, obliging, nice set of people; very ignorant, but always ready to hear. The lamas, too, are exceedingly ignorant, but they can generally read; indeed, I do not think we have met with any who cannot spell out his words. I cannot but think that there would be every encouragement for missionaries devoted to their work, and who simply desired the present and eternal welfare of the inhabitants."

The famous city of Leh, or Ladakh, was reached on the 24th of July. During his stay there, Mr. Clark very carefully collected information about the far cities of Kashgar and Yarkand. He notes:—"No people seem to be excluded from Yarkund but Europeans. If any of the latter were to penetrate to Yarkund, they say that the people would make a considerable disturbance, and turn them out, but would not kill them. The reason of their exclusiveness is that they are afraid that the English will come and take their country. The Yarkundis who gave the above information say they do not know that any European has ever been there; but they remember that when they were boys a report one day flew through the city that there was an Englishman hid in one of the houses. They described the running about of officials in every direction, to see whether or not it really were so, but they did not know what the result was.

"I tried hard to get one of them to take a Persian New Testament, with my salaam, as a present to the alum akhun [head of the Moslem theocracy], but he quite shrank from the idea. He said he was almost afraid to speak to him, much less to take so great a liberty. He said that the people were so opposed to us, that whenever they asked him at Yarkund whether he had seen any sahibs, he invariably said that he had not, to free himself from their unpleasant observations, which such a statement would produce. He even denied having seen any of us, much more, therefore, concealed what we had said. After a little, however, we succeeded in putting a Mizan-ul-Haqq and a Persian Gospel into the hands of the second one of them, which he said he might perhaps give to some mullah at Yarkund; and on leaving the tent he thrust them into his breast out of the reach of all observation. We cannot tell what the result of even these two books may be, should they ever reach Yarkund."

On 17th August the crossing of another snowy pass took Mr. Clark into the fastnesses of Little Thibet. In the territory of the Khoppali Raja, he describes the national game of Chaughan—now universally known as Polo. The return to Srinagar on the way homewards to the distant Panjab was safely accomplished by 9th September.

The story of Mr. Clark's travels is replete with interest. We may here, however, only note three great missionary outcomes: two fall immediately under our purview, the third will concern us later. During this tour Robert Clark first conceived the idea of a great chain of Missions extending from the Panjab along and beyond the British borders into Central Asia and China. The achievement of this chain of Missions marching with the frontiers became thenceforward one great aim of his life, to be steadfastly pursued.

In this connection, Mr. Clark was prompt to urge the need for the Scriptures in the various vernaculars. He observes: "A most important consideration at the present time has reference to the work of translations, and it is one which forcibly presents itself to the notice of all friends to Missions in the north of India. In the countries immediately surrounding us there are four languages spoken, all of which are but very imperfectly, or not at all, known to Europeans, viz., Gurmukhi,

Pushtu, Kashmiri, and Thibetian. The translations must, it would seem, be made. They are indispensable for the effectual carrying out of missionary work in three countries, and it is probable that very few months would elapse before they could obtain free admittance into the fourth. But, at any rate, it would appear that it is an absolute necessity that someone should be sent out at once from home for this especial work. The work is great, and it is still almost uncommenced."

Independently of missionaries appointed expressly for the Panjab, he urged the despatch of other missionaries to labour for the countries beyond the British boundaries. "These countries, it is true, are not under our own Government," he writes, "nor can any place in them be occupied as yet by an European as a permanent residence. But this does not present any real obstacle to the missionary's labours. We may, and can, act in all these countries, both directly and indirectly, without any permanent occupation of them. From the advanced frontier posts of the Panjab they may be constantly visited; and at any rate, in some of them, as in Kashmir, and I believe also in Thibet, the missionary may remain as long almost as he will. Such frontier stations ought therefore to be supplied with additional labourers for this especial work; or they might perhaps be placed there in such numbers, that some might at any rate be able—without crippling the local efforts of the Mission—to advance anywhere, wherever an important opening might present itself. Such persons would become masters of the languages spoken in the countries, and not only undertake journeys in them—which may be sometimes long in duration, and to far-distant places—but they would be ready prepared to establish missions in advance of all present ones, whenever the time might arrive for doing so. The opening in the Panjab seems to be important not only with regard to itself, but also with regard to Afghanistan, Persia, Kashmir, Thibet, and China; and we may even add, with regard to India itself."

The second outcome of these memorable wanderings was a source of the greatest thankfulness to Mr. Clark. Darkness brooded impenetrable in the lands of his sojourn, but he had the joy of seeing the day break in those far ends of the earth. That great people of God, the Moravian Brethren, were stirred up to occupy the land in Christ's name. Through the influence and liberality of Colonel Martin, they established the parent station of their widespread Western Thibetan Mission in the Himalhyan valley of Lahoul.

Robert Clark had done what he had gone forth to do; and now he once more quietly settled down again to his work at Amritsar. But it was not for long.

The waning year brought the reply of the authorities of the Church Missionary Society to the invitation sent from Peshawar at the close of 1853. They heartily responded to the call to go forward. Mr. Clark was assigned to the Mission he had promoted in its initial stages. Peshawar was to be his headquarters, and the Afghan people his cure. The veteran Pfander, king amongst missionaries to Moslems, was transferred from Agra to the work amongst Pathans. Colonel Martin had by this time definitely joined the ranks of the Church Missionary Society as a lay missionary. The new Afghan Mission had owed more to him than to any other one man while he was an officer at Peshawar, and it was greatly strengthened by his appointment to its staff.

CHAPTER XI

APOSTLE TO THE AFGHANS.

IN the beginning of 1855, Robert Clark again crossed the Indus, this time as an apostle to the Afghans. We get a glimpse of his feelings in the following letter, written at that time:—

"I am sure you will congratulate me in my preferment in having been appointed to Peshawar, the frontier Mission, and the nearest to the untouched fields of Central Asia. This is indeed an honour and a privilege. I shall again have the distinction of walking in the apostle's steps, who sought to preach the Gospel, not where Christ was named, but to those to whom He had not been spoken of, and not building on any other man's foundation. At Amritsar we were not the first in the field, as the Americans had been there before us. At Peshawur everything is as yet untouched: no missionary, to do any work, has as yet crossed the Indus, beyond which all our work will lie, and we shall be separated by that river from all India, and have to look forward to the stillness of death. I think, if you look upon the map, and take Peshawur as a centre, you may draw a very great part of a circle without going near any missionary field, and you may extend the radius to almost any length without trespassing on any man's labours. To the North you may go, I think, almost to the Arctic Ocean; to the East, almost to the Five Seaports of China; to the West, almost to Europe, that is, through the whole length of Asia, and pretty nearly the whole breadth of it, without meeting with any fellow-labourers. You will see, then, the position in which we are placed. I need only say that I feel utterly unfit for the post, and only go because I am sent. However, if you will help me with your prayers, perhaps some little use will be made even of me: otherwise, I shall not do much. You will, I am sure, not forget me in that way, although removed from you all even farther than before. Indeed, that is the very reason, I am sure, why you will wish the more to assist me, and the best way, and almost the only way, you can do so is by prayer. . . ."

The founding of the Afghan Mission made the translation of the Word of God into the vernacular an urgent matter, and in this connection a truly remarkable providence falls to be noted. In the dark days when missions were barely accorded a precarious toleration under the British flag in India, the mighty faith of Carey foresaw the time when, from the surf-beaten shores of Cape Comorin to the snows of the Himalhya, from the Bay of Bengal to the Arabian Sea, the Word of God would have free course through the length and breadth of the land, and the messengers of the Cross would run to and fro, none daring to make them afraid. He would not live to see that day, but his spirit greeted it, and he made his inheritance secure in it: with incredible labour and enterprise the Serampore missionaries translated the Holy Scriptures into the many tongues of the fast-closed lands of the North, and, amongst others, in 1818, the Pentateuch was rendered into the Pukhtu.

As we have seen, the long night at last gave place to the dawn of day for the Afghan race, but alas the book could no longer be found. It had perished unde the mordant tooth of time. All search proved unavailing. Then Herbert Edwardes remembered that he had seen a copy, in 1848, in the possession of Muhummud Ali Khan, chief of the Sunda tribe of Pathans, in the far Derajat. The book had been given to the aged chieftain, decades before, by a missionary at Hardwar, in India, and he had preserved it most carefully from "flood and fire," because of a secret conviction that one day the British sway would extend to his land, and he would then produce it. The British had come, the door was open, and the young District Officer was now Chief Commissioner of the Frontier. He despatched a special messenger on the long journey to the Khan at Kolachi, in Derajat, with a Persian Bible in exchange for the Pukhtu version. The old chief had died the day before its arrival, but he had lived long enough to preserve for the Afghan race the one copy of the Scripture extant in Pukhtu. In Oriental phrase, "Allah Ho Akbar"—Great is God!

The establishment of the Mission synchronised with remarkable developments in Frontier politics. During the winter of 1854, our old enemy, Dost Muhummud of Cabul, sought an alliance with the British. A few days after the arrival of the missionaries, also, the historic frontier city saw a significant sight. Sir John Lawrence and Hyder Ali, son of the Durrani sovereign, concluded a treaty of friendship on behalf of the contracting powers. A writer of the day notes:—"Thus the first Christian Mission to Afghanistan is opened simultaneously with an alliance with Afghanistan, sought for by the people of that country themselves. 'Dull,' writes an officer in high authority, 'must be the understanding of him who sees no significance in this coincidence—no token from above that the Lord has purposes of mercy towards that country.'"

We have a picture of the colleagues at Peshawar from the pen of Mr. Phelps, a Chaplain of the East India Company. "A better selection of men for this important post could hardly have been made. Mr. Pfander brought to bear upon the important task that lies before the Mission a considerable store of learning, great linguistic attainments, and most winning presence and manner; Mr. Clark, many years his junior, great missionary promise, combined with a singular devotedness, a most unwearied industry; Colonel Martin, an indomitable zeal and activity; and they all seemed endowed with the courage needed by all those whose work lies amongst the most fanatical of the followers of Mahommed."

The missionaries set actively to work. The broad principles which had governed the initial operations at Amritsar were adapted to the new conditions at Peshawar. Mr. Clark's first care was thoroughly to study the country, its history, and its language and tribes. The people were bold, and must be resolutely met; their teachers and leaders were men of learning; he must master their holy books, philosophies and song, and, while he entered fully into his present field, he developed a close touch with the regions beyond the Frontier. The policy he formulated can be stated in his own words. "This Mission will be one not of defence, but of attack—an outpost of Indian Missions carrying the Gospel into the midst of a hostile enemy, and bearing on Persia and Central Asia, which must also soon be unlocked. In the present time we must, I think, be no longer contented with small things, but expect great things; and indeed, whether we expect them or not, I am convinced that they are at hand, and that perhaps the most sanguine will find his expectations below the reality of that which they will shortly see."

How shall the new religion take high ground in the minds of the people? This was the pressing question. Mr. Clark's insight saw that the key to the position lay in education. Peshawar was a learned city, a seat of great religious authority, to which questions were constantly referred for authoritative decision from Cabul itself, and the Mission would therefore at once win respect if the public mind associated it with teaching. The first step in the war of God against Afghanistan was taken on the 14th May 1855, when Mr. Clark opened a high school. Prudence would seem to have demanded for the new venture some safe spot within the British lines, where, free from molestation, the work would take root in security, and in natural course expand as the people became familiarised with the missionary and his objects. Robert Clark, however, was far too astute to be misled by such superficial considerations. The institution was not to be buried in the cantonments or in a corner of the Mission compound. Christianity had come to take possession, and the school was to be in evidence, a witness in itself. Its place, therefore, was not to be in obscurity, however safe that might be; the flag must fly in the heart of the enemy's land; and, despite the perils of that deadly city, the school was established in its midst. Moreover, the object in view required that the institution should not, except for the moment, be housed in a hired building, dependent on alien kindness and an uncertain toleration. That were in itself a confession of weakness. The new departure must have all the prestige that would attach to the ownership of its own premises, and accordingly a handsome school was rapidly erected in a commanding position.

Matters such as these count for much in the East, though but few foreigners realise their importance. Robert Clark at once grasped the course best calculated to show the Pathan mind by evidence it could appreciate, that the new religion in their midst was powerful, permanent, worthy of the best consideration. As Herbert Edwardes wrote at the time: "Mr. Clark's exertions in the discouraging task of beginning a school on missionary principles in a Mahommedan city have been very great indeed, and have been rewarded with more success than could reasonably have been expected."

A few weeks after the commencement, Mr. Clark was able to report:—"Our school, not yet two months old, has some ninety pupils in regular attendance, of every country within our reach. We have one representative from Georgia, or rather whose family is from that country; some from the wandering Tartar tribes above Persia; several from Persia and from different parts of Cabul; whilst many of the people from the neighbouring mountains, and other tribes who have come here to learn at the feet of the Mullahs, also attend the different classes. There are Protestant,

Roman Catholic, and Armenian Christians, both Sunni and Sheah Mohammedans, and many Hindus. Many of the scholars are grown-up men, and some of them are from the very best families in the city; so that the school has already assumed a place of importance in missionary work."

In a letter dated 14th July, he continues, concerning the school:—"Forty-five of these scholars are in the English School, and afford sometimes hopes of their really learning something by which they may be partakers of truth and pardon through Him of whom they have been hitherto altogether ignorant. I have been much pleased lately with the altered appearance of some of them; their whole manner and character seems changing, and not only do they seem to be laying hold of and appropriating what they learn, but also to be a different class of beings from the rough, ignorant, and wild creatures they were before; some of them actually speak the truth sometimes, and some I hope generally; a virtue seemingly unknown in Peshawur, when it militates against apparent advantage. I have been also much surprised and gratified to find the boys themselves, and one or two of the masters, support a poor scholar, who is, or rather was, a workman before, and who has not the least claim upon them. It came out quite accidentally the other day that they raise a subscription monthly for him; one or two give 1s. each, and others 6d. or 3d., in order to allow the poor man time for his studies, and yet to procure his daily food. There is another boy who came from Bunnoo, who I rather think is also privately helped by some of them, which speaks well for them."

Preaching was from the first regularly carried on

in the bazaars of the cantonment. Despite the urgence of some warm friends of the Mission, the colleagues waited for some months before they began to preach in the city. They felt that the foundation-stone of Christ's Kingdom amongst the Afghans would ultimately be the better laid for the delay; and what a day that was when Dr. Pfander and Mr. Clark first published the Gospel in the streets of murderous Peshawar!

Large crowds habitually attended the preaching-places. Special honour was always shown to any Khan or great man who attended the preaching. He was given a chair, which is reckoned a high distinction, and was very properly made much of. Sometimes a frantic Afghan would literally foam at the mouth with rage, and insults might be shouted or filth thrown; or, again, the infuriated mob with violent threatenings would shout, "La illa il Allah Muhummud Rasul Allah" (There is no God but God, and Muhummud is the Prophet of God). The effect of such a cry, like the roaring of a troubled sea, is described by an officer as "most terrific." Ordinarily, however, and contrary to all expectation, the preachers were heard with patient attention. Dr. Pfander reported at the time:—

"Many of our friends, knowing the character of the people, thought it dangerous to preach in the city, and felt rather uneasy about it, but, through God's mercy and help, all has gone on well hitherto. Neither have any tumults taken place, nor has any injury or serious insult been offered to us, and the preaching has at least had the effect of making our work known, not only in the city, but in the villages and places and countries around, through those who have heard us, and seen the strange and novel sight, to them, of having the Gospel preached in the streets of Peshawur."

The subject matter at these preachings is worthy of note. Some advise, in the first instance, a whittling down of Christian truths to approximate them as far as may be to the prejudices of non-Christian faiths. Others again would, among Moslems, advocate a certain reticence concerning the facts of the Trinity and the Divinity of our Lord. But Robert Clark shrank with abhorrence from any such methods. It was not for him to try to broaden the narrow gate or do away with the offence of the Cross. Meekly, gently, lovingly, he hesitated not to declare the whole counsel of God, whether men heard or whether they forbore. He addressed himself to his high duty with "no wisdom of words," firmly "resolved to know nothing save Jesus Christ and Him crucified."

The Divinity and Sonship of Christ, His Incarnation and Atonement, were from the first freely declared to that violent and barbarous people, the Gospel being preached in its fulness and simplicity. Then, as ever, the Cross was to some foolishness, to others a stumbling-block. That Islam or the Quran should be called in question was almost more than those frantic Moslems could endure. Direct attacks, even when provoked by questions, were avoided. Those who desired to discuss were invited to the Mission, or promised a visit at their own homes should they so prefer. The colleagues observe :—"It would seem almost an impossibility for a Mahommedan of these parts to embrace the despised religion of Jesus Christ. There is a firm determination stamped on the countenance, a confidence of faith that seems never to have known a doubt, an indifference to and ignorance of every other feeling, that would lead the observer to exclaim, 'Can these dry bones live?' But the eye of faith sees more than the outward view. At God's command even these shall live, for with God nothing is impossible; and, doubtless, before the great white throne there shall stand many, even of men like these, redeemed from among men by the blood of the Lamb." Thus, without exciting violence, both teaching and preaching were introduced into that ultra-Muhummudan city by the colleagues. The Chief Commissioner observes: "That alone is a victory. Every day accustoms the people to the innovation; and soon it will seem no more strange to them that Christian doctrines should be openly taught among them, than that Hindus are worshipping idols and no true Moslem breaking them. The first step is the difficulty in these matters. After that, it is impossible that the presence of really good men, Europeans without European pride, and with all European knowledge, mixing with the natives on kindly terms, teaching their children better than they could be taught elsewhere, and radiating generally the genial influence of Christian goodwill towards all men, should not succeed in softening angry feeling, dispersing prejudice, attracting curiosity and inquiry, and winning a large amount of humanity and respect."

A great deal was done by means of visits paid and received. The distribution of books was also largely carried out. The Oriental, as we have already mentioned, has a great reverence for the printed page, because perchance the Divine Name is upon it. In addition to a large general circulation, copies of Dr.

Pfander's well-known works were sent to chiefs and leaders in religion. The colleagues report:—"The books were variously received: some sent in return their kind and respectful salaam; others simply returned the books; and the first among them, a man famous among his people for his learning and devotion, returned them with the following characteristic note, written in Arabic: 'To the renowned Priest, the Padre-Sahib, Dr. Pfander—The books on religious controversy you sent me for perusal I return herewith, without having read them. The great God has placed us firmly on the right way, and our knowledge is solid truth, established by reason and revelation, and by external and internal proofs, and we have no wish whatever to call our religion in question. What have we therefore to do with false books, belonging to such a people as have turned from the right way, and in behalf of whom it is said (in the Quran), "God has sealed up their hearts, and a veil is over their eyes"? And again it is said, "Theirs is a severe punishment for what they have forged;" and, further, "For them is their religion, and for us is our religion." To write more there is no need: for the wise, a hint is enough.—Hafiz Mohammed Azim, Waiz.'" Hafiz was his title as a reciter by heart of the Quran, and Waiz his office as preacher.

Mr. Clark had studied with such diligence, that by the end of the year he was able to preach with great fluency to the Pathans in their own tongue. To him also belongs the honour of publishing the first Christian work in the Pukhtu language.

The close of this eventful year found the Mission firmly established. Not only had there been no opposition, but here, too, as at Amritsar, the harvest followed quick on the sowing. There were three baptisms during the year. The first man to be baptized was a Syud, or descendant of Muhummud, from Central Asia. He was a merchant, of mature age, a man of education and polish, and held in high esteem alike for his sacred descent and personal worth. While on pilgrimage at Mecca, he was taught of God in a dream that he must follow Christ, and he set out to learn the truth more fully from Dr. Pfander, whom he found in Peshawar. Haji Syud Muhummud Yahya Baqar there professed the faith with great joy and boldness. A few days afterwards he was murderously assaulted by a Pathan, sore wounded, and left for dead; but he recovered, with the loss of two fingers. He afterwards returned to his distant home in Central Asia; where he held fast by the faith of Christ, and witnessed for Him amongst his own bigoted people. He had wonderful escapes and adventures, but despite Moslem fury he lived the full tale of his days, and years afterwards fell asleep while on a trading venture at Shikarpur, in Sindh.

It was the writer's privilege in 1902 to instruct an Afghan gentleman, a relative of the Amir, in the truths of Christianity. This Afghan said that he had as a lad seen the Haji reciting Christian truth in the streets of Cabul, where none dared to molest him; for the command was, "Touch him not; the hand of God is on him." A notable convert, Dilawar Khan, followed later in sequence of time. He was the first Afghan to be baptized from the vicinity of Peshawar, Mr. Fitzpatrick being the officiating minister. He had been a famous brigand, a terror to the countryside for years, but eventually entered the famed regiment of the Guides, and rapidly rose to the highest rank open to him, that of Subhadar, or centurion. He was a rigid Moslem. The truth of Christ, however, laid hold of his heart, and he, who among even his fanatical people would have seemed to be the least likely to serve the Prince of Peace, was the first to bow the neck to His yoke. A number of Afghans banded themselves together, as certain of the Jews did against Paul, "and bound themselves under a curse, saying that they would neither eat nor drink until they had killed" Dilawar Khan; but that tough old warrior recked naught of such trifles. "Pray you that my faith fail not," said he to his friends the missionaries; and he grimly added, "As for my head, my hand will keep *that* well enough." He went about as usual, stout of heart and quick of eye, a perfect walking arsenal of weapons. To the stranger who approached, his greeting was, "An ye be a friend, bide where you are; if an enemy, come on!" The avengers of Islam had to be absolved from their vow; old Dilawar, or "The Valiant Chief," as his name signifies, was too hard a nut to crack.

Years afterwards, the Governor-General, Lord Mayo, had a delicate matter of statecraft to adjust with the Amir of Cabul, and the man chosen from all broad India for this mission was the Christian Subhadar, Dilawar Khan. He started from Peshawar for Cabul in the depth of winter. The passes were bad enough in any case at this season, but the ruler of Chitral, by treachery, lured him into yet more dangerous paths. When the Subhadar regained the proper road he was stricken by mortal sickness, but he gallantly kept on his way till the sands of life ran out. He lay down to die in the deep snows of the mountain passes a few days' march from Cabul, and delivered his despatches intact to his escort to take back to Peshawar. His farewell was, "Say to the Commissioner I went as far as man could go; I could fare no farther, for the hand of God was on me. I am glad to die a good soldier of the Queen. I die also a true soldier of Jesus Christ." Then he turned in the snow, and covered his face.

As the months sped, Robert Clark's thoughts turned to the villages that dot the plain of Peshawar, and evangelistic tours were undertaken in various directions. The Afghans are above all things hospitable; the guest is sacred, his privileges are great and many; each village has its hujrah, or guest-house. In these things Mr. Clark saw a potent engine for furthering the Gospel amongst the rural Pathans.

The importance of a fixed preaching-place in the city was also realised, and in time the "Martin Chapel" occupied a site, the best in Peshawar for the purpose.

Colonel Martin was the first layman in the Panjab to join the Church Missionary Society. Robert Clark was greatly impressed, as the result of Peshawar experience, by the value of the work that could be done by an unordained missionary, and the development of such agencies became a fixed principle with him in Mission policy. In the local report the colleagues observe of Colonel Martin:—

"The erection of our Chapel in the city, and its adjoining room, the new buildings of the school, the purchase of the residences of the missionaries and of the station chapel, the distribution of the alms to the poor, and searching out separately each deserving case, the procuring funds for the publication of Dr. Pfander's works, the establishment of the general library, the whole correspondence of the Mission, and the management of the accounts, are some of the labours in which he is engaged. In the necessary absence of the missionaries from Peshawar, he has supplied their places in the school, and has accompanied the catechists to preach. The happy results of the association of a lay missionary with ordained ones has thus been witnessed; and the Mission may serve as an example of what may be done by Christian laymen in direct missionary labours."

With the further progress of the work, the question as to how he might best get in touch with his parishioners increasingly pressed on Mr. Clark's mind. The one adequate solution, to his thinking, was to quit the British quarters, and live among the Pathans, within the walls of the city itself. But was that feasible?

The Frontier is yet on occasion none too safe, even in such places as the cantonments at Peshawar. Vigilant watch and ward is incessant. On a dark night, with a nervous sentry at the charge, it is well to obviate the risk of swelling the tale of regrettable incidents by a prompt reply to the challenge. In the days of which we write, Europeans literally carried their lives in their hand. They went armed, and under military escort. The city and country were extremely dangerous. In the cantonments, though there was a measure of protection, every house was under the care of its own armed watchman.

Night and day the unceasing tramp of sentinels, patrols, and guards was borne on the ear. They shot at sight, but, despite all that could be done, only assured a moderate safety against an enemy of reckless valour, malignant in ferocity and cunning. Scarce a day passed without an alarm or an attack. Dropping shots or a regular fusillade would arouse the residents in the depth of the night. They turned over to slumber again as unconcernedly as if the rifle reports were but the serenading of so many cats. It was only the guard engaged with some Afghan marauder or assassin; he might be killed or captured, or the honours might be divided, and he get off scot free; they would hear all about it soon enough, in the morning.

Even in the daytime the vicinity of the cantonments was not without hazard. On one occasion Sir John Lawrence and Colonel Edwardes, driving under a strong escort, were greatly startled to find Mr. Clark a few hundred yards beyond cantonment limits. He was enjoying a quiet stroll, unarmed and unaccompanied, as was his wont. They rated him soundly on his rashness, insisted on taking him back to safety in their carriage, and were not satisfied until he promised to be more careful in the future. They had reason; murders of Europeans by shooting and stabbing were of frequent occurrence. Instances could be given in lamentable abundance, but one may suffice. A young lieutenant, Mr. Hands, was shot while riding with a lady in the vicinity of the cantonments. His head and hands were severed from the body, the horses were stolen, and the lady, frantic with horror, after wandering about all day, eventually reached the cantonments in a dazed condition.

Mr. Clark had his own share of peril. One day he sat at a table in school engaged in the usual teaching. As an Afghan approached to present a petition, a sharp-eyed schoolboy caught the gleam of the long dagger, naked in the folds of his belt. He promptly warned the teacher by a look, for the exigency did not admit of words. Refusing the petition, Mr. Clark moved slightly backwards; the knife was hurled at him and cut his waistcoat, and the man fled. The affair was one of moments.

On another occasion, Mr. Clark was travelling under escort towards Bunnu with Captain Minchin. They marched by night, because of the heat. At a halt, the straying of one of his camels hindered Mr. Clark from marching at the usual hour. The friends dined together, and at ten at night Captain Minchin went on, while Mr. Clark stayed to allow of a search for the truant, hoping to rejoin his companion at the morning halt. They never met again, however. Captain Minchin was shot by his own escort within an hour of leaving camp.

Obviously it was no light matter for any European, let alone a missionary, to make the experiment of residing within the walls of Peshawar.

Sweet reasonableness was a ruling feature of the solid bed-rock of Robert Clark's character. It preserved him from both the forms of folly, widely divergent though they be, that are peculiarly apt to beset the endeavours of Christians in the service of God, and from them the wreck of many a good cause has resulted. There was no trace in him of that soulless calculation of chances, sadly miscalled caution, that hesitates in abject doubt, when the call of God is to go forward,—his was no timid, laggard heart that could not enter into the promises "because of unbelief." On the other hand, he was equally free from the harebrained temerity that, under the specious guise of faith, tempts Providence,—he was not of the number of those who "run though they have not been sent," and "so fall by the way."

After judicious ponderings on the question in all its bearings, he was convinced that it was feasible to live in the city, and therefore, as circumstances stood, it must be done. The problem now was, Where should he place his home?

In the early centuries of our era, Peshawar was the capital of the great Buddhist empire of King Kanishka. It was a holy city of far renown in the Buddhist world, because of the stupa wherein was enshrined that precious relic, the begging bowl of Buddha. Vast numbers of pilgrims from all Buddhist lands thronged the city to worship at that glory of the Buddhist world, the stupa. It was encircled by an extensive Buddhist rail of wondrous workmanship, wrought in pure gold, and a vast monastery, or vihara, surrounded the shrine. The piety of the king and the munificence of the pilgrims made the buildings and all connected with them of the best. Scarcely inferior in sanctity to the begging bowl itself was a mighty Bodhi drūm, or tree of Buddha, even in those days a thing of great age. Ten centuries later, Baber's march to the conquest of India brought him to Peshawar. He visited "the famous great tree of Begram." The stupa was gone; but his memoirs give a graphic account of the immense quantities of human hair with which the cells of the vihara were bestrewn. It came from the heads of countless pilgrims, who, in pursuance of their vows, had their locks shorn at this holy place.

In the East, with changes of religion, the holy places of the old faiths continue their reign uninterruptedly, under the auspices of the new. This rule is universal. The Kaaba at Mecca, for instance, the central spot of Islam to-day, was the holy place of the Arabs "in the days of darkness," as Moslems call the period of pre-Muhummudan idolatry. The erstwhile resort of the Buddhist world in like manner was now the place of pilgrimage of rejuvenated Hinduism. In Baber's day all memory of dead and gone Buddhism was already lost; but tradition, with the undying tenacity of the East, called the old vihara, Gorkhatri, the grave of the Kshatriya, or Rajput, the warrior caste from which the princely line of Buddha had sprung.

When, centuries later, Robert Clark acquired it to make it the citadel of Christian operations amongst the Afghans, it was still known as the Gorkhatri. The choice was dictated by sound principles. The Gorkhatri was the most prominent object in Peshawar. Quartered in it, Christianity was emphatically in visible evidence. It stood on the highest ground in the city, and was therefore in the most healthy situation possible. It was neither crowded in by other buildings nor overlooked; it was open on all sides to the free play of the breeze; and the surface and deep drainage flowed away from it. There was ample room in the valuable building for present work and future developments, and it had this manifest advantage also that the Gorkhatri was famous throughout the country. Strangers could easily find their way to the missionary without incurring the suspicion and hostility inseparable from inquiries as to his whereabouts.

In going to live in the city, Mr. Clark had no intention of shortening his days by trying to live after the manner of a native of the land. He planned, altered, and built with a primary regard to health. The external surroundings of the new residence were dealt with in the same methodical way as the internal arrangements. Mr. Clark's principle was to let nothing be wasted. Order, beauty, utility were carefully considered. A garden was laid out, open spaces were planted with suitable trees and shrubs, and the refreshment and advantages that trees bring in the East were thus secured. The compounds of Europeans in India often present a picture of desolation. The neglected ground is a noisome void, unsightly, cheerless, and inimical to health. Grass, trees, and gardens are so much the everyday of life in the West that the points here emphasised may appear trivial. It is otherwise in India, and Mr. Clark's habitual thoroughness and careful forethought was in nothing more apparent than in his comprehensive grasp of just such matters of detail. The conservation of energy for his holy calling by the removal of preventable strain and the reduction of every risk to a minimum were, to Robert Clark's robust common sense, not only the truest economy but simple duty. When he had flitted to his new home, he came and went throughout the city, preaching, teaching, visiting, unarmed, unescorted, careful only to discharge his office. Under God's shadow he lived openly among the heathen. Sometimes it was known that danger was near, but no harm was permitted to befall him or his, and the step he had been led to take was abundantly justified.

Before Mr. Clark left cantonments, a pleasant little incident befell him that is worth recording. One day, as a new regiment marched in, a private fell out of the ranks and approached him at the salute with a cheery "I think you know me, sir." To Mr. Clark's "I am afraid I do not," he responded, "But indeed you do, sir," and forthwith introduced himself as a Harmston lad, a pupil in the schools Mr. Clark had built, and an ex-scholar of his Sunday class. The soldier wrote home in high glee to his native village, telling how Mr. Clark had given him a hearty welcome and a cordial handshake, and, obtaining leave for him there and then, took him to his house and said to his servants, "Prepare everything quickly, for I have a very great guest to-day." And a joyous day it was that he had with Mr. Clark. When the writer was told of this incident at Harmston, the narrator's eyes sparkled with pleasure for all her ninety years, and she described vividly the joy the great news had brought to the folk—"ay, to be sure."

Mr. Clark was greatly cheered by the devotion of some of the private soldiers in the British regiments. A number of godly men had built themselves a prayer-room at their own charges, and five hundred private soldiers annually subscribed sums varying from three to twenty-five shillings each, to further the Mission amongst the Afghans. Most of them prayed as well as gave. One of the privates said to Mr. Clark, "We never meet, sir, without praying for your work amongst the heathen;" and Mr. Clark adds, "And they meet every night for prayer."

The first period of his service now drew to a close, and Mr. Clark quitted Peshawar on furlough on 24th February 1857. He travelled home with Dr. Dealtry, Bishop of Madras, to whom he had been appointed Chaplain, and arrived safely in London, after an uneventful journey, on 2nd May. We need not dwell on the home-coming, or the reunion with friends.

While on furlough, Mr. Clark forwarded the Panjab Mission by much counsel with the authorities of the Church Missionary Society, and although he did not undertake the work of deputation, he found time to deepen the enthusiasm of friends of Missions.

An address to the members of the University of Oxford while he was at home is memorable for its marshalling of facts, its cogent reasoning, and its ardent appeal to the young manhood of England to enlist for service in "the wars of the Lord." His youngest brother, Roger Edmund, then a Cambridge undergraduate, dedicated himself as a missionary.

Harmston bore yet further fruit: an old pupil of Robert Clark's Sunday class entered the missionary ranks of the Church Missionary Society. After years of self-sacrificing service in the cold lone lands of the North-West of Canada he is still full of labours abundant, as the Right Rev. Dr. Reeve, Bishop of Mackenzie River, Canada. While on furlough, Mr. Clark took his M.A. degree at Cambridge.

The year was one of national anxiety and wide-spread sorrow, and in this Robert Clark had a special share. He had scarcely landed in England when there came news of the outbreak of the Indian Mutiny, on 23rd May. Europeans and natives alike, for their sins, trod the winepress of the fierce anger of God. But in wrath He still remembered mercy. When the calamities were overpast, a purified India emerged, freely open to the Gospel under the sceptre of the Queen. The story of that terrible time does not belong to the present narrative, but the reader will understand the anxiety that pressed on Mr. Clark while the tempest raged. Though there was no mutiny at Peshawar, the position was perilous in the extreme. The state of affairs will be evident from the following letters. A friend wrote on 2nd August :—"An interval of a month has occurred since I commenced this letter. The disturbing nature of the events happening around us renders communication quite uncertain, not to speak of its absorbing much of one's thoughts. Even while I write, the rumour is abroad that, at the conclusion of the feast now being celebrated by the Mussulmans—the Beiram—the fanatical Hill Tribes around us are to surround and destroy us. I am kept, however, by God's goodness, in great peace of mind, and have not had one uneasy night, except from dyspepsia, since the beginning of the Mutiny. A few months ago, Peshawur was looked upon as a place to be shunned and dreaded, not only as one of the most unhealthy, but also as one of the most dangerous stations in this country. Now it has turned out to be one of the safest. Through the admirable management of Colonel Edwardes, every plot has been discovered and thwarted. Time after time we have been devoted to the sword; letter after letter has been intercepted, and from great men among the Mohammedans to our Sepoys, counselling indiscriminate murder of men, women, and children. Colonel Edwardes has himself been prepared to fly at a moment's warning, so imminent has been the danger. Twice, within the last three days, the Artillery have limbered up, on some false alarm; and only yesterday a letter was intercepted, inculpating the only Sepoy regiment in Peshawur which was thought trustworthy. In common with others, I have a few shirts, and papers, and money, made up, ready at any alarm to betake myself to the Residency, which is the appointed rendezvous in case of an emergency."

Another correspondent, writing on 23rd August, says:—"The Sepoy Mutiny is an event of such unparalleled magnitude that people in India find their thoughts and pens almost exclusively occupied by it. The horrors and dangers of that movement have been brought to our very doors, and we feel as if there was nothing else going on throughout the whole world. Here, in Peshawur, though surrounded with dangers, we have hitherto been wonderfully preserved. It seems as if God had put the fear of us in the hearts of the ferocious people around us. 'Surely they had swallowed us up quick,' if they had risen up against us. And that they were fully disposed to do this, they have themselves candidly avowed. It was passed from mouth to mouth in the city of Peshawur that, when our Sepoys should mutiny, all the people of the city would join them in exterminating the Sahibs. A letter was intercepted purporting to be from the King of Delhi; and in reply to a question asked him by the Peshawur Sepoys, 'What should they do with the women and children of the English?' the answer was to the point, 'Kill every one.' Colonel Edwardes has intercepted numbers of letters of a similar kind, in which a tiger-like thirsting for the blood of the Christians was manifested. The impression among thoughtful men relative to this movement is, that it is the death-throe of Mohammedanism. The Hindu soldiers have been nothing more than tools in the hands of the more energetic Mussulmans."

The reader will remember our friend the officer

who subscribed one rupee for the purchase of a revolver wherewith to protect the missionary. He had gone with his regiment from turbulent Peshawar to the profound security of the coveted station of Meerut; yet he was the first man killed by the mutineers, being cut down by his own troopers on that fatal Sunday in May.

Throughout the Mutiny, the Peshawar Mission quietly continued its work. Dr. Pfander preached daily, according to his custom, in the bazaars, and had only to discontinue this for three days.

We must now glance at matters more personal, and refer to one who now entered into Robert Clark's life and became an important factor in all his work and all his plans. There was at this time a certain Dr. Robert Browne living in London. He came of an excellent Scottish stock. Though there was a Highland strain in their blood, his forbears were, in the main, Lowlanders, and included a staunch Covenanting ancestry. Dr. Browne himself was a son of the manse. His father had been minister of Falkirk for many years, and there Robert Browne had been born and bred. After he had taken his degree of Doctor of Medicine in the University of Edinburgh, the East had attracted him, and eventually he had settled in Calcutta, where he amassed a fortune, large even according to modern ideas. Having completed forty-five years of honourable professional life, he had retired from India, but continued to keep up a lively interest in the land and people he had so long and arduously served. The sorrow of the Mutiny came to his home; for he had lost one son, an officer, at the Alam Bagh, in the course of Havelock's relief of Lucknow. It is with his eldest daughter, Elizabeth Mary, that we have here to deal.

Miss Browne was endowed with rare talents and force of character, and of her many gifts, one was a marvellous aptitude for languages. She acquired the classical tongues as a girl; French, German, and Italian were as familiar to her as was English itself; and she read Sanskrit and Urdu with her brother John, who became a prominent Bengal civilian. Christian work claimed her deepest interest, and at the stage our story has reached she had been a prison and hospital worker for some years. The cause of Missions, however, appealed powerfully to her heart. She had for some years collected for the Peshawar Mission, and had corresponded with Robert Clark. He was anxious to see her, and secured an introduction through his friend Dr. Baddley, the first meeting taking place at King's College Hospital, where Miss Browne had been working as a Sister of St. John. Soon afterwards, Robert Clark sought her hand. Dr. Browne was very unwilling to let his daughter go out to India at such a time; but, after long delay, he gave his consent, and the marriage took place at Marylebone Church on 14th May 1858.

Robert Clark received his instructions from the Church Missionary Society on the 8th of June, and, a week later, on the 15th, he and Mrs. Clark sailed from Portsmouth in the Indiaman *Nile*. After a long voyage, they reached Calcutta in December 1858, and Peshawar on 8th February 1859. As Dr. Pfander had meanwhile returned to Europe, Mr. Clark now became the senior missionary at Peshawar.

CHAPTER XII.

THE AFGHAN MISSION.

STEADY development, born of patient continuance in well-doing, marked the progress of the Afghan Mission. Mr. Clark was able to report:—"We have many encouragements. Your heart would have been warmed had you been with me to-day when . . . But I have found by experience that the less said about such cases the better. Those converts whose names are never known grow in grace and Christian virtues. I went to the house of one of the Christians, the Qazi, and saw there a sight I had never seen before in Peshawur—seventeen men, Persians and Afghans, from both city and country, sitting round him, while he explained to them, most beautifully, in Persian, 1 Cor. xv.; they listening with the deepest attention, and apparently assenting to everything he said."

The difficulties of residence in the city were greatly intensified in the case of a lady, but Mrs. Clark faced them with high courage and unflinching resolution. Her presence, moreover, was a civilising and humanising agency of immense value. It need scarcely be remarked that from the first Mr. Clark had been alive to the extreme importance of work amongst the women. That now became possible. Amongst the ultra-fanatical Moslems of Peshawar, any effort of this kind required the exercise of the greatest discrimination, and not a little courage. Mrs. Clark, however, was soon an honoured visitor in the homes of the nobility and educated classes. Her medical skill won her entrance and secured friends, and she was ever ready to adopt in work the line of least resistance. Books in zenanas were prohibited by the men; but, finding that the wives of the mullahs recited the Quran and the *Arabian Nights*, she speedily delighted all hearts by reciting the Gospels in like fashion. The zenanas were full of bright, intelligent ladies, and Mrs. Clark was a welcome guest in their monotonous life. Mr. Clark was frequently away from Peshawar, and on one such occasion Mrs. Clark spent a fortnight in a zenana, and, in Moslem garb, witnessed a marriage and a funeral. The foundations of friendships that have endured to this day were securely laid. She had her adventures also; as, for instance, when, on a hot-weather evening, she rode out towards the Khyber Pass, was fired at twice, and had to gallop back in hot haste.

In September of 1859 sorrow came to Mr. and Mrs. Clark in the loss of their first-born child, a daughter.

In the closing months of 1859, Mr. Clark set out on a journey of exploration, accompanied by the Rev. Isodore Loewenthal, a member of the American Presbyterian Mission in the Panjab. The object of the itineration was to ascertain missionary possibilities in a hitherto untouched tract of country. Mr. Clark explored the whole course of the Indus, from the point where it touches the Peshawar District to its majestic confluence with the Panjnad River, formed by the combined five waters of the Panjab, below the historic city of Multan.

MRS. CLARK.

He followed the course of the Frontier through the Trans-Indus districts that comprise Makhud, Kalabagh, Kohat, Bunnu, and the Derajat,—the first to preach the Gospel through this extensive stretch of territory. There was no opposition on the part of either authorities or people, and he evangelised freely in every town and village. Large numbers of books were likewise put in circulation by sale at nominal prices. The door was found to be widely open, and it was clear that the Gospel could be proclaimed throughout the whole course of the Border with no more serious difficulty than in Peshawar. The British residents extended a cordial welcome on all hands, and the great garrisons of Bunnu and Dera Ismail Khan raised considerable sums in aid of the Afghan Mission. This was done without solicitation, in one case even without the missionary's knowledge. Many pleasant, helpful, and permanent friendships were formed during the tour. One such was with Major Hugh Hayley, a well-known Frontier officer, whose career of brilliant promise was prematurely cut short by death. His aged father's parting words to his son had been that he should "be good to the missionaries," and when he met Mr. Clark at Bunnu, he remembered this injunction. Mr. Clark was loaded with kindness that did not cease with his stay. When he parted from his host and was well on his way, the Major's orderly overtook him; he had been sent in hot haste with a present of Hayley's own valuable fur coat to provide against the bleak cold of the Frontier.

The journey resulted in fruitful plans. Mr. Clark outlined two chains of Missions through this country. They were to be connecting links between the Frontier, the Central Panjab, and onwards through Sindh to the sea,—the Panjab would thus be fully grasped. One line stretched from Pind Dadan Khan to Kalabagh; the other ran through the country Trans-Indus amongst the Afghans from Peshawar to Multan, with its centre at Dera Ismail Khan. The realisation of this scheme became one of the ambitions of Robert Clark's missionary policy.

The Peshawar staff was reinforced by the arrival, first of the Rev. T. Tuting, B.A., of Lincoln College, Oxford, and afterwards of Mr. Clark's brother, the Rev. Roger Edmund Clark, B.A., of Trinity College, Cambridge. The Secretariat of the Mission and the work of evangelisation in the city and villages were Mr. Tuting's special sphere. Roger Clark, who had been eight years a master at Harrow, took charge of the school.

Mr. Clark was now free to follow up a work of peculiar promise in a Panjabi regiment then stationed at Peshawar. Converts to Sikhism from the scavenger class of outcastes are known as Mahzabis; their co-religionists will not fraternise with them, and the sense of degradation augments their natural ferocity and misanthropy. Thuggee, for instance, though prevalent in India proper, was unknown in the Panjab, until it was introduced by a Mahzabi called Wazir Singh. Indeed, the class has always been depraved material, and has contributed largely to the criminal population of the Panjab. During the Mutiny, however, the soldierly qualities of the Mahzabis were recognised. Lieutenant Home, leader of the historic assault on the Cashmere Gate of Delhi, recruited the first regiment from amongst them, and it did excellent service in the grim days spent before the rebel capital.

On the fall of that city, some Christian books, part of the spoil, came into the hands of the men of the Mahzabi Regiment, the 24th, known later as the 32nd Panjab Infantry. The books were eagerly read, and when they were exhausted the men begged information from their officers. The inquiry was further stimulated at Amritsar, where one man was baptized. When the regiment moved beyond the reach of the missionaries, some of the officers instructed the Christian converts, and united with them in worship on the Lord's Day. Eventually, the 24th Panjab Infantry became a portion of the Peshawar garrison. The deepening spirit of inquiry rapidly pervaded all ranks of native officers as well as the privates, and there were forty-nine baptisms. Very soon the whole regiment was far on its way towards embracing Christianity. The Sikh priest officially attached to the soldiers, was himself ready to conduct the Christian services.

Robert Clark devoted himself to the requirements of these stirring events. He marched with the regiment in its transfers to various frontier posts, the while keeping in steady touch with the Peshawar work, and not forgetting the towns and villages where he found himself quartered. We find him living at Khairabad and at Attock, and he systematically evangelised both places. At Attock a church, a school for boys, and another for girls, were erected, and the place became a permanent branch of the Peshawar Mission. When the regiment was transferred to Abbotabad, it became Mr. Clark's privilege to be the first to preach Christ to the people of the Hazara.

The Commandant of the regiment, Colonel Morgan,

and some of his staff were unfortunately not in sympathy with the movement; but the real opposition came from the wildly alarmed Supreme Government in India. Orders were issued from Calcutta cautioning the officers against taking any part whatever in the spread of Christianity in the regiment. In Mr. Clark's own words:—"It was an unchristian order and an impolitic one; for the officers were doing nothing more than Christian men should do, and were in noways unduly using their official influence to the prejudice of the native religions. The effects of the order have been, however, most unfavourable to Christianity." He goes on, in a letter dated 2nd November 1857:—"Before it came, the men were pressing forward, eagerly and earnestly inquiring into the subject of Christianity; but from the moment they heard that the Governor-General in Council had interfered, and had written through official channels to their officers about it, they naturally understood this to mean that the English Government directly discouraged the spirit of inquiry, and were averse to any further baptisms in the corps: from that time to the present not one soldier has come forward to ask for either instruction or baptism. The Christians stand dismayed at seeing the interest in their spiritual welfare suddenly lost, and the school has dwindled down to less than half its numbers. The officers may not converse with the native Christians about Christianity; they may not hold a service for them, or even worship God with them, although they are their fellow-Christians, much less speak to any who are not yet baptized.

"Everything is in a state of doubt and uncertainty,

even as regards what a missionary may do in the corps: whether he may enter the lines at all, and if so, whether he may hold a service in a native Christian's house; and, above all, whether he may admit those to his services who are still heathen. I was certainly grieved to find that the orders were of such a nature as to leave everyone in doubt whether a missionary might or might not visit, as a pastor, a large native Christian flock of thirty persons, because they happened to live in the lines of a regiment; but it was thought better that our services should be held away from the lines, in one of the officers' quarters. I held one full service and two shorter ones with them, and administered the Lord's Supper to five adults. I also married two native Christians belonging to the regimental band; but even there the officers could not be present, although they take much interest in the parties, and although none but Christians were present at the wedding.

"Our Government cannot surely know the consequences which such orders lead to, or they would be more careful in making them. No rule had been ever transgressed, and nothing had been done to call for such an order. The only apparent fact was, that some of the soldiers had been baptized; and no sooner does the Government hear of this, than it steps in with its veto, and checks the whole proceeding, as if the baptism of ten Sepoys was something dangerous or something out of order; and a summons is forthwith sent, not to this regiment alone, but to every Panjab regiment, for every officer to hold himself clear of such untoward events. If it had been another plot against their very existence they could hardly have done more."

The order constituted an intolerable violation of personal rights, and Mr. Clark had to face the battle for the private rights of British officers and of native soldiers. The controversy does not concern us here, further than in its result. The publication of the correspondence at home led to important modifications; but the inimical spirit remained, and evangelisation was only permitted within certain limitations. The Government disclaimed any intention of interfering with the private actions of their officers; still, by that time, the favourable moment for the mass movement had gone by. The work in the regiment, however, continued for years afterwards.

The action of the Government was politically a blunder of the first magnitude. Robert Clark was quick to see the great gains that had been foolishly sacrificed, by an interference as uncalled for as it was unreasonable. He saw that the bond of a common religion between rulers and ruled was the surest guarantee of loyalty. The body of converts was loyal to a man in the dark days when, to all appearance, the British power in India was reeling to irretrievable ruin. The fruit of Missions, therefore, meant immovably loyal subjects, and, in proportion, India would require fewer British bayonets. What would not regiments of Christian Sepoys have been worth in the storm through which India had come? The Mahzabis were recruited from the Manjha tract of the Panjab, the cradle of the finest soldiers of that warlike land; Christianity carried to their homes would spread fast on family and tribal lines; a villainous clan would be transformed into a law-abiding people. Christianity established in the Manjha in fact, would mean a tremendous loyal reserve and a progressive force in the heart of the Panjab. Events barely past had witnessed to the effects of timorous anti-Christian policies. The Mutiny was not due to the propagation of the true religion, but to the lack of it. Had Christianity had free course, stories of cartridges greased with the fat of swine or of kine would have been powerless to rouse the Sepoys to the murderous frenzies of 1857.

Robert Clark sought no relaxations of the wise and eminently just policy of neutrality in religion, but he wished the neutrality to be real, and, above all, he desired that the neutral attitude should not be confounded with a widely different thing—discouragement of the propagation or acceptance of the Christian faith.

Since that day, it is to be noted, the rulers of India have repeatedly and unreservedly acknowledged the enormous debt they owe to Christian Missions. The principles Robert Clark maintained will yet command adherence to the full.

We must now turn to some other results of Mr. Clark's sojournings with the regiment. The towns of Khairabad and Attock face each other on the banks of the Indus close to the spot where "The Father of Waters," as Pathans call that majestic waterway, is joined by the river of Cabul. The towns were important points on the one great highway that ran north and south between India and Central Asia. While here, Robert Clark was brought into contact with peoples of many lands, but on a day there came a visitor stranger than any that had come and gone.

The sullen roar of the mighty river told of heavy floods in its course through unknown lands. The dead cattle and household débris that raced madly by in the swirling eddies of the turgid waters witnessed to many a ruined homestead. By and by, a haystack swept down with a living woman perched precariously upon it. She was rescued, and proved to be a handsome matron, exceeding fair, clad in skins, who spoke no word of any known tongue. The District Officer placed the poor waif under the tender care of Mrs. Clark. She was a difficult person, this castaway, and would sit mute for hours gazing in speechless grief at the blue mountains of Afghanistan. Then her glance would fall on the baby in Mrs. Clark's lap, and she would beat her breast in a paroxysm of tears, and lament the while in her unknown tongue. The only thing that interested her in the great city of Peshawar was a packet of needles. It was conjectured from the words "Sardar Khan," "Istandan," "Kaffirastan," which she uttered in her sorrowings, that she was the wife of a chief at some place called Istandan in Kaffirastan, and that she had lost in the flood just such a child as the baby Robert. This was corroborated in measure by some Kaffirs of the lower lands in service at Peshawar, but as every valley of Kaffirastan seems to have its own speech, the communication between them and this remote uplander amounted to very little.

Mr. Clark was thus vividly confronted with the far regions of the remotest Hindu Kush, termed Kaffirastan, or "The Lands of the Unbelievers," by the encircling Moslem powers. Entrenched amongst the ramparts of tremendous mountains, these highlanders had defended their native uplands and glens against the powers of Islam. Implacable hatred to the Moslem was the mainspring of their religious and national polity. No male of the race was accorded the privileges of manhood until he could bring a tale of twenty Muhummudans slain. The Kaffirs were at that time supposed to be the descendants of the Greeks of Alexander who elected not to face the perils of the homeward march to Macedonia; they are now known to be a fragment of the Aryan people who in their remote fastnesses have maintained the primitive ethnic type and faith in its purity. One day the stranger disappeared with the infant Robert, and when the hue and cry was raised, she was captured in full flight for the hills. Later, she slipped away, and was heard of no more. The problem of the evangelisation of Kaffirastan, however, remained in the steadfast heart and kindly brain of Robert Clark.

Access to that distant land was absolutely impossible for the European or the Indian. A Moslem Afghan could reach its borders with ease, thereafter certain death awaited him. If a Christian Afghan could in any wise traverse the zone of fire of the intervening Pathan countries, he might have some chance of life in Kaffirastan itself. The perils were stupendous, but the true Afghan convert is tough metal, as strong in the service of God as he has been fearless in that of the Devil. The following may serve as illustrations:—

A young Afghan mullah from Swat had been baptized, the first of his nation, in the Medical Mission at Amritsar. As the writer was preaching at a fair, a Panjabi Moslem asked a question, and at this the convert said, "My father, my heart is so full of love to Christ that I beseech thee to let me enlighten this man." The request was gladly granted, and the writer turned away to another group. In a few minutes there was a yell. The Moslem was prostrate on the ground, howling, "I'm dead! He has killed me! Call this Christianity!" Undeterred by a surrounding mob of Moslems, the irate Afghan towered over him, shouting, "Just say that again!" and then explained, "This scum said Christ was not the Son of God; so, of course, I knocked him down." "Call this Christianity!" again spluttered the injured "true believer." "Yea, verily," responded the writer, "had this youth been a Muhummudan Afghan, thy life alone would have satisfied him—inasmuch as he is a Christian, rejoice that the loosening of a few of thy teeth hath sufficed." "Verily the words of our doctor sahib be the words of truth and wisdom," exclaimed the crowd. "Fool, what demon drove thee to affront the Afghan? Knowest thou not the race?" they added to their discomfited co-religionist, who continued to listen to the preaching, but asked no further questions.

A stranger from the depths of Afghanistan on a visit to Peshawar stood spell-bound at the sight of a convert preaching in that city. "What man is this, in our garb and of our lineage and tongue," he queried, "who proclaims not the truth of Muhummud?" When he heard the man was an Afghan, now a renegade, a Nazarene, he said, with withering contempt, to the Moslems, "And you swine let him live?" "These be the lands of the Faranghi, not Afghanistan," they muttered, abashed. The Afghan walked up to the catechist, breathing threatenings and slaughter, and then, maddened with fury, he yelled, with violent revilings, "English or no English, say but one word against the blessed Prophet of God, and may I be accursed root and branch if I do not at once despatch thee to hell!" The catechist, however, was also an

Afghan of the Afghans. In a moment the hot Pathan blood in him was aflame. With eyes ablaze, he shouted, "Wilt thou indeed lay down thy life for that lying camel-driver of Mecca, dead and gone, with his very bones mouldered into dust, who never did a hand's turn for thee, and shall I do less for the Lord who ever liveth, and bought me with His own blood? Come on!" The two powerful men were instantly in close grips, and Christians and Moslems alike had much ado to separate the champions. "Could I do less for the Lord?" was, for long, all that the Afghan replied to the remonstrances of his friends.

In 1859, a fine young Afghan, by name Fazl i Haqq, accosted Mr. Clark after the bazaar preaching. He was full of questions, anxious for instruction, and received the Faith as a little child. His brave, gentle, loving heart went out to the Kaffirs. Another Pathan convert, by name Nurullah, joined him in volunteering to carry the Gospel to the men of the Hindu Kush. After such preparations as were possible, this forlorn hope set forth on its errand of mercy to Kaffirastan. The innumerable perils of the way, the thrilling adventures and hairbreadth escapes of the comrades, cannot be touched on in this place, nor may we dwell on the entrancing theme of the secluded land and people now first brought within our ken; suffice it to say that the missioners returned safely, after having accomplished their purpose. Concerning Kaffirastan, Mr. Clark observes, in his valuable book, *Missions in the Panjab and Sindh*:—"The first Christian missionary to that country was an Afghan. He took some medicines with him, and wrote an amusing account of his reception as a medical man, although he had only received one hour's instruction, together with some labelled bottles, from Mrs. Clark. In one place he doctored a girl who was ill with neuralgia, but the girl still went on crying; on which the mother boxed her ears, saying that if she was not well she ought to be, for she had had her medicine. In another place he witnessed the slaughter of twenty-eight unarmed Mohammedans by the Kaffirs. 'The Kaffirs brought a drum and pipes, and began to dance and sing, throwing their hands and feet about, the women looking on; then, suddenly, without one moment's warning, each Kaffir's knife was unsheathed, and seen poised high above his head; and, with a loud whistle, four or five Kaffirs rushed on each Mohammedan, stabbing him in every part. The whole was over in a minute, and all had sunk down dead, covered with wounds. They then beheaded them, and threw them all down into the river below.'"

Fazl i Haqq reported that the wild highlanders had given them a joyous welcome. They had begged for a visit from Europeans, in whom they acknowledged, according to their traditions, "brothers from the far West." On two subsequent occasions an Afghan Christian, Syud Shah, the hero of the episode in Peshawar bazaar, already narrated, followed in the footsteps of the gallant pioneer, Fazl i Haqq, with like success. A "Kaffirastan and Border Mission" was formed, and those valleys of the Hindu Kush were never forgotten in Robert Clark's plans. For the present, the star of hope set when the recent British Boundary Commission handed over the land to the sphere of influence of the Amir of Cabul.

In 1860, the perils of Peshawar were again startlingly

SYUD SHAH KHAN.

emphasised. At a bazaar preaching, Roger Clark had finished his address. As Mr. Tuting rose in his turn, an Afridi ran up, and, in a trice, the long razor-edged Afghan knife was descending with murderous precision. The stroke was foiled by the promptitude of a bystander, and the man was secured. He was a soldier with three years' good service in the famous Guide Corps. Mr. Tuting finished his address as if nothing extraordinary had occurred.

The case of the Rev. Isodore Loewenthal, Mr. Clark's companion in a former exploration, was lamentably tragic. That distinguished linguist had been lent by the Presbyterian Mission to the Afghan work. His charge was to translate the New Testament into Pukhtu. He laboured diligently at his task, working far into the night. Wearied on one such occasion, he wandered into the garden of his house in the cantonments. Lost in thought, he failed to reply to the challenge of his own armed Sikh watchman. Thereupon the man promptly fired, mortally wounding his master, who in a few minutes passed away—the only missionary ever killed in civil life on the Frontier. The text on his monument was, "Well done, good and faithful servant" (*sic!*). That inscription no longer exists: some have it that it was never there; others that its incongruity led to its removal; and yet others that it was noted against the entry in the burial register by a chaplain lacking in a sense of proportion. However this may be, the story has a firm hold on the Frontier. *A priori* there is nothing to militate against it, for all have not the saving grace of humour. In a certain Panjab church the low vestry door by which the clergy enter to minister in holy things was adorned with "The Lord shall go before thee." Immediately underneath followed, "Mind your head"! Nearer home, in the parish church of Portsmouth, may be seen a window in memory of a number of gallant chaplains who fell in the Crimean War. One of the panels represents Balaam and his ass!

CHAPTER XIII.

TRIALS, LOSSES, AND GAINS—CASHMERE.

THE closing of the year 1861 witnessed the gathering in Lahore of the first General Missionary Conference of the Panjab.

Belief in the need of constant mutual intercourse between colleagues was an axiom with Mr. Clark. Those who have no experience of Indian life cannot conceive the disastrous effects of isolation in a land where the environment differs radically from that of our own. It makes men self-centred, dwarfs their horizon, and breeds incredible mischief even between fellow-workers. Mutual confidence can only result from sympathetic understanding born of free intercourse. That is difficult to maintain in India, for it must not be forgotten that the lives of most Europeans are crowded with responsible duties, in a climate which is intensely trying. When the day's work is done, there is a paresis of body and a lethargy of spirits that disincline men, in a manner not understandable in our own land, for even the smallest extra exertion.

Robert Clark, therefore, regarded the assiduous cultivation of courteous personal intercourse with others, and an interchange of the sweet charities of life, not only as a privilege and a duty, but also as a means of grace and a paramount requirement of missionary policy. Thus only were cobwebs to be swept away from weary brains, and pernicious estrangements between brethren nipped in the bud. He strenuously taught these principles throughout life. Those "who only England know" may think that in emphasising these things we are merely apostles of the obvious, but the truth is—as witness the wreck of promising missions and the roots of bitterness that are constantly springing up to defile—that the lesson has still to be learned at the present day.

Mr. Clark considered it peculiarly lamentable that there should be any lack of touch between the various Christian agencies, or strife between the rival herdsmen of Abraham and Lot, while "the Canaanite dwelt in the land." He took a large share in promoting the Conference, and the gathering was held with the happiest results; the wisdom of the whole body of the missionaries of the Panjab was brought to bear on various types of work and on all future plans. The members separated, feeling it had been good for them to be together. Mr. Clark's special work at the Lahore gathering will concern us later.

The little seed planted by Robert Clark and his comrades in 1861 has developed into the stately tree under whose shadow all the scattered tribes of our common Israel now gather in the Decennial Missionary Conference of India. That great Conference has commanded the allegiance of all Protestant missionary bodies, except only the Society for the Propagation of the Gospel, whose episcopal proclivities did not allow of such fraternising, even in the mission field, until the latest Conference, held in Madras.

The year 1862 was a period of sorrow that was

sorely to test Robert Clark. A three-years' struggle with attacks of the terrible Peshawar fever so weakened Mrs. Clark, that in February of that year she was compelled to voyage home. The same hot season brought Mr. Clark the news of his father's death. The Rev. Henry Clark had resigned the cure of Harmston on 16th June, after an incumbency of forty years, and on the 2nd of July he died at Torquay. His last words were, "Christ, Christ, Christ." Grief followed hard on grief. On the 27th of October the beloved Mr. Tuting also passed away. The first pang of that sorrow was scarce spent ere the deadly climate again claimed its toll in Roger Clark, who fell asleep in great peace on 14th January 1863, rejoicing and thanking God with his latest breath that he had been called to be a missionary.

A striking testimony to the worth of those who had gone was borne by the tears of many non-Christians as they followed the funerals of these brethren. To the end of his days, whenever Mr. Clark spoke of Roger, the unconscious wistfulness of his voice told of a love that many waters could not quench, nor years dim.

The condition of the widowed Mrs. Tuting was most precarious. Her constitution had been shattered by Peshawar fever, and death had robbed her of two infant sons within a month, shortly before her supreme loss. She still remembers Mr. Clark's brotherly care of her husband during his illness, and his tender solicitude in arranging her affairs and furthering her journey home. In all things he proved "the most perfect type of Christian gentleman" she ever met.

Sorely bereaved and broken-hearted, Robert Clark carried on the stricken Mission with a dauntless courage born of unflagging faith. He endured hardness as seeing Him who is unseen; and to him the sorrows were not disasters, but pledges of the joy that "cometh in the morning." He was persuaded that "great trials and losses are the very earnest of great spiritual strength and life when at length a mission arrives at manhood. The graveyard that contains the bodies of the missionaries is the garden where the seeds of great missionary success are sown; for our Lord's own promise is that when corns of wheat fall into the ground and die, they abide no longer alone; but when they die, they bring forth much fruit."

He wrote at the time to his wife:—"I felt so much for Mrs. Tuting I cannot tell you. . . . We have all been upset—one burst of tears has succeeded another, and it was only with some difficulty that we could get through the burial service. We have had a season of much heartfelt prayer and communion. . . . And now, how about the future? It was said in my hearing by one that sooner would he live on eighty or a hundred pounds a year at home than in this wretched country, where *the rule*, not the exception, is that friends are torn from one, and husbands, wives, and children are always being separated. If it was *not for our work* he would go home. Yes, that is it, 'if it was not for our work.' What would become of the heathen if we Christians were faint-hearted enough to leave them because stronger men than we are cut off by death and we may any moment follow them? I thought at the time, that we must just be content to suffer and to die—in God's name for the sake of the heathen—to conquer through death as Christ did before us. Yes, we too may be called to give up our lives. Can we do it? We can, God strengthening us. We must just give ourselves to His work—for life—or for death. Let the world call us fools—we will live through death, and let them laugh, but we will win. Pray that we may be faithful—faithful to our Lord. It is He; we will not be afraid. Let us walk closely with Him, and in our union with our brethren, even as He loved us—let us be their servants, as He was ours—and we too shall be received at last into the mansions of light above."

The Rev. Thomas Russell Wade now joined the Peshawar Mission. He is still in the field—the present *doyen* of the Panjab Missions. In him Robert Clark found a steadfast friend and good comrade in the fight. The arrival of Mrs. Clark's youngest brother, James Browne, was also a great solace to Mr. Clark. They lived together in the city, and in the sterling qualities of the young officer of Royal Engineers Mr. Clark foresaw a great future. When, as Government examiner in Pukhtu, he congratulated his brother-in-law on scoring a good pass in that tongue, he added, "I shall see you 'Sir James' yet." Nor was he wrong, for Sir James Browne, universally known by his sobriquet "Buster Browne," had a brilliant career, and has left an honoured name in the annals of Empire builders in India.

The first-fruits from amongst the women were now garnered. On the 27th July 1863, Mr. Clark writes to his wife:—"Another woman has just been here who wants to be baptized together with her husband. The latter is an old Afghan soldier who has long been an inquirer, and the old woman was in a great state about it. She first abused him, then she tried to starve him by not cooking his food, then declared that she was going to leave him, and going to do I don't know what; she would never stay with an infidel, not she! However, she has thought better of it, and came this morning, very humbly, and said her husband after all had been very good to her, and it was no use vexing herself and him about it, and that, if he must become a Christian, why, the best thing would be for her to become one too. I, of course, told her that there was to be no compulsion in the matter, and that if she wished she was quite at liberty to go; and so, being a veritable woman, she was at once ready and eager to stay. However, she wanted to make a bargain, that we were to see she never starved for becoming a Christian. I told her that was a bargain she must make with God, and not with us, and that we could not be responsible about her in any way whatever. These, however, are only the outward features of the story. She seems much humbled and softened, and one cannot but hope that having been, as she has, for now several weeks under the influence of the Gospel, she might be in the way to becoming a good Christian body. She looks honest. How strange that when we had four missionaries' wives we had no native women in the Mission, and now that we are only two bachelors we have so many! I'm thankful I married one of them off yesterday—but we have two unmarried young ladies still, and I am trying hard to get them nice husbands."

The work amongst the men continued full of encouragement. The following incident illustrates Robert Clark's soulful method of considering the claims of each individual case, instead of being hide-bound, as is all too common, in the blighting trammels of routine. An inquirer, well recommended, was brought to him from Amritsar. Mr. Clark says:—"I examined him; he knew the Creed, Lord's Prayer, and Ten Commandments, and not only so, but he appeared to understand them fully, and to believe in them with all his heart. I promised to baptize him shortly. 'But why not now?' was the reply. 'I have been waiting and learning for months.' I told him to wait at any rate one week. 'And who knows that I may live a week?' he said. I was silent for a minute or two, when he broke out with the words, 'The truth is, Sahib, *I am thirsty, and I want to drink.*' The way was quite plain, and although it was Saturday, and I had only seen him twice before, I baptized him on the Sunday. His state was very clear: 'Like as the heart panteth after the water brooks,' so his soul was longing after Christ."

We will let Mr. Clark speak in some detail about an Afghan convert. He calls him "a true Christian, a man whose biography will be written some day in another world, because he is a remarkable instance of great grace." The story shows us how Mr. Clark dealt with these strong Pathans. We note the blossoming of true belief into fruitful deeds under the systematic teaching of God's Word—a marvellous instance truly of the power of the Gospel in its simplicity over that apparently most unpromising of mankind, a ferocious, fanatical, Muhummudan Afghan.

On the evening of the Sunday that witnessed the baptism of the convert already referred to, one Shah Munir came to Mr. Clark. They had met once, over a year before, in February of 1862, at Khairabad. He had inquired into Christianity, and departed with some Christian books. Mr. Clark's notes run:—"He is a

Mullik, or chief man, from Zeyda, a large village in Yusufzai. He had walked four days' journey to inquire about the way to heaven. He is a fine handsome man, about thirty years old, grave and dignified, with the medal of Mooltan and Gujrat hanging from his neck, for he had served as Havildar in the Guide Corps in those engagements. On his arrival he said at once, 'I am a great sinner, and I am in search of God's grace and mercy, and have been so for some years; I am terribly afraid of God's judgment.' His state was that of Christian in the *Pilgrim's Progress*, for he had read a little in the New Testament, and felt the burden of his sins, and his only cry and only thought was, 'What shall I do to be saved?' I asked him if he ever thought of Jesus, and he said he was always thinking of Him. He pointed to the chief artery in his neck, and then put his hand on his heart, and said, 'As quick as this blood passes to my heart, so quickly and as constantly do my thoughts pass to Jesus.'

"15*th June.* During our evening family prayer the subject brought before us was charity, and the necessity of every Christian man laying something by, to give to God, according as God prospered him. The next time I saw him alone, he professed his intention of doing so, and asked to whom, and how, he was to give it, adding that his income was not in money but in kind, and chiefly in wheat from his fields. When one remembers how hardly an Afghan will let one anna leave his hand in charity, this was to me a most encouraging sign. . . .

"17*th June.* A plain avowal from Shah Munir: 'I believe Jesus Christ to be the Son of God, and I look for pardon and life and mercy from Him, and from

Him only.' Long conversations have taken place on all the last days, in which light comes flashing before his eyes, and he seems to see all so clearly. His earnest look of deep thought as he puts down his book to take in some doctrine of Scripture, and then the bright, quiet flash of the eye, showing that the word had hit its mark and the arrow had gone quite home, was greatly cheering.

"19*th June.* Reading St. Matt. chap. v. 39–48, I was almost wishing for his sake that these verses had come later on in the Gospel, knowing an Afghan's sacred duty of *revenge.* I hardly knew what I should say, but I dare not leave it out, as it came in the ordinary place. However, I had (as it happened) nothing at all to say; the word was quite enough alone. His whole face brightened up, as he concluded the few verses and put down the book. 'I have read quite enough to-day,' he said; 'I want no more.' I looked at him, and he then told me why. 'This word,' he said, 'has been medicine to my heart. Look here.' He then slowly took off his turban, which was torn and ragged. 'The people of my village did this,' he said; 'they have only left me this.' He then showed his coat, which had also been torn and mended. 'When I went home, after seeing you at Khairabad in February 1862, I went straight to my village with those books, and called the people round me and showed them to the people, and told them to answer them, or to find out with me whether they were right or wrong. They would not look at them, and told me to give them up. I would not, and they abused me and tore my clothes. Whenever I put on a new suit, they tore it also. I had my eye on them, and marked five or six of them, and meant to have my revenge quietly. I knew I could pay them off. But now, after reading these verses, I see it all plainly. I must do no such thing. I will bear it all, and worse than all this.' A long conversation followed, when he rose up and said, 'Now kneel down and pray for me and with me.' For many days he had now knelt with us—always taking off his turban in the most reverential manner. 'I was a great man in my village before I read these books and knew my power. They dare not have done anything to me then. But my mind is quite changed now; I feel low and much humbled.'"

In writing of this delightful event to his wife, Mr. Clark adds the caution—"Don't let any of this get published, by any means. Converts seem always to go wrong as soon as their names get into print. You may tell everyone who will to *pray* for him."

The returning heat is in India the signal that awakens slumbering legions of tormentors of mankind into vigorous life. With "the voice of the turtle" in the land comes also the hum of the mosquito, the vanguard of a host fraught with pain and peril. In a letter, Mr. Clark refers incidentally to an event by no means uncommon in Indian life. "People are beginning now to go away to the hills, but the weather is very pleasant. I sleep often with two blankets on my bed, and cannot yet keep the windows open at nights. I had a strange visitor two mornings ago—a snake which climbed twenty-five feet up from the ground, up the spout literally, they say, and hid himself under the matting close to my washing-stand. I neither saw nor heard anything of him, however, till I found him dead on my return from school. I have in consequence had the spout stopped up and all the matting taken up until these creatures get underground again. How a snake can crawl twenty-five feet up a smooth perpendicular wall I know not. I thought we were quite out of the reach of all such creatures."

With the passing of the year 1863 new prospects began to loom in the near future for Robert Clark. It was once again to be his lot to relinquish established work, and go forth to be the founder of a Mission in yet another nation and land—namely, in Cashmere. In the hot weather of 1863 he wrote to Mrs. Clark:—

"It is blowing fire here, but I keep cool in my underground room—alone most of the day with my old dog Tohfa ('Delicious'), you called him 'the stuffed crocodile,' and two cats, Spina and Tora ('White' and 'Black'),—one a very large long-haired Persian a native brought me as a present. They like cool places, and wisely never go upstairs till evening. I miss Roger sadly. . . . How I have been longing lately to remain at Peshawur! I love it more and more, the work is so great here, so important. There is so much to be done for the women and girls; unless we gain the women, we do little or nothing; we want you badly, for they take to you, and are, through the men, always asking for you. I am sick of fresh beginnings. In Cashmere, no house, no schools, no converts; no church, no friends, and natives I do not take to. However, it must be; like Abraham, we must strike our tents, and live by faith, build houses for others to live in, sow for others to reap. All last year I was living in native quarters and settling to my Pushtoo work, then came Tuting's and Roger's death and changes, and now others are to come here, and we wander off to Cashmere, and probably Amritsar. It is trying, but if it is God's will we must be content to have no abiding city or continuous work. I have kept up your Sunday almsgiving and preaching,—we had two hundred and ten poor to-day,—several catechists preached very earnestly. Shah Munir and Fazl Kadir are often with me. I feel more real brotherhood with Pathans. So do you and James, who gets on splendidly with them."

In August Mr. Clark set out from Peshawar to preach in and further explore the new land to which he was shortly to be accredited. We shall refrain in these pages from entering into the deep things of Robert Clark's inner personal life. The following letter written to Mrs. Clark on 22nd August from Khanda, on the road to Cashmere, must serve to outline the nature of his thoughts :—

"To-day's march was a short one, and I got in about ten a.m., instead of at twelve, as usual, after breakfasting on the road. A wash and dress soon follows arrival, and a half-hour's snooze, which soon takes off all the fatigue of travelling, and comes naturally after a ride and walk of from five to seven hours daily, over the most wonderfully rough roads imaginable ; then a Pushtu book and one or two other books (of course after one's daily reading of the Bible), then dinner at four, and after dinner preaching. However, to-night it is raining, and besides there is no one here to preach to—and I have had my reading and a talk with the old munshi [teacher] who is with me, and Nunda has just been putting up curtains on the side of the house (for it is only enclosed on three sides, the fourth being open), and I have been walking listlessly about with my hands in my pockets, thinking of all kinds of things—or rather, especially of Elsie and the little ones, and wondering where and how they are, and what they are doing, and how nice it would be if they were here. How I wish you were here to talk to me, and to spend to-morrow (Sunday) with me. Will it be so . . . in a few months? Will Robbie and Henry be coming here too, and playing about on the floor? I hope to find letters from you waiting for me at Sirinagar. Let me see,—this letter will reach England, I suppose, about 1st October. When do you sail? Will it be of any use writing any more? Except, of course, to Alexandria and Aden. But this will probably be mentioned in your letter. May God guide you in everything relating to the time and manner of your journey. It is both safe and pleasant to be led entirely by Him and to seek to do His will. That is, after all, the true secret of happiness—to do His will, and then the end! I always think of the coming of Jesus with more and more joy—the more so as I see more of myself or of others, or of the world generally. Long has the Curse been on the ground and blighted God's creation—but then there will be no more Curse. Long has there been pain and sorrow, but then there will be no more sorrow or crying, for He will wipe away all tears. Long have we been groaning by reason of sin within and without, but then there will be no more sin or death. Long has the world been in darkness, but then will the whole earth see the glory of our God.

"I have been thinking a great deal lately of these railroads; means of communication, and new roads opening out every country, as preparing the way of our Lord. Every valley shall be exalted and every mountain shall be made low, and the crooked made straight, and the rough places plain. Seeing all this is being now done and the whole world is coming together. Journeys will soon be mere nothings. What a glorious world this would be if sin was taken away! But as it is, sin and darkness everywhere prevail. How hard it is for a single person to see and receive the truth! Take the case of the old Nunda, a good old soul as ever lived, and a true help and comfort. He has heard the Gospel for years, and says yes to everything—not as if he never cared or thought about it, but gravely and solemnly, and without the least excuse for not receiving it. Why does he not become a Christian? Then this old munshi who translated the New Testament into Pushtu with Loewenthal, and knows it almost as well as I do,—a nice, simple, unsophisticated old man,—who is always bewailing the state of Mohammedans generally. Why does he not come out and declare himself on the side of Christ? The only answer I can make is by looking into my own heart, and see how hard it was to become a disciple of Christ myself, and how long it was before the seed which had been sown for years took any effect, and then I had nothing to lose—and it was nothing but the hardness and desperate wickedness of my own heart—and here how many other adversaries rise up in a land like this on every side against a man in whose heart the light is struggling for an entrance. However, some day, perhaps, they too will feel in their hearts that the darkness is past and the True Light now shineth. There are doubtless in every country many of those who, like the Eunuch (Acts viii.), of whom we have just been reading with Imam Masih and Jelaluddin, at our evening prayers, who are living up to the light they profess, and will in due time receive more. I am beginning to give up making *plans*. It seems better in every way just to be guided every day and hour by God as the time comes, seeking His aid and guidance in everything, and seeking to have no other desire but His will."

The record of these journeys into Cashmere will occupy us elsewhere in the narrative, and we here only chronicle a single episode. The question that Mr. Clark propounds is one that the British people may well ponder. It bears an intimate relation to their national dignity and material interests abroad, alike in subjected and in foreign lands.

"This evening had quite a gathering and a long talk with the people, and they were civil and listened well, till a man, a sepoy of the Maharajah's, interrupted us rudely and boldly, told my hearers that all the sahibs were bound for hell. I was annoyed, but found that this man had heard missionaries preach in the Panjab, and treated us in Cashmere as he had seen the natives treat us in our own territory. This set me thinking. Why is it that we often meet with rudeness under the English Government, and very seldom in a native state? How is it that natives treat us whenever they dare do so with impunity in a way they would never attempt with their own officials? How far is our Government right in allowing this? An English officer would most likely have knocked the man down, and would be called to account for it. And this only four years after the Mutiny! The natives do not understand our ways."

At the New Year of 1864, Mrs. Clark arrived in Peshawar, and in the spring Mr. and Mrs. Clark bade farewell to the beloved work amongst the Pathans, and took their way as heralds of the Cross to far-famed Cashmere.

CHAPTER XIV.

EARLY DAYS IN CASHMERE.

THE new land that now became the theatre of the Missionary war demands no description in this volume, for "who has not heard of the vale of Cashmere," transcendent in its loveliness, abject in the degradation of its people? It has been aptly written of Cashmere, "Poets have sung of it, historians have commended it, pilgrims have directed their wearied steps to this snow-girt shrine of peculiar sanctity, kings and emperors have deemed their glory incomplete until they have added Cashmere as another jewel to their diadem. Thus, like the Koh-i-Nur, or Mountain of Light, it has been ever coveted, and ever changing hands; with each new master deteriorating more and more, becoming more spoiled, more impoverished, until, bereft of everything, save those grand features of natural beauty which the great Creator had bestowed upon her, Cashmere sits as a weeping widow, until she shall be delivered from the bondage of corruption into the glorious liberty of the children of God."

Mr. Clark writes in his journal:—"The ignorance, darkness, and wickedness of Cashmere seems to be beyond all conception. It is like the dirt in their own city, that lies in the dark winding narrow lanes untouched and unremoved. It is even unnoticed, and is best expressed by the story in one of the Pushtu books which describes the comfort with which a tanner can live all day, and even eat his food with relish, in his own tanyard, whilst strangers are sickened by the sight and smell, and are obliged to leave it because it is to them beyond endurance. The Cashmerees are unconscious of the filth, either physical or moral. 'We have been brought up in it,' they say themselves, 'and so we do not mind it, but if anyone comes from the country, it makes him ill.' The people have been so long imprisoned in the cage that confines the powers and capacities of body, mind, and soul, that, like caged birds, they love their captivity, and have no desire to burst through the bars that enslave them, and become free. Brought up in the dark dungeons of vice and ignorance, they cannot bear the light; and if but one spark appears, they try to exclude it, or else they flee back again from it into their dark abode. Like blind men who have never seen the wonders of creation, they have not the faintest idea of the glories of redemption and sanctification."

The degradation of the Cashmeri in his own fairest of lands is the more profound, in that his intellectual and physical endowments are of the highest order. He is a by-word and a reproach. "Kick him first, then speak, an you would be practical in dealing with the Cashmeri," says the Panjabi proverb, while another declares him to be "abandoned, neither salt nor sweet."

The new land greatly exercised Robert Clark's spirit. "The state of Cashmere," he tells us, "dwells heavily on my mind. The only source of comfort is the Angel's question, 'Is anything too hard for the Lord?' But does it not seem passing strange and wonderful that for generation after generation this country and people should almost seem to have been overlooked and uncared for by their Creator? Yet what a country! Can the choicest gifts of nature have been unsparingly heaped together here; can every advantage of position and climate and fertility and beauty have been crowded together into one little spot,—only that the inhabitants might be given over to ignorance and wickedness, and to Satan for him to work his will on them? It would seem that as man's creation occupied so much more of the Creator's thought and care than that of other creatures, more time and care must have been spent on the adorning of Cashmere than in other lands. Then why neglected, why given up to the spoilers of so many lands and ages, who successively have stripped and degraded it, till it has become a base country, a proverb amongst all surrounding nations? Why do ignorance and vice hold revel here, and why should Satan be allowed to plant his throne so firmly here? With what wonder and surprise do we regard this land! With what wrestling prayers and bold remonstrances may we not besiege the throne of heaven on its behalf! Are Jesus' wounds on His hands and feet no more beheld in heaven? Is that pity which brought down the Son of God to earth no longer manifested? He could not then dwell in heaven, and yet see man perishing on earth. And so He became a man, and dwelt with us, and suffered and died for us. Does this love and pity now remain the same? Can Christ see this land, and not come down with all His Spirit's power? Then why is Cashmere thus given over? In the midst of wondrous natural beauties, when every hill and plain and tree seems to shout aloud for gladness and in praise, has He ceased to care for the people of the land? Is not man here cursed? Are the Cashmerees given up for some former sins, so that God leaves them alone to themselves?"

The sins and ignorance of the people were to Robert Clark the loudest of all calls for help, for "the greater their misery the more their need. Mohammedans though they be, yet Ishmael, when driven out as it were from the Church of God, was not excluded from God's care and left to perish in the wilderness. When dying beneath the desert shrub, his need and misery was the cry which reached heaven, and God heard the voice of the lad." Though Robert Clark felt his ministry was to be "even where Satan's seat is," he went unwaveringly forward with indomitable hope. He states his conviction that "The Lord shall yet arise and have mercy on Cashmere; for it is time that He have mercy on her, yea the set time is come; for why, His servants think upon her stones, and it pitieth them to see her in the dust. . . . We believe, therefore, and doubt not, that these mountains of difficulties shall all be thrown into the sea, and that this garden of the earth shall yet become a garden of heaven. Though, humanly speaking, there seems little hope, yet Jesus is enthroned and has all power in earth and in heaven, and has made known His will that the Gospel shall be preached. Though we see as yet not all things placed under Him, yet we see Him crowned."

The Mission was the third direct outcome of Mr. Clark's journeyings in 1854, and an account of the incidents which took place then, and in subsequent visits in 1862 and 1863, will fitly precede our record of the present developments. His observations convinced him that every opportunity existed in Cashmere for the preaching of the Gospel. He wrote in 1854 :—"All that is attempted in direct missionary work must be carried on under immediate European superintendence. I believe that a native would not be suffered to work alone; but in connection with an English clergyman they may do, I think, as much as they"—the Europeans—"can, even in the capital itself, as well as in the villages and towns. In the present condition of the country, missionary stations cannot be established, nor houses or schoolrooms built; but such are not essential to the carrying out of missionary work. The climate is such that, at any rate during the six or eight summer months, there are the same opportunities of living in tents as, during the cold months, there are in the plains. There are also houses at almost every principal place, expressly set apart for the convenience of European travellers. There can be no difficulty in travelling about with little hill tents to any part of the valley, and spending some weeks, and even months, in each important city and town. The climate is almost an English one, even if not preferable to it, and provisions as yet are everywhere very cheap and plentiful. Any missionaries appointed to this particular sphere of labour would of course learn Cashmeri."

He continues :—"We can go from the Panjab, and with the languages already at our command, which are known either to ourselves or our catechists and readers, we can preach in a manner intelligible to very many of the inhabitants; and if we also have some knowledge of Persian, we can address the greater part of them, or certainly all the better classes, in a language which they can understand."

The pitfalls in the way of the missionary were clear to Mr. Clark. "Our work must be set about warily and discreetly. Many hindrances might arise from influential quarters. The changing, fickle, native mind cannot be trusted for a day, except where self-interest is concerned, and is not above stooping to the meanest and most roundabout ways to accomplish its end." Unremitting caution was necessary. A perfectly simple question, or a remark neither injudicious nor indiscreet, would, on the slightest pretext, be laid hold of by emissaries who were lying in wait to catch the missionary in his words. The traducers would come in all guises—as attendants at the preachings, as inquirers into Christianity, as casual questioners, or as ostensible friends.

One instance of the care which Mr. Clark exercised will suffice. The Deluge was his subject when preaching in the bazaar. He pointed out that, "It was illustrative of a day yet to come, when there would be another, though a different kind of deluge. All sinners whose sins were unremoved would then likewise perish. 'That day has come!' a man cried out from the crowd: 'it came three years ago; and we have hardly been able to get a handful of rice to fill our bellies since.' We said that we alluded to the destruction of the wicked in hell. 'And this, too, is now a kind of earthly hell,' he replied, and then went on with a long story, a great part of which I did not understand. We did not venture to inquire into the details of the deluge which he referred to, as it would not have been wise to do so in the streets of the city, in which other persons besides the sufferers would probably be acquainted with what was meant."

The simplest inquiry would readily have been distorted into an event of political omen, and the report that the missionary was stirring up the people against their rulers, or undermining the Government with the British power, would have gone to the Maharajah, with such amplifications as are a fine art in the East.

Mr. Clark's first interview with Maharajah Gulab Singh took place five days after his arrival in Cashmere. He wrote on 25th May 1854 :—"To-day we had the honour of an interview with the Maharajah. The hour specified was after four o'clock; and so, about a quarter past six, the Maharajah's boat arrived for us. It was a very long boat, with a great many rowers, and towards the fore-part of it was an immense hood, to screen us from the sun, on which account the boat was called the 'buggy.' Beneath the hood was a wide silk-cushioned seat, on which we were all four of us to sit: another cushion lay at our feet. The babu who attends to the sahibs, and who was to introduce us, sat on a carpet upon the floor just before us. We then started, but our pace soon slackened, for we heard that the Maharajah had arranged to meet us in one of his state barges on the river, instead of in his palace, and he was coming up to meet us. In a short time we saw him approaching, propelled, they said, by sixty rowers, with horsemen on each bank, and one bank lined with part of a regiment of soldiers. He was sitting on an arm-chair on a raised dais in the centre of the barge, with a large ornamented canopy over his head. We were invited to enter, and he came to meet us at the side of the barge, and shook hands with each of us. There were arm-chairs placed for us, one on each side of his, and two a little in front, on which we were to sit. Immediately before him, and on his right-hand side, sat the wuzier, or diwan, Jawala Sahai, on the carpet, which was covered with white cloth, with several of the other ministers and attendants, some of them munshis. In the fore part of the barge were some handsomely dressed officers, with shields and pistols and ornamented swords; and beyond them, again, the rowers. The Maharajah was dressed in a neat silk dress, with gold-embroidered turban, and white trousers and sash, and large jewelled earrings. His beard and hair, dyed jet black, were quite shining and glossy, and gave him the appearance of being a much younger man than he really is.

"As soon as we were seated, the barge proceeded. The Maharajah was most affable and courteous: he had a kind word for everybody, and inquired about each one severally. The conversation soon became general, and turned, first, on the beauty of the scenery around us, the mountains, and valley, and river; and then due mention was made of the kindness of his providing houses for us, and sending us daily supplies of bread, etc.; and he seemed much pleased at the appreciation of his attention to English travellers. It then led to steamboats, railways, and electric telegraph; and some actual facts which Major Martin and Captain —— told him as having occurred personally to themselves seemed a little to astonish him, although he had, no doubt, often heard general accounts of them before. One gentleman suggested how nice it would be for him to have a little steamer on the Jhelum for his personal comfort and convenience. He replied that he did not think that it would be of any very great advantage, as he had always two hundred rowers ready to take him anywhere he pleased.

"The news just brought by the telegraph relating to the Russian War was then discussed. He asked how it was that all these telegraphs and railways in England were not made by the Government; and this led us to speak of the number of Companies established in England for almost every purpose. We then told him that there were Companies for religious as well as secular purposes. There was the Bible Society, which yearly circulates thousands of copies of the Scriptures; and there was the Church Missionary Society, which sent Padres to every part of the world, to make known to all men the doctrines of Christianity, and that I was one of these Padres.

"The conversation then assumed altogether a religious tone. He asked what were the principal doctrines of the Gospel, and was told they were the sinfulness of fallen man, and his restitution to the favour of God by the merits of Christ. He then wished to know what became of men after death, and added that their belief was that good men would be saved by the merits of their own works: and, without waiting for a reply, he went on to speak of the attributes of God; that, as He was never created, the world was also never created, for God was in the world, and the world was in God; the Deity being the soul, and the matter the body, which could do nothing, and could not exist, without the all-pervading energy of the spiritual being within. We told him that, as the maker of the house was distinct from the house itself, so was the Deity distinct from the work which His hands had made.

"He then asked why God had made men so different in this life; why one man suffered, and another enjoyed the good things of life; referring, we supposed, to the transmigration of souls, and to their reward or punishment in this life for the actions of a prior state of existence. He went on to try and prove the reasonableness of idolatry, by the usual argument that, as one sun is reflected a thousand times in as many basins of water, so everything that exists is but the reflection of the Deity, who is the Sun of all light and glory; and then he added, that all religions are true, although they may be distinct; a proof of which is that all human faces are faces of men, however distinct one face may be from another. We answered him, in each respect, with the best proofs that occurred to us at the time, and referred especially to the love of God, and also as to the necessity of being prepared for death; and then took our leave, and returned to the buggy, much pleased with his kindness and cordiality, and with a great desire to renew the conversation at some future time. The buggy soon carried us home, and the Maharajah proceeded up the river by torch-light."

The next day was memorable. Gulab Singh had seen the missionary; Mr. Clark now arranged that he should see Panjabi Christians. It was a fine piece of Christian statesmanship. For the first time, a Sikh sovereign ruler was brought into contact with the Christian converts from Amritsar, one of whom, it will be remembered, had himself been a Sikh priest. That these apostate outcastes should be honourably received by the Maharajah was a lesson to the kingdom, while the Maharajah himself could not but be impressed with the reality of the faith that had been brought to his dominions. We are fortunate in possessing Mr. Clark's description of this interview also.

"We yesterday presented the robe of many colours to the Maharajah. It was taken by the three Christians, who, all together, with the bearer who carried it, were ushered into the room where the Maharajah was sitting. Their account is that there were a hundred people present, together with two sahibs,—probably two Englishmen in the Maharajah's service, who translate the papers to him, etc.,—and Dr. Honingberger, and his usual attendants. The report is that His Highness and his Court were examining it for half an hour; that he was most graciously pleased to accept it, and gave five rupees to each of the Christians and also to the bearer. They were told to be seated, and he called them one by one to him, asking them who they were. They told him that they were Christians. He asked them why?—and what Christianity was? They told him about the two great commandments, love to God and man; and said that the reason why they became Christians was that no religion but the Gospel revealed the Saviour who could cleanse from sin, and gave pardon and peace to the soul. He then asked them if they really believed it, or whether they were induced to become Christians for temporal advantages; and when they said that they felt its truth in their hearts, and were convinced that it was from God, he told them that if such was the case they had acted rightly, and that it was well that they had become Christians. It seems that the conversation on religious subjects was carried on for some little time, and that he was led to give them the opportunity before his whole Court, which they well made use of, to declare openly and boldly the fundamental doctrines on which they rest their faith.

"I heard afterwards that patchwork robes are usually worn by fakirs in this country, and are often of great value—*i.e.*, those possessed by the rich—and that Gulab Singh, when he first saw it, said that it was a most beautiful robe, and that 'it would do very well for a fakir.' However, when it was explained to him that our English customs were different from those in this country, and that it was sent merely as a mark of esteem and respect, he appeared much pleased. I have no doubt that its effect will be very good, and that the result will be that intended and hoped for."

On the 31st of May the Maharajah gave a public dinner to the British residents. Mr. Clark thought it well to go, on the ground that, by doing so, "we should not only show respect to the Maharajah, but also that our presence might remind him of the object of our journey, and thus bring the great subject of religion indirectly before him; at the same time that possibly we might be able to speak a word bearing upon it; and thus it would be well for us, in our character as Christian teachers, as well as that of English travellers, to be present on this public occasion.

"However, as we heard that there was to be a nautch [performance by dancing girls] before it, we told the babu that we should come after it was over, as we could not consistently be present at it. Contrary to our particular directions, the babu told the Maharajah about our scruples, and the Maharajah at once sent a special request that we would come at the usual time, and that we could remain in another room until the nautch was over. We went accordingly. On our arrival we were ushered in, and introduced in due form. The Maharajah expressed very great joy at seeing us, and immediately took Major Martin by one hand and me by the other, and took us we did not know where with him, and said, 'Well, let us go in;' and thus, hand in hand, we went in together to an open terrace, where the other officers were assembled. The carpeted ground was covered with white cloth, the stars were glittering overhead, and torches were flaming in every direction: servants and natives with rich and gaudy dresses were standing about. A large number of chairs were placed round three sides of a square, for there were fifty English officers present. The Maharajah led us to the centre of the whole, seated himself, and directed us to do the same, one on each side of him. The other officers sat down, and he turned to me and said, 'Now they will have their nautch, and we will talk together about religion.' We were completely taken in: the dancing had begun.

"Before we had been seated many minutes, the Myan Sahib, or heir apparent, Rajah Runbeer Singh, came in and took his seat next to Major Martin; and, in rising to make room for him, our places were somewhat altered, and I got next to Major Martin, and between him and the Maharajah. The Myan Sahib was on the other side of Major Martin. A conversation ensued, both with the Maharajah and the Myan Sahib, on the subject of religion, and especially with the latter. They both asked why we did not like to come, and whether the nautch was expressly forbidden in our Gospel. We told them that it was not mentioned by name, as the custom did not exist in the countries where it was written; but that Christians aimed after higher pleasures, which gave far more enjoyment, and which left no disrelish or dissatisfaction in the mind behind them. The Maharajah then said, 'I suppose you think that such amusements are hindrances which make men stop and loiter on the way to heaven, instead of pressing onward; that such things pull men backward, so that they cannot hasten forward and enjoy these pleasures too?' 'Precisely so, your Highness,' we replied. 'All true Christians wish to be freed from all such obstacles, which are the stumbling-blocks of many.' 'And then,' he said, 'the road is clear—you have no obstructions.' The Myan Sahib then asked, 'What are the Christian's pleasures?' We answered that they were spiritual ones: the Christian enjoyed Christ; Christ was present in his heart, by His Holy Spirit, to give His righteousness in the place of man's sinfulness—His wisdom instead of man's ignorance—His holiness instead of man's proneness to evil, etc. I cannot sufficiently state the value of being with Major Martin on such occasions: many such conversations, and their seeming impressions, have been entirely owing to him. He stated, also, with great force and clearness, a little time afterwards, when the conversation turned on England's greatness, that it was entirely due to England's recognition of the hand of God, and her endeavour, in some measure at least, to walk according to the commandments of God. 'Whenever,' he said, 'any country does this, it is sure to become great and prosperous; but the moment that we, or any other nation, forsake the law of God, that moment the nation begins to fall.' May such advice sink deeply into the heart of the prince who heard it!

"During all this time the dancing was going on, but the music and singing were so loud that our conversation was unheard by others. I did not observe anything improper in any degree in what was going on. The poor singers and dancers walked backwards and forwards, sat down occasionally, turned round and made grimaces, and sometimes threw about their arms a little; and their singing was not exactly in accordance with either tune or taste. All natives, it may be remarked, despise us for our way of dancing at balls, and there is, perhaps, nothing we do which makes them think evil of us more than our balls do. In the first place, they have the idea that it is improper, in the highest degree, for a man to dance with any woman, especially one not in any manner related to him; in the next place, they wonder why we give ourselves the trouble to dance, and ask why we do not pay other persons to dance instead of ourselves; for the English, they say, have always plenty of money.

"I should state that the Maharajah mentioned the robe we had presented to him. I took the opportunity of thanking him for the very kind manner in which it had been accepted. He thought it was my memsahib who had made it, and asked where she was. I told him that I was unmarried. He said he had been thinking of a present to send in return. I hoped, of course, I said, that he would not mention such a thing, as a return present was never expected. 'But I must,' he replied, 'send something to the memsahib.' 'Well,' I said, 'if it is to be for the memsahib, of course I must not say anything about it. I am sure the memsahib will consider it a very great honour to receive anything from your Highness.'

"Dinner was announced, and we all went in and found our places. We had both taken the precaution to dine beforehand, as we were not quite sure what we would meet with: however, everything was very nice, and plenty of it. When dinner was over, they drank the Maharajah's health. During the dinner he had remained in the next room. We immediately went up to him and took our leave, and returned home."

The preliminary exploration of 1854 was followed by another in the summer of 1862. On that occasion the Rev. W. Phelps, an Indian chaplain, accompanied Mr. Clark. As in the earlier campaign, they found endless opportunity for preaching. Much to rejoice their hearts mingled with the stubborn opposition to the invasion of the Gospel. In some places the people were frantically noisy, in others indifferent, and in still others shut their ears or boycotted the preacher.

An incident may suffice to illustrate the cruder forms of opposition. Mr. Clark writes:—"During our preaching the people were much excited, and again clapped and yelled us out of the place. Yesterday I partly lost my temper myself, and felt that little good was done. To-day I was enabled to keep it, although the people were far more insulting, and therefore I felt happy. There were a number of people from Kabul, brought evidently by the boy we saw yesterday. Our friend from Swat was also there, and many Cashmeris. The latter are dreadfully irascible, and seem as if they hardly knew what they were doing; they are, however, great cowards, and only bark when they know they will not be bitten. The Kabulis seem rather desperate fellows. One of them, for a considerable time together, kept crying out to our face, 'That's a lie! It's a lie, a lie, a lie!' The Cashmeris heaped insult upon insult, and talked about 'this fellow going about all Cashmere deceiving and misleading the people,' and said the English had taken every country by deceit and wickedness. However, it was a very favourable opportunity. The word was plainly spoken, and spoken in kindness, without mention of their religion, or any irritating expression. May it bring forth much fruit!"

On the same day, Mr. Clark notes an example of the encouragements that constantly cheered him. "A very nice and seemingly thoughtful pandit called on me with three questions, which he had never been able to solve. The first was, What was I before my birth? What am I now? and, What shall I be after death?—alluding, I suppose, to transmigration,—but a most important question. Another question, put from the occasion of my answer, referred to sleep. What is sleep? He then turned to another point, and said that all religions profess that men are reconciled to God through a mediator; the Hindus through Vishnu, the Mohummudans through Mohummud, the Christians through Christ. What is that reconciliation? What is it to be reunited to God? The answer I gave him from the Bible to this seemed to strike him much. He seemed a more candid and earnest inquirer after truth than I have met with for a long time."

This inquirer accompanied the missionary to the public preaching, and remained through the trying time detailed above. "Just before he left," writes Mr. Clark, "he said, 'Sir, I was born a Hindu, but my mind is not at rest. I have examined Mohummudanism, but still do not find peace. I am just now neither a Hindu nor a Mohummudan.'"

On his homeward way from Cashmere, Mr. Clark advocated the claims of that country in a sermon preached at the hill station of Murree, and it was published at the instance of Sir Robert Montgomery, then Lieutenant-Governor of the Panjab. A requisition, influentially supported, was immediately sent to the Church Missionary Society urging it to promote a Mission in the mountain kingdom, and the Lieutenant-Governor was the first to sign the invitation. His donation of a thousand rupees in aid of the proposed Mission was the nucleus of a fund that the generous liberality of friends rapidly augmented to over fourteen thousand rupees.

As we have already seen, in 1863, Mr. Clark, joined later by the Rev. W. Smith of Benares, carried out another preliminary tour of evangelisation and survey in Cashmere. During these months he matured his plans, formulated his policy, and in 1864, together with Mrs. Clark, founded the Cashmere Mission under circumstances now to be detailed.

CHAPTER XV.

THE CASHMERE MISSION.

AT the time of the British annexation of the Panjab, the leading spirit in that country was Gulab Singh. The greatest of Ranjit Singh's nobles and the powerful chief of the martial Dogras, he wielded an enormous influence over the fortunes of that distracted and war-riven land. A treaty concluded between him and the conquerors ceded the Land of the Five Rivers to the British, and secured him in the sovereignty of Jammu, Cashmere; and the Trans-Himálhyan provinces of the empire of the "Lion of the Panjab." These fair lands were consolidated into one magnificent kingdom, over which Maharajah Gulab Singh ruled as the first king of the Dogra dynasty. The winter capital of the kingdom was at Jammu, the chief town of the territories of that name. In the summer, the seat of government shifted to the great city of Srinagar, "the most honourable town," as its name implies, in the heart of the Vale of Cashmere.

The terms of the treaty between the contracting powers provided that British officers should be admitted to Cashmere during the summer months only, and then by special permission, and to a strictly limited number. They were under stringent regulations, and were restricted to certain portions of the country and specified routes of travel. Under no circumstances could a European or a British subject own landed property in the dominions of the Maharajah. Guest-houses were built at suitable spots in Cashmere for the convenience of European visitors, and a special quarter in the environs of Srinagar was set apart entirely for their residence. Agents were appointed to attend to their wants, and all business was transacted through a babu, deputed for that purpose.

This system effectually isolated visitors from the real life of the land. From the moment of their entrance into the territories of the Maharajah until they quitted the same, it placed them under an espionage none the less vigilant because intangible and unostentatious. The Maharajah thus sought to secure his domains against the dreaded encroachments of the new masters of the Panjab.

The establishment of a Mission in Cashmere roused the most uncompromising hostility on the part of the Maharajah. We have already noted the personal friendship and appreciation he had for Mr. Clark. As a Sikh, Muhummudanism was a thing abhorrent to him; he knew his subjects, and had refused to interfere with the dissemination of Christianity in their midst. That religion he knew to be good, yet he waged bitter ceaseless war against the Mission. The reason was neither spiritual nor social, but political.

The history of British India presents to the native mind nothing but a long record of strenuous insidious advances, resulting in successive absorption of independent kingdoms. The virulent Cashmeri mentioned in the preceding chapter truly voiced the certainty that dominates the Indian mind on this subject. The establishment of a permanent Mission in Cashmere was therefore looked upon as marking the first subtle steps of the British in the path of annexation, and, as such, had to be fought in the most uncompromising manner. As the result the Mission was to be founded in no halcyon days, but amidst much tribulation.

From the very beginning, Mr. Clark realised that the success of the Mission hinged on the permanence of his occupation and of residence amongst the people, and the best tribute to his discerning statesmanship was the implacable hostility with which his plans were met by Gulab Singh. His policy was to take up his abode, year in year out, in the city of Srinagar itself. A mere summer occupation, he considered, was no solid foundation on which to rear the edifice of the Cashmere Mission. To live among the visitors was to sacrifice the work. Mr. Clark puts the matter plainly in a memorandum that he drafted when the Maharajah was straining every nerve to compel him to reside in the European quarter. "This, it seems to me, is the last step to ruin our Mission. It is seen that once outside the city, I am no longer connected with the people. Let us be in a house separated from others, a house without any compound, with a river before, and an open plain behind, and they can *easily* keep everyone from us, *as they have done before.* Let us once be mixed up with visitors, and we are no longer in the eyes of the people set apart as sent *to them.* In the midst of young officers (often leading most immoral lives); in the midst of officers' servants, soldiers, spies; in a place where only a few privileged tradesmen are allowed to sell, and hardly even to come; in a spot visited nightly by the women of the town, and within hearing perhaps of the drunken song (I speak from knowledge),—it is but little indeed that can be hoped for, for the success of a Christian Mission. Who will ever visit us there? Not anyone in the Maharajah's employ, for there is an order against any servant of the Government having any communication with any sahib whatever. Not any Cashmeri, for who would dare to do so when the whole Government are against it, and people are set to keep them off. Whereas, in the city, they can, to a certain extent, come and go as they will, without observation."

Having settled on his policy, Mr. Clark brought characteristic energy and sagacity to bear on its development. French shawl merchants lived in the city, and in the absence of any local law to forbid him as a non-official European from following their example, he set about finding a suitable house. It was hopeless to make the attempt in Cashmere itself, but Amritsar is a strong Cashmeri centre, and to it Mr. Clark turned. Negotiations set on foot in that city in 1863, after long delay and disappointments, were crowned with success in 1864. Through the good offices of an Amritsar friend, Mr. Cope, a house was rented for one year from a certain Ghulam Hassan, a Cashmere merchant resident in that city. The house was well adapted for the purposes of the Mission. It was centrally situated in Srinagar city, on the river Jhelum, which with its canals and tributaries forms the highways and byways of that Venice of the East. Mr. Cope paid the three hundred rupees of rent at once, for he "considered the payment in advance a great deal more binding than the agreement." The wisdom of this course became apparent. No sooner was it generally known that the Mission was intended to be permanent, than difficulties cropped up in abundance. Ghulam Hassan, under pressure from Jammu, did his best to evade the agreement into which he had entered. When this failed, the Maharajah changed his tactics. A mob was commanded to oust the missionary from the house that had been secured.

Late on the night of 15th April, Mr. Clark's boats reached Srinagar in heavy rain. He was anxious to push on at once to the shelter of his home, but the servants he had sent forward returned with the report they had been driven back with threats and stones by four hundred men, who were determined not to allow him to set foot in his abode. The boats halted for the night at the entrance to the city. Mr. Clark, sincerely anxious to avoid unnecessary strife, had resolved to go temporarily next day to the visitors' quarters, when a new aspect was put on affairs by Shah Munir Khan.

That prompt and fearless Afghan, who had accompanied his beloved teacher from Peshawar, had gone on an exploration on his own account. As a result of his observations in the city, he reported the house prepared and vacant, and the neighbourhood quiet. Though sentinels were on the watch, Mr. Clark thought good generalship might effect a landing. Early next morning, according to his wont, he broke camp, and the boats arrived without let or hindrance at his own doorstep. The enemy, not expecting him to move till later, were completely forestalled. But the guile of the East is a bottomless pit, and its wiles are many and crafty. Though the compound was open, the house was locked. The gardener promptly went off "to fetch the keys," a euphemism for running post haste to inform the authorities that the Mission had stolen a march on the mob. The party waited in the rain. To them came Monsieur Gosselin, a French shawl merchant, their neighbour across the river. "Mrs. Clark cannot wait out here in the rain," said he; "the bungalow is yours, and should have been open to receive you." At his command, one of his servants speedily broke open the native padlock with a small hatchet, and, having done what he could, this kindly neighbour left the missionary party to settle into the new home.

While the boats were being unloaded, the enemy opened his next attack. A certain Sheikh Aziz arrived and demanded what Mr. Clark was doing in his house. He did his best to rouse an altercation, but, unable to make headway against the dignified reasoning of Mr. Clark, had to retire discomfited. Then came the grand assault planned by the myrmidons of the Maharajah.

An hour or two after the aforesaid Aziz went away, "the house was literally besieged with men and noisy boys. They stood by hundreds on the bridge, and lined the river on both sides, shouting, and one man striking a gong to collect the people. Not a chuprasse, or police officer, or soldier, or official of any kind appeared. The tumult quickly increased, and no efforts were made to stop it. The people began to throw stones, and some of them broke down the wall of the compound and stables. Our servants became greatly alarmed, for they threatened to burn the house down. The number present was between one thousand and one thousand five hundred.

"In the midst of all, my surprise was great to see Monsieur Gosselin crossing over the bridge from the other side, alone, with a hunting whip in his hand, which, however, he never used. The people fled from him like sheep; but at last, returning, they surrounded him, shouting and gesticulating, and throwing their hands wildly about over his head. My first thought was to go out and join him, as I had great fears for his safety, but I felt that my doing so would only greatly increase the tumult. I feared they would crowd and press round him; and as the bridge had no protection on the sides, I knew that the least push would precipitate him into the swollen river below. He told me afterwards that *his* only fear was that the bridge would give way under the weight of so great a crowd, as one of them last year did, when many people were killed in its fall. However, on he went, and I sent three men to him to urge him to come in, and not to expose himself in such a way."

This gallant French gentleman went to the chief Maulvie, or Moslem divine, to induce him to still the tumult, but in the meantime the mob continued to swell and grow in violence. "The native Christians were all with me," says Mr. Clark, "and it was suggested that we should join in prayer to ask for God's protection. I read Acts iv. 18–33, and we then commended ourselves into our Heavenly Father's hands. The words were full of comfort and encouragement, for we too were being 'threatened' for having come to Cashmere 'to speak in the name of Jesus.' But 'why do the heathen rage, and the kings of the earth stand up, and the rulers gather themselves together against the Lord and against His Christ?' It calmed every thought when we could tell the Lord to 'behold their threatenings' and ask Him to 'grant unto His servants that with all boldness we might speak His Word, and that great power and grace might be upon us all.' Not till we had concluded did Monsieur Gosselin return."

The Maulvie professed himself unable to deal with the uproar, for who dared interfere with a riot instigated by the authorities? Monsieur Gosselin "told us that the matter was becoming serious; and that it was far worse than he had imagined, for the mob had been let loose, and some of them were much excited."

During that year the wily Maharajah had remained in his winter capital of Jammu, and the British Resident had not yet arrived in Srinagar. Prompt action was therefore necessary. Mr. Clark notes in his journal:—"I took my determination at once. Monsieur Gosselin promised to remain with my wife and children to protect them, and, if necessary, to take them across the river to his own house. I opened the river door, and, amidst the yells of the people, got slowly into a boat, so that they might not think I was running away from them, and then went off, as quickly as the rowers could convey me, to the Wazeer, at the palace in the Sher Gharri."

The situation required deep knowledge of the East. Instead of waiting in the boat until he was announced, Mr. Clark nipped all subterfuges in the bud by at once following the usher into the Court of Justice, where sat the disconcerted Lala Shankar Dass, deputy of the Wazeer. The Prime Minister was not himself visible. Messengers reported him to be asleep. He could not be awakened, that would be against all etiquette; and, contrary to his usual custom, on that particular day he had retired for his slumbers into the women's apartments, where no message dare follow him. It was all part of the official scheme. The authorities had carefully planned a rising of the populace. They could not be held responsible for the occurrence of a sudden peril, of which, moreover, they had no knowledge. They would deplore the untoward results of a riot they disclaimed, and punishments would be zealously meted out with liberal hand. In this way there would be a splendid opportunity for officials to profit by mulcting the rich; and as for the rest, what mattered any number of Cashmeris, less or more, so that, in time to come, the missionary was effectually barred from a foothold in the city?

Mr. Clark's unexpected appearance, however, forced their hands, to the destruction of their hopes. Messengers sped to various parts of the city, and the deputy instructed the Chief of the Police to take instant action.

The writer has a vivid recollection of that day. His mother watched the howling mob with an amused smile, and so interested her children in the doings of the crowd that they forgot to be terrified. The huge gathering swayed and surged round her house and at her doors, threatening, yelling, hooting as only Cashmeris can, while she faced them with unruffled mien. Suddenly a hush came over the assembly, then all was calm, and in a few minutes the mob had silently melted away. The word had come from Headquarters.

Mr. Clark waited while successive messengers reported that the Wazeer still slumbered. He was treated with the studied contumely and insolence that Orientals excel in barbing with a surface politeness. He sat neglected, on the ground, like the humblest native petitioner, and this in the very palace where he had been an honoured guest, and at the hands of officials whose royal master had showered signal favours upon him. Further extracts from Mr. Clark's journal will best tell the story.

"My anxiety may be imagined, as half-hour after half-hour passed away. I had left my wife and children in the midst of a yelling, excited mob, and knew not what might be happening to them. At one time I rose, and was about to proceed myself to the Wazeer's house, but was told that it was impossible. Other messengers were despatched to see if he was awake, and some were sent to different parts of the city. In about an hour and a half the Kotwal's—the Chief Constable's—report arrived that he had been to the house, and had himself cleared the streets. This was a relief indeed; but I had still long to wait. I knew that I must see the Wazeer. Had I returned without doing so, the whole city would have said that the Padre Sahib had been himself to the Wazeer, and that he had refused to see him. The consequences would have been even worse than before, for the people would have felt that they might treat us as they would.

"My patience was at last rewarded. There was a hum in the crowded Court that the Wazeer was on his way to the Durbar. I rose from my seat on the ground, and at once followed him there. He even did not give me a chair. His manner outwardly was kind enough, as he assured me, apparently with much concern, that whatever was the cause of the disturbance, a Governor's first duty was to put it down, and he had done so. It was hard to see how he could have done this when asleep the whole time in the recesses of the women's apartments, where no one dared to go either to tell him of the disturbance or of my having come to see him; but of course nothing was said of this, and I simply told him of the strange reception we had met with at our own hired house, and claimed his protection for an English lady and two little English children. We had just arrived when we met with this demonstration and anything but a friendly welcome. He said in reply that there were many houses outside the city especially set apart for European visitors, any one of which was at my service. I told him the object of my coming to Cashmere, which was not that of other visitors, but was to teach God's Word to the people. He replied that other sahibs did not go to live in the city. I reminded him of Monsieur Gosselin, whose house is exactly opposite to ours. 'Yes,' said he, 'but he is a merchant, and his work lies in the city.' 'And our work too,' I replied, 'lies also in the city, with the people to whom we have been sent.' Someone then whispered at some length into his ear, and he then said he would send a guard down to our house *for two days*, but he could not send it always. I took my leave, and he still appeared very friendly."

Needless to add, the guard never came. In the afternoon the people reported the Wazeer as being "angry with them for allowing us to occupy the house at all, and is still more angry for [their] making the disturbance to no purpose after we had done so. We feel that we owe our preservation and our present possession of this house, under God, to the kindness and courage of Monsieur Gosselin. Mr. Budge, the English gardener of the Maharajah, also came down to render assistance the moment he heard of the disturbance, and he sleeps to-night at Mr. Gosselin's to be ready at hand in case of further alarms."

The efforts to nullify the lease had been nugatory, the attempt to frustrate entry into the house had broken down, and mob intimidation had signally failed. But the Maharajah well understood the deep issues at stake. He returned to the charge, and, as is the custom in the Orient, the next attempt was to be deadly. A report was industriously circulated that the missionary had pledged himself in open court to vacate the house within two days. Plans were concerted. The Wazeer departed to a distant part of the Valley; and the authorities gave battle.

We find from Mr. Clark's journal, that on the morning of 18th April "Two messengers, one after another, appeared from the palace to say that the Wazeer had gone away for a few days from Srinagar, and requesting me to keep the promise that I had made to him to leave this house in two days' time. The message was from Lala Shunkar Dass, the Wazeer's deputy, who informed me that although he had been able to keep the people quiet by telling them of my own promise to leave the neighbourhood, yet it was impossible that he would be able to restrain them much longer. As an additional reason for our leaving, the messengers reported that Lala Shunkar Dass had heard that we had broken into a room in our own house and had removed some property of the owner. We must indeed be surrounded by spies who watch our every step." A few worthless pieces of furniture had been removed from one room to another, "and that," continues Mr. Clark, "is brought against us by the chief authority in Srinagar as an act of violence on our part, although, having rented the whole of the house, we were clearly entitled to the use of any room we pleased. We had all heard the Wazeer promise to send a guard down to the house for two days (which he had never done), but no other promise had been heard or had been given. As regards the implied threat of renewed disturbances if we did not leave, I reminded Lala Shunkar Dass that a single word had before at once removed every annoyance; that there could hardly be any difficulty in affording protection from an unwarlike, timid people like the Cashmerees; and that it would be creditable neither to them as rulers of the country, nor to me as an Englishman, to leave the house by the order and intimidation of a noisy mob. I told him also that the Resident would be here in a few days, when the whole matter would be decided. The reason of this reply was that we felt perfectly sure that if we once left the house, we never again should be allowed to occupy it. The slightest concession is always misunderstood by natives. Reasons are misinterpreted; the best motives are attributed as mere excuses put forward to hide weakness; so that, however desirous of giving way and conciliating them by every justifiable measure, there is nothing more damaging, nothing that more multiplies difficulties, or leads to more ruinous consequences, than voluntarily to give up that which belongs to one as a right, when no good can follow from it, merely to satisfy the wishes of a native's mind."

It was clear that the Wazeer had left simply to be out of the way. The Moslems were being put forward to achieve the purpose of the Government, and mischief was determined against the missionary. The authorities would plead that they had restrained the mob as long as they could. Mr. Clark had the warning of the previous riot; they had sent him urgent messages; he deliberately chose to incur the swift-coming dangers of Moslem fanaticism, and his, therefore, would be the blame. Mr. Gosselin came in after the messengers had left. In his opinion "there was a very fair chance of the house being really attacked, and perhaps even burnt, and a probability that we might lose everything and run considerable risk of personal safety. Affairs again began to appear very serious, and for a few moments we almost doubted whether it would not be necessary to leave the house until the Resident arrived."

The fateful moment in the history of the Cashmere Mission had come. Everything now depended on the course adopted. Mr. Clark tells us:—"My dear wife was the person to decide the matter, by declaring that we would not go, that we were in the path of duty, that she was not afraid either for herself or the children, but was confident that God could and would protect us, and that at any risk we ought to remain. M. Gosselin then turned to me, and asked if that was my opinion too. I replied that I could not feel comfortable in leaving, for I felt that it would be shrinking from a difficulty, instead of trusting to God to bear us through it; that there was, after all, no present necessity for leaving; and that I too thought that we ought at any rate to try to remain. 'Then my determination,' he said, 'is taken. I shall ride down to the Shekh Bagh as fast as my horse can carry me, and collect all the Europeans I can find to come and protect you.' An hour and a half afterwards he returned, bringing with him Mr. Budge and Mr. O'Reilly, both in the Maharajah's service. They were the only Englishmen in Srinagar, for though he had heard that two English officers had arrived, he found on going to the spot that it was not so. He had explained to them what was going on, and all three had gone straight to the palace and had told Lala Shunkar Dass that they had resolved to stand by us, and that they threw on him the whole responsibility of whatever might occur. This bold appeal turned at once the whole course of affairs. It was like a thunderbolt amongst them. Orders were sent to the Kotwal to allow of no gathering of people whatever, and very soon the Kotwal himself appeared at our house, and left with us one of his men to send him word at once of the slightest appearance of uproar. Thus has Monsieur Gosselin, a French gentleman and a Roman Catholic, been the means under God of again preserving us. I cannot sufficiently admire also the bold and noble action of Messrs. Budge and O'Reilly, who, although both of them in the Maharajah's service, thought neither of possible injury to their private prospects nor of any personal danger to themselves, but went straight with Monsieur Gosselin to the highest officer in the palace to tell him what they were going to do, and then came down to us with the determination to protect an unarmed missionary, together with his wife and children, from every attack. Thus God provides for and defends His people."

The Government now prepared to deliver the next attack. Meanwhile a close blockade was established. On 20th April, Mr. Clark notes: "Men are again stationed on the bridge, as they were for weeks together last year, to prevent anyone from coming to us. Our servants cannot buy the mere necessaries of life, and we have to send strangers to the other end of the city to purchase flour."

Force had been foiled, the authorities now resorted to diplomacy. They struck a crushing blow on 24th April. On that day, Robert Clark chronicles the receipt of the following letter from Mr. Cooper, the British Resident, who was on his way to Cashmere: "My dear Sir,—The Maharajah of Cashmere has addressed me to-day in regard to a slight disturbance which appears to have occurred in regard to your obtaining possession of a house for rent in the city, and he begs me to request that you will have the kindness to occupy one of the bungalows set apart for European visitors. I should feel obliged by your regarding the wishes of the Maharajah on this subject. I hope very soon to have the pleasure of making your acquaintance, when I will do my best to smooth all difficulties in your way, with the nature of which I am of course at present not accurately acquainted."

"So the native Government," comments Mr. Clark, "having itself created a disturbance against us, is making use of it to seek to remove us from the city, through the English authorities. They have succeeded in influencing the Resident to request us to leave it. If we do so, their point is gained; and if we do not leave, they think they have put us in direct opposition to our own Government. It is a skilful move. In either case it seems as if our great object of living amongst the people, and teaching them by example as well as by word, by constant intercourse, must be defeated. It was thought that the tumult would itself expel us. If it did not, the fact of there having been a disturbance still remained, and it could still be represented in such a manner as to show that our remaining in the city was impracticable, or at the least inexpedient. The whole country is against us, and it would seem as if we were becoming involved with our own Government too. Which way shall we turn, and what shall we do? Our eyes are on Him who sent us here. He is a great and a wise Captain, and we will leave it with Him to order the fight with all our foes, even principalities and powers though they be. If He means us to remain, they cannot expel us from it. Yet if He would have us retire, it is not we, but He, who retires and leaves one position to take up a better. His eye is over all, and can take in all with a simple glance. Our horizon is contracted, our wisdom and forethought is folly. We therefore only follow Him wherever He leads, whether in advance or retreat. Wherever He goes or stays, we are with Him.

"We cannot trust to our English Government, Christian though it be. It is better to trust in the Lord than to put confidences in princes. We stand here alone, sent and upheld by Him. . . . We therefore lie down and rise up in peace and tranquil joy. The Lord is our Keeper, our Shade from the sun, our Shield from the foe, our Guide, and Guard, and our eternal Reward."

In his reply to the Resident, Mr. Clark traced the sequence of events from the execution of the lease to that date, 26th April. He sent extracts from his journals. "I will simply state my firm belief," he wrote, "that when you are acquainted with the whole facts of the case . . . you would yourself wish me to remain in the bungalow until a full investigation has been made. I feel sure that you will not deem it to be a want of respect to you, as the representative of a Government which is honoured by every friend of Missions both in this country and at home, to ask you most kindly to permit us to remain here until then. We ask for no injustice to others; we ask for no unfair favour to ourselves. But I cannot but feel that your decision in this matter will stamp the character of this Mission, perhaps for many years, in the minds of the natives; and that on your action may depend the very existence of an infant Mission that is already surrounded with difficulties. I have had it hinted to me that no means will be left untried to prevent our return to this house, if vacated even for a few days, which may make it difficult or perhaps impossible for even an English Resident to reinstate us, should he desire to do so. If excluded from this house, there is no other one that we can hope to obtain in which a family can spend the winter. I may add that there is now no disturbance here whatever, nor are the people likely to make one against the Maharajah's wishes."

Robert Clark adopted no mere defensive policy, but with the highest state-craft carried the war into the enemy's camp. In conclusion, he expressed his hope "that this request of the Maharajah himself, intended plainly either to oblige us to leave the city altogether or else to place us in seeming antagonism with our own Government, and lead both you and them to regard us unfavourably on account of our not at once complying with your wishes, expressed to us in so kind a manner, may be the means of leading both you and our Government not only to decline to interfere in this matter, but to do more than we even thought of asking, and to resolve that we shall not be unjustly hindered in all prudent and lawful efforts to make the Gospel known. We will pay all respect to the Maharajah and his native Government, and we daily pray for Divine guidance, that in all our actions we may be gentle and conciliatory, and guided with much wisdom to enable us always to perform Christian duties in a Christian manner."

The messenger who had brought the Resident's letter refused to take the reply—he had no orders to receive one; but two of the Christians were entrusted with it, and accompanied the orderly on his return. "On their arrival at the palace, Lala Shunkar Dass was very angry. He had orders, he said, not to receive any letters, but for me to go. He turned to the messenger, and asked him how he dared to bring back any letter contrary to his orders. The man replied that he was not the bearer of it, but the Christians. Lala Shunkar Dass would not receive it, but told them to take it to the Wazeer, who undertook to forward it.

"It appears that Lala Shunkar Dass really had orders to expel us. When he found out that we had not gone, he threatened us openly with another disturbance, telling the Christians that the people would certainly rise again. 'The people will never rise,' replied Shah Munir, with all the grave and noble dignity of a genuine Pathan, 'unless you tell them. What can Cashmerees do without the orders of their Government?' Several of the chief Maulvies and shawl-weavers were sitting with Lala Shunkar Dass, and it seemed as if they all thought that we *must* leave instantly on the receipt of Mr. Cooper's letter (which by the bye was brought to us open, and which they had no doubt read), and they had all come together to make merry and congratulate each other on our discomfiture. Verily there is something very ridiculous as well as serious in it all."

The Resident replied on the 28th of April:—"I read your letter with much interest, and also great concern that matters should have assumed so threatening an aspect. . . . Until we have arrived at a satisfactory adjustment of the case (and especially under the detailed circumstances you so obligingly gave me in your note), I request that you will not think of stirring from your present residence, on account of any previous communication, which was addressed, as I mentioned to you, in ignorance of the whole bearing of the facts. I hope to be in Srinagar some time on Thursday, and will take the first opportunity of paying you my respects. The deportment of your European friends, and especially of Monsieur Gosselin, seems to have combined that firmness and temperance which always tells with effect upon an Asiatic mob."

On Mr. Cooper's arrival in Srinagar the authorities pressed their request. They offered to indemnify Mr. Clark for rent and all further charges of removal to one of the houses outside the city. They thought "it could not make much matter to do so, as it was only for a few months that we could remain here. Mr. Cooper at once told them that we wished to remain here altogether. They were quite staggered, or professed to be so, at the very idea of the Mission becoming a permanent one. I am thankful that this subject has been brought plainly before them; so that the Maharajah can now make any objections to it that he may think fit before our English Government, and the matter will be decided before the Resident returns to the Panjab, and we are left alone at the beginning of a winter season."

The 2nd of May was a red letter day. "Mr. Cooper called, and told us that after careful consideration he had decided not to interfere in any way about this house; that we were in possession of it, and that as far as he, as Resident, was concerned, he had no wish for us to leave. He told us that he has spoken to the Wazeer about it, and complimented him on the successful manner in which he had put down the disturbance. There was no doubt, he said, that the Government able to do this so quickly and so effectually was powerful and wise; and that, this being the case, there was in his opinion no reason whatever for us to leave. He was quite sure of their ability to protect us; yet should any emergency arise by reason of our remaining here, or any mob assemble which it might be difficult to control, he would be happy to lend him the whole of his support.

"Thus has this matter been terminated, I hope for ever, and our difficulties have all been removed. We cried unto the Lord, and were delivered; we trusted in Him, and were not confounded. It seems that we have little or nothing to do. It is God who is working, acting each moment in the best manner for us, or rather for His own glory. Occasionally He makes some use of us to do some little thing, to be one little link in the chain; but generally He works through others, and we have only to sit still to see what He is doing. How humbling is this! how it takes off the thoughts from men, to fix them on Him and His salvation! Blows and attacks come on us one after the other, unexpectedly from unseen foes; and I may add that the internal conflicts are even greater than those that appear, and each blow seems as if it would annihilate us. In a few hours we look around, and the storm has passed away, and the sun again shines bright. Surely God is about to work a great work in this land."

In truth, all the strenuous opposition of the Maharajah had immensely furthered the cause of the Gospel. The Mission had been superbly published throughout Cashmere. It had been brought prominently under the notice of the British authorities. The discreditable tactics of the Cashmere Government had been dragged into the light, the footing of the missionary in the city was placed on a firm basis, and the question of permanent residence had been raised in the most effective way. The Maharajah stood defeated all along the line. Even the timorous Cashmeri realised that he might dare to consider the claims of the new religion, if he so pleased. Mr. Clark learnt that "some of the best informed people look on the establishment of this Mission as the commencement of the Maharajah's downfall. It is the first time, they say, that he has been contradicted or crossed in anything. Their conclusion is arrived at, I suppose, by the same method of reasoning as when they were quite sure that the Commander-in-Chief had come to make arrangements to take Cashmere when he visited the country last month, because one morning he looked out of the same window three times, and each time exclaimed, 'What a beautiful country this is!'"

The storm of battle had not hindered Robert Clark

from the work he had come to do. "More and more do I feel the necessity in missionary work of boldly carrying out the plain commands of God, and of using every means that lies in human power in accordance with the teaching of the Bible, even in the midst of difficulties and opposition, and however conscious of great personal weakness. It is such efforts and endeavours which God honours and particularly blesses, when they are according to His Word and will. What then? though they seem to be impossibilities, let us undertake them. It is useless to sit still when we are told to act. We have no right to expect any success or blessing, any remarkable extension of our work, any protection from human or spiritual adversaries, until we have in faith and prayer done all that lies in our power, and left no proper means untried. We have no right to look at all to the difficulties and impossibilities, when we ought to look to God. The command to the man with the withered hand was 'Stretch forth thy hand,' a thing he was quite unable to do; but with the command there was a promise implied, and obedience gives strength, and in the endeavour to obey we received power to do things of which in ourselves we were altogether incapable."

The very uncertainty of tenure spurred Mr. Clark to steady use of every opportunity, and there was indeed good cheer. He was able to report:—"It is a cause of great thankfulness that our inquirers of last year have all returned to us. The first was Husn Shah, who came as soon as he heard of our arrival, and appeared amongst us in the midst of the tumult. They have all suffered imprisonments, and scourgings, and persecutions of many kinds, and have been brought before rulers and governors, 'for Christ's sake and the Gospel's.'"

Amidst the anxieties of that critical day, the 18th of April, the missionary commenced a school and regular work with the native Christians.

The 2nd of May is a date memorable in the missionary annals of Cashmere, not only for an event already noted, but for one of yet wider import. On that day Mrs. Clark opened a dispensary. It speedily attracted patients in crowds, and the homes of the people began to open to her. The ignorance of the people was almost incredible. One day, when Mrs. Clark was dispensing medicine, "a Cashmeree, who was standing by, asked if it was not made of the hairs of dead sahibs? The idea naturally provoked a smile, when the man declared that everybody said it was so, and that was the reason of its great power." On another occasion, a boy had lost four rupees at a fair, and came to Mrs. Clark to ask her who had stolen it. He had heard, he said, that the memsahib knew everything, and could at once tell him.

As we have already seen, visits to men of influence were a special feature of Mr. Clark's method of evangelising. We may tell of one such, noted in his journal:—"In the afternoon, called on Raj Kar, the Finance Minister. He received us in state, in his large and handsome room upstairs, which was neatly carpeted, and was lined on both sides with great numbers of his retainers. There must have been two hundred persons present. As soon as we were seated together on the soft carpet at the upper end of the room, leaning against the large round cushions in front of all his followers, who were seated on both sides, up to the very end of the spacious hall, he at once turned the conversation to religious subjects, and especially to the time of the second coming of the Lord. I told him that of that day and that hour no man knew anything; that Jesus would suddenly descend from heaven when no one expected Him, with all His angels, and in the glory of God. 'But when do Christians generally think that He will come?' he replied. I said that there were many learned and holy men who, after much study of God's Word and prayer, had come to the conclusion that He might soon appear; and that there was beginning to be a general expectation of His coming, in the same manner as there was when He first came down from heaven. We went on conversing for some time, and before leaving I took notice of his little son, who was seated next him, and asked him if he were learning English. He seemed to be a clever little boy, and I offered to teach him myself, if he would send him to me. 'But what advantage will there be in his learning English,' Raj Kar replied, 'if Christ is to appear soon? If the end of the world is at hand, it will hardly be of any use!'"

CHAPTER XVI.

THE CASHMERE MISSION—*continued.*

THE astute Gulab Singh now sought to secure the abandonment of the Mission in another way. The Resident wrote to Mr. Clark on July 19th:—"The Maharajah requests me to intimate that the location of Europeans, or even the establishment of a Mission at Jammoo, the chief city of His Highness' government and residence, would yield him no anxiety, as His Highness could there exercise immediate control over the discipline of his civil officers, and would feel no solicitude as to the temper and demeanour of his subjects." Needless to say, the offer was not made in good faith, and the king counted on a refusal. To the Maharajah's consternation, Mr. Clark at once accepted the invitation, "so kindly and voluntarily accorded." He wrote to Gulab Singh, as was but courteous and right, and, through the Resident, acquainted him with his plans and purpose. "It will be my earnest desire to endeavour at Jammoo, as everywhere in your Highness's dominions, to meet your wishes in every possible way, and to show all deference and respect to the established Government. This is indeed enjoined upon us by our Christian religion, which requires us to be 'subject to the higher powers for conscience' sake,' as far as in us lies, because they are 'ministers ordained by God, to whom all honour is due.' It is in this way, amongst others, that we are taught 'to put to silence the ignorance of foolish men,' by showing submission to the king as supreme, for the Lord's sake, as well as unto the governors, who are sent by Him 'for the punishment of evil-doers, and for the praise of them that do well.' My desire will be to seek in every way your Highness' welfare, and the real benefit of the people. I will obey the laws of the country. I will endeavour to give no offence by improperly wounding the feelings of anyone, and will seek, by God's help, to maintain the character of a minister of Christ. I ask for your kind favour to myself, and for your countenance in the work which has been entrusted to me."

The Maharajah made no further overtures. Mr. Cooper was succeeded by Mr. Birch, as Resident in Cashmere. Then the latter was informed, writes Mr. Clark, "that we could not possibly go to Jammoo; and, in fact, that the mere idea of it was quite out of the question altogether. Since then, we have waited day by day for the official reply to my letter to the Maharajah, but we have been favoured with none. No reason is given why his own invitation, voluntarily given, is thus retracted; we only hear that it is so. Mr. Birch will leave to-morrow; and to-day, after an interview with the Dewan, he has with much regret positively forbidden me, on the part of the Dewan, to go there. The prohibition is so strong, that he would feel obliged to order us back, should we set out."

The Maharajah's implacable opposition evidenced itself in many ways. Inquirers were seized, flogged, imprisoned, and subjected to domiciliary visits. The pupils were withdrawn from the school *en masse*, by the Government order; as suddenly all were ordered back again to school; and then one day, without warning or cause assigned, the whole of the parents, including many principal natives, were clapped into prison.

It is evident from Mr. Clark's narrative that the poor were debarred even from charity. "There was a large fire near us the other night, when several houses were burnt down and many poor people lost their little all, and some persons lost their lives. The next morning we collected, from our native Christians and some others, thirty-two rupees for the sufferers. It was known that, if given to them openly, it would probably be taken from them, and so the poor people came to us to receive it between eight and nine o'clock at night. It appears that they could not keep their own counsel, and that some of them went and talked about it, for to-day they have all come again to give back the money. For Cashmerees to give up thirty-two rupees seems something wonderful; but they say that the whole Muhalla [quarter] rose against them, and began to beat them and to call them Christians and Kafirs for receiving the Christian's aid; and yet poor people come here every Sunday morning to receive the Christian's alms. It seems like the old tactics over again, and that the Cashmerees are again put forward, as if it was their wish not to receive any favour or kindness from us. We received the money, and when the crowd stood back they all thanked us for our kindness, which they said they felt, although their own people would not allow them to take advantage of it."

It is not possible to describe in detail the attacks that succeeded one another in wild profusion and great variety. An account of the crowning attempt must suffice to illustrate the tactics of the baffled Government. This was entrusted to Dewan Kirpa Ram, the greatest dignitary in the kingdom, who came in person from Jammu to Srinagar to promote the plot. On 20th July, Husn Shah, the first Cashmeri convert of the Mission, had been baptized. Mr. Clark notes concerning him:—"He has been with us now nearly a year; has been imprisoned continually, and had logs of wood tied to his feet; has been beaten, threatened, and promised all sorts of things by the Wazeer himself, if he would leave us. Never has he been left in peace. Day after day has he been tried and tempted by mother and friends, and coaxed and punished by those in authority, but apparently in vain; for he has hitherto resisted or endured all. For months has he earnestly asked for baptism, which we no longer could refuse. Yusaf (for so he is now called) is, however, still very ignorant, and but a timid Cashmeree." This young Christian became the pivot on which Kirpa Ram's plans turned.

The story of the Dewan's machinations is best told in Mr. Clark's own words:—"A most remarkable interposition of God's providence has occurred to-day. On Thursday evening last, our convert Yusaf (Husn Shah), after his return with us to Srinagar, requested permission to go home to see his mother. I cautioned him against going alone, but he thought there was no danger, and went. On Friday he had not returned, and I sent to his mother's house to inquire about him; but all declared they had never seen him. On

Saturday morning, after our preaching, the catechists met him, with several other people, including his mother, on his way to the palace. He hung down his head, and his mother hid herself. The catechists called to him to return with them; but he gave some excuse, and after a few words went on his way, with the people with him.

"This led me to make his case one of earnest prayer, that this helpless ignorant lamb might be saved out of the paw of the lion. He was quite alone, a weak Cashmeree boy, and against him were arrayed all the power and skill and wealth in Cashmere, and, we may truly say, all the malignity and subtlety of the god of this world. We prayed that, for the glory of Christ's name amongst the heathen, he might be delivered, and that the people might themselves confess that He is Lord. We did nothing, we had nothing we could do; we only prayed.

"Now mark the consequences. In the evening, we had several visits to pay after our return to Srinagar, and the first one was to Mrs. Birch. The Dewan's boat was at the gate, but we went in to see Mrs. Birch, who begged me at once to go upstairs and see the Dewan and Mr. Birch. I knew nothing that was going on, but went. I was asked to sit down, although I excused myself, thinking they were engaged; when, to my great astonishment, I learned that they were talking about myself, and about a very grave charge which the Dewan, the highest personage in Cashmere, had himself preferred against me. It was stated that I had compelled Yusaf to become a Christian by force; that the memsahib had drugged him; that he had been made a Christian when intoxicated; and that we had ill-treated him, and almost made a slave of him. The documents were all on the table—the charge and evidence in Urdu, and also in badly worded but intelligible English, and a long letter from the Dewan himself. They were handed to me, the Dewan sitting gravely by. I begged Mr. Birch to go on with the case, and to sift it to the utmost, and so Yusaf was called up. The charges were all brought forward, and Yusaf questioned.

"'Did Mr. Clark ever drug you?'

"'*No*' (in a bold, straightforward voice).

"'Or the memsahib?'

"'*No.*'

"'Did they ever give you wine to drink?'

"'*No.*'

"'Or ill-treat you?'

"'*No.*'

"'Or use any force whatever to make you a Christian?'

"'*No.*'

"He said he had become a Christian of his own accord, and that the people had put those charges in his mouth. He was asked what he was? He replied, a Christian. When did he become one? Had he received anything for becoming one? He became a Christian, he said, of his own accord, because he thought Christianity to be right, and he had received not one pice for it.

"Mr. Birch looked at the Dewan. He was speechless, and had nothing to say. He was asked if there was any reason for this grave charge which he himself had brought. He could give none. He was then asked if there was any reason that prevented Yusaf from going away with me. The answer to this was that he might go with me and leave the country with me, and he only requested that he might never come back again to it. Mr. Birch hoped he would not insist on this latter point, as it would be banishing him from his native country without the commission of any fault. Yusaf was released; but in the conversation that followed, the Dewan said, in my presence and that of Mr. Birch, that the Maharajah's desires were that I should neither remain in Cashmere nor return to it next year, nor go to Jammu; nor in fact carry on any missionary work whatever in future in His Highness' dominions. He was evidently angry, and had quite lost himself. Mr. Birch asked him whether he said this of himself, or whether he was requested to say it on the part of the Maharajah. He said he said it *on the part of the Maharajah.* Mr. Birch requested him to give it him in writing, when he would at once take official action on it. (This, of course, was never given.)

"The Dewan then accused me of writing in the *Lahore Chronicle* the article (which seems to have given such great offence) of the 31st August. I assured him that so far from having been the author of it, I had not even *seen it*, and had no idea whatever who the writer was. 'But you wrote to the Government,' he said, 'before Mr. Cooper's arrival.' As he seemed incredulous, I assured him, on the word of an Englishman and a Christian minister, that I had never addressed Government on the subject of this Mission before Mr. Cooper's arrival at all, and never after his arrival, *except in answer to communications received from them.* I said this, as my conversation with Mr. Cooper on the 17th of June, when Husn Shah was lying in prison at the very time on account of his Christianity, and the letter that followed, were merely of a private nature, and that was the *only occasion on which information has ever been volunteered by me to any official connected* with Cashmere. I assured the Dewan of my earnest desire to show all respect and deference to the Maharajah and his Government, as I was bound by my religion to do so; and I ventured to tell him that he had himself been a witness of the utter absurdity of the charges brought against me, and that, as possibly they might some day he repeated, I hoped that he would in future give me the credit of *at once* believing that I was incapable of them.

"He became more friendly, and at last offered to come to my house to visit me. I answered that, as the representative of the Maharajah, it was rather my part to call first on him, which I would gladly do. But no, he said he would call on me; in fact, *he wished to consult the memsahib about his illness*!!

"How wonderfully has God's hand been apparent in the whole of this matter! I did not know that any charge had been brought against me; did not even know that Yusaf had been brought before the Dewan; did not know that the Dewan was visiting Mr. Birch; when all at once, suddenly and unexpectedly, I am confronted with him, and the whole matter fell in pieces at once, without my having to say one word. Mr. Birch said to me that the charge was so manifestly false and absurd that it would be almost an insult even to ask me for any explanations. Yusaf was set at liberty before all the wondering train of the Dewan, including Colonel Gardiner, the Kotwal, etc., and went back with me to the city in my boat. His mother, as the Dewan left, asked if he was not going with the Dewan Sahib. 'No; I am going with the Padre Sahib,' was the reply; and they all walked slowly away without him. The Lord had stood by him, and had enabled him to witness a good confession before the Dewan himself. False witnesses did rise up; they laid to our charge things that we knew not. They digged a pit before us, and are fallen into the midst of it themselves. The Lord kept not silent, He was not far from us. He awoke to judgment, to plead and defend our cause; so that they are ashamed and brought to confusion that wished our hurt. Our help is the name of the Lord; who has brought great good out of evil, and made their own desires only to expose their great wickedness."

The scheme had been no secret in the city, for in the East everything is known in a manner that is positively weird. There is, however, always a conspiracy of silence, never broken unless a plan miscarries or a favourite falls. The day after the fiasco, abundant information poured in to both Mr. Clark and the Resident. It revealed a deep-laid plot to induce the British Government to effect the permanent removal of the missionary from the Maharajah's territory. The details given in Mr. Clark's official memorandum, submitted on the 18th September to the Resident, throw an interesting light on the ways of the unchanging East.

"Secret agents disguised as fakirs, deputed to watch Yusaf, tracked him to his mother's house. On their report, a high officer, by name Rajkol, followed him, and brought him to his own headquarters. Rajkol there offered him four hundred rupees, which were actually given to him, and left for two days in his possession; he was offered any girl he might choose in marriage; and a certain amount of grain year by year; together with ten rupees a month. The next morning he was taken privately before the Dewan himself, who repeated the offer, it is said, with his hand over water [a solemn form of oath], in the presence of Colonel Gardiner (in the Maharajah's employ) and Rajkol also placing their hand on their sacred books [another solemn oath]; the conditions being that Yusaf should follow out the Dewan's instructions to the letter, which were, to apply to him for justice next morning in full Durbar; and *not to him only, but through him to the English Government*, for the charges against us, as stated in the document you yesterday showed me.

"Yusaf, to say the least, showed great weakness, and a want of manly courage, if not of faith. He is only a timid Cashmeree. His own account is that he felt that he was in their hands; that he was terrified, and saw no way of escape, except in allowing them to do with him what they would, and then, when once in your presence, declaring to you that what he had done was by constraint, and that the whole charges were false. He certainly allowed them to write the document, and was present when the cry 'Duhai' [Justice, O King] was made in the Kutcherri [Court]. It was there that the word 'drugs' was substituted by —— for 'wine,' as it was feared you would ask him why he had consented to drink wine. Karim Bakhsh (the news-writer) was the only one in the Kutcherri who came forward to say that no constraint had been used when Yusaf became a Christian; but he was told by the Dewan to attend to his own concerns. Ramtan the

Wukeel (Advocate) encouraged Yusaf not to mind, even if you spoke to him in a loud and firm voice; 'for we are all,' he said, 'round you, to help to carry you through;' and the Dewan had, the morning before, insisted strongly on the necessity of his carrying out his instructions *to the very letter*.

"When all was carefully arranged, with the whole skill and power of the Cashmere Government, it was then brought before you. The Dewan was to clench the matter by his visit in the afternoon; when, most providentially, the spell was broken through by my arrival; when we were brought to your house at the very crisis of time; by accident, some would say, but evidently by the guidance of One who rose up to plead for us and defend our cause. Well may we now say, 'If the Lord Himself had not been on our side when men rose up against us, they had swallowed us up quick. But praised be the Lord, who has not given us over as a prey to their teeth; our soul has escaped as a bird out of the snare of the fowler; the snare is broken, and we are delivered.'

"If only they could have proved the charge, and got Yusaf to swear to it, backed as it was by all the weight and influence of the country, what a strong reason would they have had, according to their own ideas, for requesting our Government to interfere. If only they could show that we even had acted without judgment and rashly, it would have been sufficient to prove that we were unfit for the position in which we are here placed. As regards their own people, too, if only these charges could have been *proved* (no matter whether truly or falsely) the news would have spread like wildfire over the country that we forcibly made men Christians, and even baptized them when they were drugged, and the whole people would be set against us, and shun us as a plague. They thought that their bribes and their threats were sufficient to make them sure of their man; but they have only fallen into the pit which they themselves dug for us.

"Shall I tell you how the cries and tears in the Dewan's court were created, on which so much stress was laid, in my presence, by the Dewan and Colonel Gardiner. Yusaf was told that he must begin to cry as soon as he came publicly before the Dewan. He professed inability to do so, or to command tears at pleasure. So the Head and Superintendent of the Cashmere Police himself smeared some red pepper on his sleeve, telling him to rub it into his eyes when the time came to weep!! The Dewan has told Yusaf that if he played him false, not only he, but all his family, would suffer for it, and that he would bring him back again from Baramulla whoever he went away with. I am perfectly well aware that it is impossible to prove many of the things contained in this letter, especially as much took place in private, on purpose, in order that it may never be proved."

The position now was humiliating in the extreme for the Dewan. Further relations would have been sorely strained but for the judicious action of Robert Clark. In his journal of 26th September we find an entry:—

"The Dewan has not fulfilled his promise of calling on me, even to ask the Memsahib's advice about his illness. This morning, after prayer and thought, I determined to call on him. He received me most kindly. I told him plainly our object, which was solely a spiritual one, and had nothing whatever to do with politics or secular concerns. I promised to meet the Maharajah's wishes in every possible way; I agreed to leave the city if he wished it, and would appoint any other place where we could live and quietly carry on our work; and even said that, if he desired it, we would not establish a school, *for the present.* I told him plainly that, when all the world was opening out to Missions—including Constantinople, Egypt, Persia, China, India, and Burmah—it was *impossible* to exclude them from Cashmere; that the work was not mine, not even that of a Committee, but of the whole Church, who undertook it in God's strength, and therefore it must succeed. I told him that he had himself seen the view taken of it in public notices of it, and begged of him, for the sake of the Maharajah's honour and interest, to cease to oppose it; for it would only lead to His Highness's injury. Looking at it in a merely interested view, it would add much to his honour to gain the good opinion of every Christian, and be praised (instead of the contrary); whereas opposition could do no good; for even if we left Cashmere this year, the probability was that we would remain next. I asked, therefore, for his friendship, and the favour of the Maharajah.

"He listened to everything with the greatest attention; and of course all this came out in conversation, and after I had repeatedly asked him whether he wished me to open out my whole thoughts. He begged me to go on and tell him all that was in my mind. I did so. He promised to help us, to write to Jammu, and to further our cause on his return there. But I have no faith in him or in them. Their words are softer than oil, but *swords are in their hearts.* I had many opportunities of dwelling practically (at his own request) on 'temperance, righteousness, and judgment to come;' for he sought to draw me out to speak of Christ and His Gospel, and here too I told him all that was in my heart. He read me a manuscript account of a visit of Andrew the apostle [!] to Jammu (containing, by the way, an anachronism of some nine hundred years), in which there was a prophecy that all India would be subject to Christian rule, including *Jammu and Cashmere.* A learned Mullah came in towards the end of the conversation (I fancy, by order), who had known Joseph Wolff, and wanted to discuss on the nature of God, independently of His attributes and actions. I tried to make the matter *practical* and *personal.* The Dewan was most cordial, and on my leaving shook hands as if I had been a friend of twenty years' standing, and asked me to come again. But *cui bono?* I shall, however, of course go, should it seem desirable."

An itineration undertaken about this time in the north end of the Valley revealed many encouragements. Large and attentive congregations were secured in places that had in former tours proved most unfriendly. Some of the best work was done in towns where, to quote Mr. Clark, the Christians had previously "been swept out of the place."

As the eventful summer of 1864 drew to a close, the settlement of the second point Mr. Clark had formulated in his policy—that of a winter residence in Cashmere—became a matter of urgency. The Maharajah would have none of it. The British Government, before whom the subject had been brought, was distinctly non-committal. The Secretary of the Lieutenant-

Governor of the Panjab wrote, "I am directed to say that the Government will not insist on your leaving the country, although no officers in the service of the Government are allowed to remain there after the departure of the Political Officer deputed for the season as the Government representative. The Lieutenant-Governor, however, understands that you agree to depart at once, should the Maharajah require you to do so. At the same time, I am to state that if you remain in the Valley it must be entirely at your own risk."

The missionary had now friends amongst the Cashmeris. Their plan to compass the desired end was characteristic. He tells us :—"Mrs. Clark has been asked twice by the natives to remain here in Cashmere alone during the winter. They tell her that there is no order for her to leave, and that they would like her to remain. They say no one would dare to interfere with her. She has expressed her willingness and even rather a desire to remain if I will consent to it. I have not the least fear for the result; she is quite able to do it, and would, I feel, be borne out in any such attempt, did God's guidance lead us to it; but it seems to me like a native underhand way of gaining our point, rather than a straightforward open one. God is well able to make the way plain for both to stay when He thinks fit."

The Maharajah pressed for Mr. Clark's departure from his territories. Mr. Clark writes :—"On 28th October a native officer was sent to me by the Wazeer, together with the Baboo, to tell me to leave. I was not at home, so they came straight into the room where my wife was sitting, without any invitation, the native officer calling out in a loud and most impertinent manner, 'Well, what does she say? Are they going or not going?' Mrs. Clark said not one word, but rose and left the room, and sent a servant to request them to leave."

Two days later, yet another emissary was sent:—"Colonel Gardiner called to say that I *must* leave. I said there were plenty of other sahibs in Cashmere, and it was strange that I was to be obliged to leave before them. He said I *must* leave, and the fact was that the local Government would have nothing whatever of Christianity in Cashmere. He said that overland news through Central Asia had reached the Maharajah, to say that the Turkish Government had closed all Mission houses and bookshops in Turkey, and that the Maharajah meant to do the same in Cashmere."

At one time Mr. Clark thought of sending his family away for the winter, while he himself remained in Srinagar; but, on a full review of the circumstances, the most helpful course to adopt seemed to be that of retiring, for the moment. The Mission had originally been undertaken for six months only. In that stirring half-year much strenuous work had been done. The foundations had been securely laid, and every outwork had been triumphantly carried and held in the brilliant campaign that now lay behind him. He had realised that a permanent residence in Cashmere was essential for his purpose; it was equally plain to his robust commonsense that the inevitable battle involved could not be fought to a finish at that late season of the year. The exodus from the Valley had begun; the Resident himself was already on his return march to India.

As regarded Cashmere itself, Mr. Clark saw the vital issue raised by the Maharajah's determination :—"Any native, of whatever country in Asia, may live in Cashmere all the year round, and may occupy a house in the city; but Europeans are not treated with the same consideration as other nations, and are not allowed equal privileges with them. If the question be brought forward publicly, a hundred reasons are at hand with which to blind the eyes of Englishmen; but the true fact is that the Maharajah's object is to show to his own subjects that he can insult or injure a European at his own pleasure, and believes that he can do so with impunity, either because he thinks we are too weak to retaliate, or too dense to see what every native knows to be a gross indignity."

Time was required to form a mature judgment and to perfect plans; for the question had a far deeper side than has yet appeared, and this we shall presently consider. Mr. Clark was ever ready to change a view or a plan for one that was better. His decision was made, and on 2nd November he left Srinagar. "Our house was occupied the moment we vacated it. As we were dropping down the river, I heard a shout behind us that the Kotwal was following us. I looked round and found that he was close on us, in a swift boat, and that runners and horsemen were with him on the bank. It appeared that, *without my knowing it*, a young man, who for some days had been an inquirer, and wished to be a Christian, had taken refuge in the boat of the native Christians. He was seized and dragged away. They were going to beat him on the spot, when the Mayor forbade it. He was carried away, before my very face, to answer before the

Wazeer, and to suffer imprisonment, for wishing to be a Christian and visiting the missionary. No other crime was ever spoken of."

The authorities removed the property Mr. Clark had left in his house, pending his return, to a bungalow outside the city. The Lieutenant-Governor of the Panjab took very serious notice of this act, which he termed "an insult to the British Government," as well as exceedingly "improper behaviour to an English gentleman."

To the superficial observer it may seem that the victory now lay with Gulab Singh; that his triumph had obliterated every reverse; and that he had swept away all the precious gains of the missionary's agony, patience, and endurance. As a matter of fact, it was far otherwise. The Maharajah never rendered a weightier service to the cause he opposed than when, on that November day in Srinagar, he secured the departure of Robert Clark. "God writes straight on crooked lines," says the Portuguese proverb. The wrath of the heathen was to be found to His praise in exceeding great results that the Maharajah himself was all unwittingly to secure.

Robert Clark had been quick to realise that the effects of this act of the hostile Gulab Singh was very far-reaching. The question now was no longer limited by the borders of Cashmere; its boundaries had become immensely enlarged, and it was evident to him that the precedent established in the greatest feudatory kingdom of the British Empire would govern the event in all other feudatory and tributary states of India. The Divine purpose was clear in the apparent check to Mr. Clark's plans. Had he been permitted to remain unchallenged in Cashmere, no question would have been raised, no principles settled. A great issue, however, was now at stake between himself and Gulab Singh, and he realised it in all its wideness of detail and in all its consequences to the bodies and souls of millions of men. He had done his best to obviate a struggle, but from this he could now no longer stand aside; it became alike his duty and his privilege to take up the wager of battle in a strenuous war for civil and religious liberty throughout the native kingdoms of India.

"As in political, so in religious matters," wrote Mr. Clark, "there are legitimate means, which may be used, and which in many cases ought to be used, to remove disabilities and to pave the way for the introduction of measures that are fraught with great benefits to large communities. The question will not then be merely whether a single country like Cashmere can bar her gates to the Gospel for the half of every year, imprison converts, and prevent the establishment of schools. It will refer not to one Church, but to all Christian Churches; and not to one province, but to many native states. The question will then be whether the Queen's Proclamation is merely a dead letter, or really is in force, in all tributary and feudatory states; whether the native rulers of these states have the power or the right of expelling missionaries from their territories, and preventing the Church of Christ from exercising any religious influence, in a judicious manner, in their dominions.

"Granted, as it will be on every side, that every Prince may rightly prefer his own religion, and show his preference by favouring and aiding it by all resources at his command, yet the question will then be, whether he may make the reception of another religion by any of his subjects a crime for which a convert is liable to punishment; whether he may officially oppose, by the influence and power of his Government, private efforts, such as the introduction of schools or hospitals, which are believed to be beneficial to his people; whether he may insist on the European or the native teachers of the Christian religion being banished from his territories during any time of the year, simply at his will and pleasure. Should anything be done in the effort to propagate Christianity whereby the peace of the country is endangered, or should any scheme be undertaken injudiciously, or carried on without due regard to the circumstances either of the native Government or people; should the peaceable Gospel of Christ be taught at wrong places and times, offensively to the religious feelings of the inhabitants generally, or in a purely polemical spirit, it is doubtless the duty of every ruler to check such schemes and to preserve the peace. But it is not to such exceptional cases that the question now refers, but to the large and general question of Religious Toleration, so forcibly dwelt on in the Queen's Proclamation."

Before leaving this subject in the meantime, we may quote a pertinent paragraph from that historical declaration of religious liberty in India:—

"Firmly relying ourselves on the truth of Christianity, and acknowledging with gratitude the solace of religion, we disclaim alike the right and the desire to impose our convictions on any of our subjects. We declare it to be the Royal will and pleasure that none be in any wise favoured, none molested or disquieted, by reason of their religious faith and observances; but that all shall alike enjoy the equal and impartial protection of the law. . . . In their prosperity will be our strength, in their contentment our security, and in their gratitude our best regard. And may the God of all power grant unto us, and to those in authority under us, strength to carry out these our wishes for the good of our people."

CHAPTER XVII.

DEVELOPMENT OF THE PANJAB MISSION.

ON leaving Cashmere, Robert Clark returned to Peshawar, but that beloved sphere was not to retain him long, for he was soon called back to his first field at Amritsar.

The soundness of the principles on which that Mission had been founded was abundantly evidenced by its prosperity. A senior missionary was now required, one not only able for the heavy responsibilities of Amritsar, but also qualified to fill the position of adviser to the whole of the Panjab Missions. It was clear that Robert Clark was the man for the post. By the close of the winter his colleagues were well established in Peshawar, and on the 15th of March 1865 he set out for the Central Panjab. The interests of Cashmere, however, were steadily borne in mind, and the trend of events in that country now centred round Amritsar. In this connection it is now time to consider Mr. Clark's special task at the first meeting in 1863 of the Panjab Missionary Conference already referred to. His main work had been to advocate ardently before that representative Assembly the claims of what at that time was considered to be a startlingly novel method of missionary work, namely, that of Medical Missions.

The inestimable value of this arm of missionary service is now so universally admitted, that it would be preposterous to enlarge upon either the warrant on which Medical Missions rest, or the power they have wielded. At the time of which we write, however, the Churches were blind alike to the place and value in their operations of this most Christlike agency. The very idea was practically non-existent. It is doubtful whether there was a single Medical Mission in existence in India in connection with any Church. There may have been in South India. In the North, there were none.

One Medical Mission, unconnected with any Church, did exist, and is worthy of record. The missionary was Dr. John Newton, eldest son of the revered Newton of the Panjab, and his work was carried on under the auspices of the ruling sovereign of one of the Sikh states in the Panjab. The Rajah of Kapurthalla, second in position in the Panjab only to the Maharajah of Cashmere and the Maharajah of Patiala, was far in advance of all the feudatory chiefs of India in the clearness and soundness of his religious and political views. This enlightened ruler, in the matter of his own personal faith, was a zealous student of Holy Scripture, took his Bible wherever he went, conducted family worship in the palace—in a word, did everything short of seeking actual baptism into the Church of Christ, though his children received that sacrament. He, in great measure, supported two Christian Missions: one in his own capital, and the other in his territories in Oudh, at a cost of about twelve hundred rupees a month. This was in addition to many other contributions to Christian benevolent objects. He opened a hospital, and supported it on a liberal scale. In this Dr. John Newton worked as a medical missionary.

Even the stirring spectacle of a Sikh ruler who had advanced beyond Christians in work for suffering humanity, and was using Christ's own means of evangelising the people, conveyed no lesson to the Church at large. It was given to Robert Clark's large mind to grasp the importance and urgency of the ministry of the medical missionary. Among his manifold labours for the bodies and souls of men, none ranked higher in his estimation than his plea for the employment of this agency. From the moment that he realised the necessity of the healer-preacher, onward through life, he advocated Medical Missions with whole-souled enthusiasm. The ignorance and prejudice he had to combat are scarce credible. Some of the staunchest battles of his strenuous life were fought on behalf of just this very cause, and that, *mirabile dictu*, not against foes but against some of the most earnest and self-sacrificing friends of Christ's cause. At a later period of this narrative we shall consider the difficulties he encountered, as well as the principles he laid down. Meanwhile, we note that the germ of Medical Missions lay for Robert Clark in the medical chest his mother had kept for the villagers of Harmston. The seed took root in the wanderings through High Asia, where he saw the important results that accrued from Colonel Martin's box of medicines.

At the time that the Peshawar Mission was founded, one or two friends were inclined to think that a knowledge of medicine "might prove of use" amongst the Afghans. With the advent of Mrs. Clark it became evident to Robert Clark how readily the fast-shut doors flew open at a touch of that magic key. He had heard also what Mrs. Clark's pupil, Fazl i Haqq, was able to do in Kaffirastan. As he himself stood on the threshold of a permanent occupation of Cashmere, he was convinced of the paramount importance of a Medical Mission in that country.

Thus by a gradual development, Medical Missions had taken shape in Robert Clark's mind. His survey of missionary methods was world-wide, and the dawn of the same idea and the efforts to realise it, now evident in another quarter, interested him intensely. In a land far distant from the Panjab, a movement was on foot to restore the long-neglected ministry of healing to its right place in missionary enterprise. It is to the glory of Scotland that her Churches were the first to awaken to the value of Medical Missions, and it is the abiding honour of her capital city to have been the home of the gifted men who initiated the movement on a world-wide scale. At the time of which we write, the Edinburgh Medical Missionary Society had been recently founded, and in that Society Robert Clark's hopes centred for the beginning of Medical Missions in the Panjab.

The Panjab Missionary Conference lent a willing ear to Mr. Clark's plans. His labours in that Assembly, and a notable sermon which he preached at Lahore on the 24th of January 1864, resulted in the formation of a Panjab Medical Missionary Association. The objects in view were to make known in the Panjab the Edinburgh Society, to co-operate and associate with that Society by collecting funds on its behalf, and, by means of it, to promote a Medical Mission in the Valley of Cashmere. The Society was unable to undertake the work for lack of funds, but the hour had come, and in the

Divine Providence the man was ready. That was the contribution of the Edinburgh Society to the Panjab; the Church Missionary Society saw to the rest.

The man who offered himself was an Aberdonian, a loyal Presbyterian, trained in the world-famed Medical School of Edinburgh—Dr. William Jackson Elmslie. In him the Church Missionary Society sent out their first medical missionary; appointed to Cashmere, in 1865. He joined Mr. Clark at Amritsar. That city, with its enormous population of Cashmeris, its touch with the kingdom of the Maharajah, and above all its possession of Robert Clark, made it an ideal base of operations for that semi-closed land. Cashmere now became a station of Amritsar. Dr. Elmslie arranged to spend the summers in Srinagar and the winters at the base; and although Mr. Clark's multifarious new responsibilities only permitted him to pay occasional visits to Cashmere, Dr. Elmslie found in him a tower of strength, wise in counsel, and a true comrade in the war. Mr. Clark's lofty soul was free from every trace of self. All that was in him was placed unreservedly and with perfect simplicity at his colleague's service. He bent every energy towards assisting Dr. Elmslie in the tremendous struggles that awaited him in the dominions of Gulab Singh. The issue the Maharajah had forced was unceasingly fought. The result will come before us in due course.

On taking command of the Amritsar Mission, Mr. Clark first carefully reviewed the existing situation. A new order had resulted from the faithful and fruitful labours of those who had succeeded him. A readjustment of plans, a further adaptation of principles naturally followed. This survey completed, he, as ever, laid a clear course on which to sail the ship of missionary enterprise. He determined that his policy should be one of conservation, consolidation, and expansion.

The individual convert could not receive too much attention, for he was the unit from which all else was to be built up. He must be developed by loving, watchful, faithful care to the fullest of which he was capable. It would only be a splendid failure to lead men in by one door to the Church of Christ, if there were to be a constant exodus by another. Robert Clark, moreover, was not forgetful of the fact that man has a body as well as a soul. The perplexing problems involved in the furtherance of the material and social welfare of converts were not to be lost sight of in concern for the weightier matters spiritual.

The conservation of the individual was to march with the consolidation of the scattered units as a body of believers. Very large questions would naturally arise, but Robert Clark was content that the Panjabi Church should face them for itself in the fulness of time. The Panjab for Christ, not for any specific branch of the Church, that was his guiding star. Until an indigenous Church was established, converts had of necessity to be shepherded in the nurture and discipline of the section of Christ's Church that had brought them to the knowledge of the Gospel, for it was the missionary's bounden duty to give them what he deemed the best in matters ecclesiastical. That stage of tutelage, however, was but transitory. Robert Clark was jealous that there should be no infringement of the glorious liberty of the Panjabi children of God. Let them ultimately order their national Church as they deemed best, within the compass of their Master's will.

Ecclesiastical divisions that had their roots in the strifes and circumstances of foreign lands were, he held, out of place in the Panjab. God might, he believed, be preparing His people for the extinction of differences in Christian lands by showing them their unreasonableness in the Mission Field. A loyal member and minister of his own beloved Church, he yet abhorred the irrational, unchristian spirit that, in pitiable narrowness, relegates vast sections of the Church of Christ, for lack of Episcopacy, to "the uncovenanted mercies of God." Robert Clark saw to it that Panjab Christians should realise that, by whatsoever instrumentality it had pleased God to gather them in to Himself, they were brethren—one in the one Lord, one faith, one baptism, one God, and one Father of them all. Uniformity or corporate union might or might not be in the future, his labours for consolidation were steadfastly undertaken "in the unity of the Spirit," and for a federal union.

Again, Mr. Clark held a constant expansion to be the surest evidence and prime requirement of a truly living Church. The highest good of the individual Christian, and the only hope for the land, lay in a steady and healthy advance. He was instant to impress upon converts that they had received of God that they might give. They were the leaven and the salt, the lighted candle set on the candlestick. Their destiny was not always to be that of a feeble folk, poor and despised. It was their high calling to become the dominant factor in a regenerated national life.

As a first step, Robert Clark took up his abode in the native city. The moment was opportune. Converts had evinced a natural tendency to congregate round the mission compounds outside the city. A colony had established itself, and quite a little village had sprung up in the European civil lines. Sanitary objections apart, Mr. Clark considered it an altogether retrograde step that Christians should be so assembled in houses expressly built for them in mission compounds. The system was one of an artificial hothouse culture. It stunted free development, fostered certain characteristic faults, and crushed independence by reducing men to the unnatural condition of children in leading-strings. The healthy, spontaneous, rational development of Christianity required that converts should live as ordinary citizens amongst their fellow-countrymen. Strengthened by the fierce blasts of persecutions and the rubs of daily life that go to making of character, the converts must become living epistles known and read by non-Christians. These considerations lent added weight to the reasons, already detailed, that had induced him to make his home in the city of Peshawar, and to some extent in that of Srinagar. He used his influence to scatter the Christians throughout the city —each home a centre of light in the encircling night. He did more, he went himself to dwell among the people.

The castle of Maha Singh, surrounded by an ample demesne, stood within the city walls. This Mr. Clark acquired from the authorities in exchange for the piece of land in the civil lines occupied by the converts. He also supplemented the funds raised for the projected buildings by well-nigh a thousand pounds of his private means, and the City Mission House in the Katra Maha Singh soon became an accomplished fact. He brought his great experience to bear on every detail of the stately building and its surroundings. The upper storey was for occupation during the winter; while to the lower, designed for the hot weather, he added an underground chamber, as is the custom in Central Asia, for use during the fierce heats. Thus the citadel of Christianity in the Holy City of the Panjab rose on the site of the fortress whence Maharajah Ranjit Singh's father wielded the power that was the foundation of the son's greatness.

Gratifying results speedily accrued from residence in the City Mission House. The leading men of Amritsar regarded their neighbour as a true friend, and the current of their daily lives was drawn into a closeness of touch that brought Christianity very near to each of them. This kindly union of hearts was evidenced in many ways. The son of the leading Moslem magnate of the city lay desperately ill. The stricken father vowed large sums in charity, if Heaven would spare the hope of his house. That vow was sacredly kept on the lad's recovery; lavish donations were showered on Hindus, Moslems, and Sikhs, and a large sum of money and presents in kind were laid at Mr. Clark's feet for distribution amongst the Christian community.

The late Mr. Ishan Chandar Singha, one of Dr. Duff's converts, and a well-beloved father of the Panjab Church, has given us a picture of these early days. His reminiscences of Mr. Clark, the outcome of many years of intimate association, have been placed at our disposal by the editor of a vernacular paper, the *Masihi*, in which they were published.

Mr. Singha writes:—"Having built his house, Mr. Clark was ever mindful that he had placed it there because it was the best means of benefiting non-

Christians. So his door was never shut to any visitor, and the heathen were not slow to profit by this love and friendship; for, during the hot weather, they thronged to him in such numbers that he had no time for even his necessary rest, and his health would have suffered seriously had it not been that, unknown to him, for a couple of hours every day, the Christians locked the door of the staircase which led to his study."

In the same quarter of the city, Mr. Clark built a pastor's house and an inn. The latter was the outcome of his quick appreciation of existing needs. The building, a caravanserai of true Oriental pattern, was erected to obviate the indignities and inconveniences which travel entailed upon Christians. It was a place of rest for converts from various parts of the district when they resorted to Amritsar for business or worship, and it was a haven of refuge for inquirers and their families, where, safe from molestation, they could receive instruction.

Mr. Clark, on the completion of these buildings, had the satisfaction of noting:—"The arrangements connected with the location of the native Christians in the city have now been completed. The native pastor is living in his own parsonage in the city, with his congregation around him. Opposite to his house is the Christian serai, where travellers and inquirers are entertained. A handsome frontage of a row of shops has been added to the serai opening into the bazaar, where Christians who wish to be shopkeepers may at any time carry on their trades, without experiencing any of the difficulties and annoyances to which at times they are liable when renting houses from Hindus or Muhummudans. Two of the shops have been fitted up as a reading-room for the Christians, where they can meet their friends, and where, in due time, they may have a library. Two more are intended for shops for religious books, where it is proposed that every kind of Christian vernacular literature may be on hand for sale, and may be always procured by those who desire such books. The rent of the remaining six shops will provide subsistence allowance for inquirers, hospitality for strangers, and funds for repairs. Behind the pastor's house, in a large separate compound, opening into his, a row of four houses (which may at any time be added to) has been erected for young men, or for any Christians whom it is not thought desirable to expose to the temptations of life in the bazaar. A native Christian burial-ground has lately been made in a convenient spot in the neighbourhood. . . .

"The preliminary outwork has thus been accomplished. The work of keeping themselves unspotted from the world, and of holding out the light of God's truth to their countrymen from a more favourable standpoint, now commences. The future of their Church must in a great measure depend upon themselves."

Later, a hall was built in close proximity to the inn and pastor's house. It has an interesting history. Throughout the city of Amritsar the eye is arrested by the flutter of flags of various shape and hue, and each flag indicates that under it dwells a professor of some one or other of the multifarious religious beliefs of the land. The day came when Shamaun, erstwhile Kaiser Singh, first convert of Amritsar, having kept the faith, was to finish his course, the first to rest in the new God's acre "till the day break." His dying words were: "I see many flags for many gods and religions all over the city, but none for the Truth. Take my property, and let there be raised a flag for Christ, that my countrymen may know He too has come to Amritsar." His house was used in accordance with his wish until it was acquired for city improvements. At this juncture the Christians desired to have a hall for congregational purposes, hitherto served by accommodation in Mr. Clark's own house. We learn from Mr. Singha, that on hearing of their wish Mr. Clark said, "If you consider the hall necessary, pray, do what you can, and God will help you." The proceeds of Shamaun's jewellery and house were supplemented by the collections of the native congregation, and Mr. Clark added further sums raised "here and there." The hall was built with these monies, and upon it, years afterwards, it was given to the writer to erect, on what is now the Medical Mission Hospital, the flagstaff from which Shamaun's "Flag for Christ," with its white cross on a red ground, now floats over Amritsar.

The educational work of the Mission stood so high that the Panjab Government, through Mr. Arnold, the Director of Public Instruction, a son of Arnold of Rugby, had been prepared not only to make a substantial grant in aid, but also to withdraw their own school in favour of that of the Mission. The proposal fell through for reasons that do not concern us here. But, in 1865, Mr. Clark felt that the time had come for a forward step. He advocated the affiliation of the school to the University of Calcutta, and its development into a college for undergraduates. Higher education had begun to loom large, and he recognised that it would be a serious loss to let promising boys pass from the good influence exerted over them, solely because their educational needs could not be further met in Amritsar. The affiliation was also necessary to stamp the character of the greatest centre of missionary education in the Panjab in connection with the Church of England.

In the sphere of evangelisation in the villages Mr. Clark formulated large plans. Previously the method had been that a missionary wandered about over the whole district. The villages could, as a rule, only be revisited at very prolonged intervals, and the attention they then received was of necessity limited. This manner of evangelisation was all that circumstances admitted of until this time, but Robert Clark now felt that the tactics could be improved. His proposal was to divide the district into sections of manageable dimensions, grouped round important towns. These sub-districts were to be occupied by itinerating parties, and every village in them was to be frequently visited and systematically worked. He anticipated the day when these sub-districts would themselves become Mission centres. A European missionary, with a suitable staff of fellow-labourers, would reside in each district, and so be the friend and adviser of the heathen, and exhibit to them, in his family and himself, the beauty of Christian life, and thus be a visible centre of all that was good.

On the 8th of December 1865, Mr. and Mrs. Clark lost their second son, Roger, at Amritsar.

CHAPTER XVIII.

FOUNDING A NATIVE CHURCH.

IN 1866 a great sorrow befell the Amritsar Mission in the death of one of the staff, the Rev. Frederick Wathen. While mourning for his friend, Mr. Clark was led to express his feelings on the subject of the missionary call. Let him who would follow "count well the cost. A missionary's task is no easy one. His life must be in his hand, and he must be willing and ready to give it up when the Master calls for it. I have heard it said at home by a young minister, 'Look at ——; he went out, and he died in two years;' and of another, 'He died, and his wife and child both died; I cannot run this risk.' I have heard parents say, 'We cannot thus send our sons.' Then let such stay at home. They are not worthy. They can come themselves, and send their children to India for other professions, but not for God, nor for the souls of men. It is the missionary's lot to 'bear about in his body the dying of the Lord Jesus,' and to be 'always delivered to death for Jesus' sake.' There are times when with St. Paul 'he dies daily,' when he feels he is standing on the extreme edge of a precipice, very near indeed to death, with danger to soul and body all round; when he knows not what a single moment may bring forth. There are times when he is harassed, perplexed, disappointed, troubled, and weighed down. Friends fail him; converts disappoint him. He is in a position where he feels his utter weakness and ignorance, where he is tried, tempted above other men. Flesh and heart often fail, and he is overburdened, and feels almost as if he must give up the strife, or else *die*. But let us reverse the picture, and we see him 'always rejoicing, filled with peace,' upheld by 'the everlasting arms,' 'with the life of Jesus so manifested in his body' that he feels in perfect security and ease, 'full of comfort' and 'abounding in peace.' 'I am at peace, through Jesus,' were amongst the last words of Frederick Wathen; 'Jesus has washed all my sins away.' The same living and dying testimony was given by his four predecessors, who have died in the Panjab, at Mooltan, and Amritsar, and Peshawur. There was not one that regretted that he had been a missionary—not one who was not ready to accept a missionary's lot again, with all its trials and its early death. They loved not their lives unto the death, and they now rest from their labours, and their works do follow them; and never will one pang of regret be felt by them or theirs, when Christ returns again to reign, and awards to them the crown of victory. They were more than conquerors; and Christ and the Church now call on others to fill their places. Who, then, will follow them, and answer the oft-repeated cry, 'Why stand ye in the market-place all the day idle?' 'Go work to-day in the Master's vineyard,' 'Go forth into all the world, and preach the Gospel'?"

Through sunshine or storm, Robert Clark's mind was ever attuned to read the lesson contained in the providences of God. The meaning of losses such as those he refers to was clear: "But God's providence calls us to view His dispensations in still another light. In fourteen years, fourteen missionaries have laboured in Amritsar. Of these, two have died, and nine have returned on account of sickness to their native land, or been removed to other stations. In the Peshawur Mission the losses in eleven years have been equally great. We see, therefore, that the missionary comes and goes; his average life in India has been as yet but very small indeed; and as far as the Panjab is concerned, only the native Christians remain long and permanently at the same place. The language of the people is the native Christian's own language; and the customs of the people are their own customs; they can live amongst the people, which missionaries can seldom do, and then with difficulty; in their own country they are not often ill, and but very few native Christians indeed appear to have died at Amritsar since the establishment of the Mission in 1852. It would seem to follow, then, that we *must* make them the *actors* in missionary work, and must not let them be merely the persons who are always *acted on.* We must throw responsibility on them, and throw on them difficulties too, as they occur; and, placing them in the arena, in the sight of God and man, we must let them act, and see how they will act, and encourage them to act well, and of themselves. Have we not, we may ask, made duties, and especially Mission duties, too easy for native Christians; so that they are still, even now, many of them, mere babes, without self-reliance, or ability to originate or carry out measures by themselves; so that, without any will or wish of their own, they are like the pieces at a game of chess, put forward by the player, and, when left to themselves, remain everlastingly in the same position in which they were placed? It would seem that they must begin to act for themselves; to preach for themselves; to conduct schools for themselves; to go out on itinerations for themselves; to publish books for themselves; to raise subscriptions themselves; to live by themselves; leaning on no arm but their own and God's."

The constant promotion of the self-support and self-government of the native Church was a prime factor in Mr. Clark's labours. We find him expressing the opinion that "In a few years the work of instruction alone will be such that foreign missionaries will not be able to overtake it. Even if they could be sent in sufficient numbers, it would be injurious to the native Church for them to perform it."

In 1868, Mr. Clark reports:—"The native Christians have continued to make praiseworthy efforts during the year towards the self-support of their Church. In the course of nine months they have received from their Church Fund no less than 1324 rupees, of which 401 rupees have been subscribed by natives. Compared with the amount subscribed by them in 1867, the increase in 1868 (had the collections been continued for the whole year instead of nine months) would have been seventy rupees, exclusive of forty-nine rupees received from native Christians who have lodged in the serai. The management of the Church Fund is in their own hands; and it is thought important that it should remain so; and that they should continue to make all arrangements connected with the serai, and the houses for the native Christians. When they see the special value of their own contributions, as tending to pave the way for an independent, self-supporting Christian Church, the congregation will give more liberally. They have given from their collections fifty rupees a month towards the support of their native pastor, twenty rupees of which are a grant from the Calcutta Committee for this purpose. They have also afforded relief both to inquirers and to their own poor; and have made considerable grants to the City Mission buildings that have been completed during the year. The importance of these efforts towards self-government and self-support on the part of the native Church cannot be overrated. They are worthy of every possible encouragement."

Mr. Clark heartened the Christians by being among them as one who served, not as one who was "lord over God's heritage," but we will let Mr. Singha tell the story of those times. Robert Clark, he tells us, "possessed the gift of business-like habits and organisation, in things great as in things small, to marvellous perfection." To these he added unfailing tact. "Because of the steadfast purpose and iron will of Mr. Clark, some may think that he forced others to accept his opinions,—there could be no more preposterous error, for it was ever his rule carefully to hear and consider the opinions of the poorest and humblest Christian, and it was the secret of his success that he considered all things well.

"It was not with him as it is with some missionaries, that when once they have spoken they adhere to their opinion with weary obstinacy—heaven and earth may pass away, but their word shall not change. That was not the way with Mr. Clark. Whatsoever was fitting or was acceptable to the majority was not opposed by him. He gladly gave all the opportunity of saying what they thought and of practising what they deemed best. Thus, in Amritsar, he established a Church Committee which met monthly for business. Every six months there was a gathering of the whole congregation for the consideration of the accounts and congregational affairs.

"On one such occasion a very obscure individual embodied his criticisms of the work of the Committee in a memorandum of forty pages. Against the wishes of the members, Mr. Clark carefully listened to every word, accepted all that was reasonable, and fully answered every objection that appeared otherwise.

"In similar fashion, on another occasion, when his opinion did not agree with that of the congregation concerning the pastor to be appointed for Amritsar, he followed the wishes of the congregation, and not his own; but in the end it was evident his way was right."

The relations of the Amritsar converts with those of the Presbyterian Mission were fraternal in the extreme. Mr. Clark and Mr. Newton, as was to be expected, steadfastly promoted a federal union between their respective flocks. Mr. Clark knew well that a defensive war is ever a losing war, and that the highest interests of the infant Church depended on the missionary zeal of its members. He therefore fostered every plan proposed by the Panjabi Christians for the enlightenment of their fellow-countrymen. They were bound to make the effort at the earliest moment possible. He had in 1865 baptized Maulvie Imaduddin Lahiz, the greatest of the converts to

Christ from Islam. Next year we find the City Mission House thronged by crowds of the learned of Islam, while the Maulvie, like Paul of old, disputed mightily with his ex-coreligionists. The upshot was, to quote Mr. Clark, that—"After three public sittings, an excuse was made by them for discontinuing it; thus giving an example that truth in a native's mouth can appear so strong that error can think it prudent to avoid it. The objections brought forward in the attack upon Christianity were culled from many an infidel and Roman Catholic work, and were replied to. But Muhummudans do not now generally wait to defend Muhummudanism; and when it became their turn to reply to objections against their own religion, the field was deserted. We can thank God that it was a native of India, and one in the service of no Christian Society, that stood up for the defence of the Gospel against many subtle and unscrupulous adversaries."

Again, we find Mr. Clark setting the Rev. Daud Singh free, at his own request, to go forth to preach to the Sikhs as a native, unfettered by European ideas or ways. The experiment was arduous enough, but he achieved his purpose, preaching to great numbers of people, especially to the officials of the Maharajah of Cashmere in his own capital of Jammu.

The question of work amongst the women was one that Mr. Clark steadily pushed to the front. In 1821 a Society had been formed to promote female education in Calcutta amongst the lower classes. Later, the Calcutta Normal School was inaugurated for those of better position. In 1857 both sets of schools were amalgamated. It was then decided to enlarge the operations of the Society as circumstances permitted, and so the "Indian Female Normal School and Instruction Society" entered the vast field of British India. In response to the claims of Amritsar, this Society sent Miss Jerrom and Miss Branch, the first lady missionaries to this city other than missionaries' wives.

Mrs. Clark had set actively to work on her arrival in Amritsar. An Orphanage for boys and girls had been established. In the zenanas she broadened and deepened the tracks marked out by Mrs. Fitzpatrick and other ladies of the Mission. She superintended the Lady Lawrence Girls' Schools—eight of them—that were educating and evangelising the women of Amritsar. Native ladies in numbers were her fast friends, and on all hands she was a welcome visitor. Such was her influence, that, wonderful to tell, for her sake her husband and other gentlemen were sometimes actually allowed into the jealously guarded zenanas.

The Rev. T. V. French of Lahore tells us of one such instance. After describing a visit to the house of a Bengali Christian lady, he goes on :—"We went to a Mohummudan house in the ladies' quarter, to see a poor young girl, once of the Orphanage at Amritsar, and baptized, whom, after her mother's death, an uncle or aunt carried off and married to a Mohummudan. It was a curious sight, which I had never witnessed before, the interior of a Mohummudan zenana. I suppose it was only because Mr. and Mrs. Clark had so much to do with the bringing up of them that we were allowed this privilege. It was quite a group of females; from shrivelled and aged women, through various ages down to little children. The poor young wife lives a few doors off the Bengalee lady's house, and, in her seclusion, says she goes to the top of the house sometimes to look at the roof beneath which she loves to think a Christian woman lives close to her."

Glimpses now and again into the great underworld of zenana life showed the progress of the Kingdom. On a day, in Amritsar city, a high-class lady lay mortally stricken with cholera. She confessed her faith in Christ to her assembled family, and mourned the cowardice that had hindered an earlier avowal. "Send for the Missionary and let me be baptized," she pleaded; "for though I have not lived in His name, under His banner would I die." Needless to say, the desire was not one that the relatives were prepared to gratify. On their refusal, she asked for water. Instead of drinking it, as they had anticipated, the dying woman poured it over herself, saying, "I baptize myself in the name of Christ, and if I do wrong may Christ forgive me."

As we have seen, it was Mrs. Clark's high honour to be the first to commence medical work in Peshawar and Cashmere. A like privilege now fell to her in Amritsar. The beneficent influence of her ministrations was felt generally throughout the Mission. Many strange experiences were hers, but one must suffice for this narrative. A stalwart Jat Sikh had been baptized. A few nights later, as the result probably of an overdose of some delicacy, seductive rather than digestible, he awoke to severe pains. The stentorian yells of the suffering man before her doors awoke Mrs. Clark in the small hours. He admitted that the experience was not unprecedented, and that he had occasionally suffered in that way. "What did you do for it?" she asked. "I eat a handful of caraway seeds, and it always cured me," replied the patient. To the indignant, "Well, why don't you do so again?" the astounded man rejoined, in all simplicity, "But I am a Christian now!"

CHAPTER XIX.

FACING SOCIAL PROBLEMS.

THE great subject of Industrial Missions next began to occupy Robert Clark. The thorny problem of the means whereby converts could earn their livelihood lay in the forefront of the question of a vital indigenous Church. Converts in India have to endure many things. They are despised, rejected, and cast out from home and kith and kin; they suffer loss of their goods, and are in danger of personal hurt; sometimes death is their lot, for their faith's sake.

One of the hardest of their trials is to know what to do to earn their daily bread. It is not generally understood how utterly a man is cut off from his means of livelihood by becoming a Christian. Caste rules India with a rod of iron, and a special caste means not only a religious but a worldly standing. Trades, professions, and handicrafts run in castes. A man is a carpenter or a worker in brass, not because he wishes to be, but because he is born to it. Every trade lies in the hands of a special body. To be at war with it is therefore to be at war with the world. It means a boycott, compared to which similar things in the West are the merest of child's play. An artisan on becoming a Christian will find all the springs of trade, its wealth and standing, ranged against him.

There is no employment for him; if there were, he could find no market. The mighty power of the members of the craft, down to the smallest child, grinds him hard, through every relation of life. There is but one will and purpose through the hundreds of thousands of his people. He has left the religion of his fathers, and is therefore an abomination. Outside his clan, the convert finds the rest of the world as staunchly leagued against him. As a general rule, the hand of the Hindu is against the Muhummudan; the Muhummudan is not backward to pay the debt, and mutual relations in consequence are marked by a bitterness which is apt to become savage and dangerous. But men of different faiths find a strong bond of union in hating the Christians. It is the old story: Pilate and Herod became friends in the day of the humiliation of Jesus of Nazareth; and to this hour the Pilates and the Herods close up their ranks, and forget for the time their own quarrels in their bitter hatred of the Christ and His children.

The day had yet to come when the intertrading of Christians would suffice for the maintenance of their community. In 1867 it was still far distant, and beset with multiplex difficulties. Thus, to illustrate: a barber, let us suppose, had become a Christian. As a non-Christian he had five hundred co-religionists as his customers, shaved their heads, and so earned his living. There are but a dozen Christians to take the place of the lost customers. It is not their custom to shave their heads, and, if it were, they could not have them shaved every day. Nor do they employ the family barber, as do the heathen, in the delicate negotiations of personal life, in arranging marriages and the like, as do non-Christians. The heathen barbers, further, compete for the custom of the Christians, and will undersell the convert to any extent. Trade follows its own laws. In the East as in the West, purchasers will not pay an enhanced rate for the privilege of buying from fellow-believers.

To the convert the advantages from the patronage of Europeans are limited, for here also non-Christians rule. Even where a European is prepared to trouble himself over the matter of the convert's livelihood, it is more profitable to the heathen servants to give their master's custom to men of their own stamp, for non-Christians play into the hands of each other. The Christian is a nuisance to heathen servants. He hurts their religious pride; that is bad: he hurts their pockets, and that is worse still. Here we come to the third great difficulty a Christian has to meet. Even if he can follow his trade and obtain custom, how is he to avoid the rascality on every side of him? The servants understand well how to deal with the noxious element. A Christian trader secures the custom of a European house: the master orders his servants accordingly; they bow low in humble submission. Then they set to work to insult and bully the Christian, to thwart him in every way, to play tricks with the things supplied, till the baffled master goes back to the old order of things, and the heathen triumph.

An experience or two will serve to illustrate the methods employed. A Christian milkman commenced business under happy auspices. The custom of one large household alone was almost sufficient for his wants. Under the command of their mistress, the servants were civil and anxious to further the Christian; but, though ostensibly polite, war was in their heart. All went well until, one afternoon, a very large party were having tea, when out of the milk-jug four huge earthworms squirmed into the cups. There was horror, but to the indignation of his mistress the butler meekly replied, "It is Christian milk, your ladyship, as you ordered. What knoweth thy slave of the living creatures? Christian milk—as your honour willed." Needless to add, the Christian had to dispose of his cows speedily, and at a loss.

Again, a butcher became a Christian, and was induced to follow his trade under peculiarly favourable circumstances. Shortly after his baptism one of the clan fell ill. A formidable operation was satisfactorily performed, and the delighted butchers' fraternity, in the warmth of their gratitude, paid the writer the highest compliment in their power, "You are worthy to be a butcher!" As a result, the convert baptized in connection with the Amritsar Medical Mission was not persecuted; in fact, some went beyond neutrality and actively helped him. The writer's Muhummudan cook, out of a personal regard for his master, gave the Christian butcher much good help and advice in connection with joints. Panjabis, for instance, do not use knives and forks, so all meat for their use is cut small by the butcher. It took our friend some time to realise that the taste of the British ran to legs of mutton and joints, and not to little knobs of meat. As long as the writer went about with the butcher, all went well. Left to himself, things began to follow the natural course. Customers wrote to say, "Your Christian butcher never came at ten o'clock, as ordered." The unfortunate man was there, but the servants would not let him see the lady. A very fine joint of Christian mutton, purchased before the mistress herself, was much enjoyed by the cook and his cronies. A tough piece of non-Christian meat, set instead before the master, was not relished by him or his friends. The excuse was, "Not the fault of your lordship's slave. Lo, it is Christian mutton." In another household the cook hung the meat carefully in the sun. The result at table was impressive. The dish could not be removed too quickly. The outcome of the venture, in spite of the exceptional advantages which the writer was able to command amongst non-Christians and Christians alike, was as it ever is. "Christian mutton" followed "Christian milk," and was in due time followed by "Christian tea."

The difficulties and discouragements that faced Robert Clark did not deter him. He was studiously watchful to assist men in the struggle to earn their living. He studied the individual capacities, realised what a man was best fitted for in the struggle of life, then, prompt of heart and hand, seconded to the utmost the convert's efforts to help himself. Various handicrafts and callings were promoted in the Orphanage. He unweariedly blazed the path that was in time to become a royal highway, through the tangle of the trackless jungles of Indian exclusiveness and hostility.

Mr. Clark did not rest content with the devoted furtherance of the interests of the individual. He was too great a statesman not to realise the wider aspects of the question. The work must acquire a force and permanency impossible of attainment as long as it centred in the shifting circumstances of the individual. How was that stability to be obtained? What method would best and most speedily affect the mass? What was the line of least resistance? Such were the questions over which he pondered. He found the true solution in the adoption of the village as the unit on which to base his policy. India is pre-eminently the land of villages and peasant proprietors. The great cities are but a drop in the ocean, for ninety-three per cent. of the people are villagers. Each village has been self-supporting and self-governing, and the village system has remained unchanged, though empires have risen and perished, in the years that can be counted by the thousands. Christianity, Mr. Clark saw, could have no permanent hold in the land until it gripped the rural population. A congregation that centred round Government offices and institutions in a city would cease to exist in that town if official headquarters were transferred elsewhere. It were wisdom to learn from the Moslem monarchs, who propagated Islam in the villages: their power perished, but their religion remained.

A Christian agricultural settlement with its Christian yeomen would be alike the best object-lesson to the people and the most efficient means of gripping the villagers. It would go far to emancipate the converts from the thraldom of dependence on foreign Christians. It would operate powerfully to deliver them from the cruel bondage of the yoke laid on them by their non-Christian countrymen, while the possession of land by Christians would speedily give Christianity, in the eyes of the heathen, the prestige and place of one of the recognised religions of the country.

The settlement would also solve deeper problems than those of agricultural labour. Holy Writ declares that "the king himself is served by the field." Robert Clark foresaw that round the Christian community there would be free field for the exercise by Christians of the arts, crafts, and professions. The potter, the weaver, the water-carrier, the artisan, would gain their livelihood equally with the scribe, the lawyer, the medical practitioner. The difficulties to be faced in putting his plan into action were great and many, but difficulties Mr. Clark considered to be merely things to be overcome.

Mr. Singha tells us of him :—"When, on full thought, it was clear to him that any measure was for the glory of God, then it was in him a lifelong trait that he put his hand to it with all his heart and soul, and, meeting every difficulty as conqueror, perfected the matter."

In this spirit Robert Clark undertook the task of founding the first Christian village in the Panjab. He looked for a stretch of fertile land, well watered, on main lines of communication, easily accessible; and he found what he required in the Government Reserve known as the Rakh Handal. This tract of ground, in the south-west of the Lahore district, lay on the great highway between Multan and the Panjab capital. It was irrigated by the Baree Doab Canal; the main line of rail to Karachi, the port of the Panjab, ran by it; and it was but a couple of hours' train journey from Lahore. After prolonged delays and great difficulty, nineteen hundred acres of land were acquired from Government. Four Indian gentlemen undertook the work of settlement, provided the matter was committed so entirely to them that they would be in no wise trammelled by Europeans. Mr. Clark was heartily glad that they should have the opportunity they desired. He constantly kept in mind the advice of an eminent Indian civilian: "Carry the people with you; aid their efforts, rather than remove from them all stimulus to exertion by making the effort yourself." The quartette received every help and encouragement from Mr. Clark. He notes: "With a perfect knowledge of the country and of the people, and possessing as they do the confidence of the native Christians, they will have the management of the whole undertaking in their own hands. . . . The experiment will be made by natives. We shall now prove whether they are able to carry it out. If by their tact and prudence, and by the means of their personal influence and resources, even a small Christian community can be attracted together, who will live together in harmony, supported by their own labour, without any foreign support, they will accomplish a work which will be greatly beneficial to the interests of Christianity in the country, as well as profitable to themselves."

Robert Clark was too profound a statesman to be ruffled by the chances of the failures that dog the efforts of beginners in novel tasks. He recognised the truth of the dictum, "He never made anything who never made a mistake." Such errors and miscarriage of plans were to him but the premiums that have to be paid to experience, rungs in the ladder whereby the heights are eventually scaled; for, as the Panjabi hath it, "Many tumbles go to the making of the rider."

The Christians established the village, which they named Clarkabad, in honour of the beloved leader. Some years went by, and the efforts put forth resulted in a melancholy failure. The specific reasons do not concern our narrative. The very few Christians who had settled on the land showed neither unity nor brotherly love. The place was a desolation in every sense. Mr. Clark readdressed himself to the task on fresh lines. The Rev. Daud Singh was sent from Amritsar to Clarkabad; later on, the Rev. Roland Bateman followed, and his indomitable labours re-created the place. The great results he achieved were broadened and deepened by the self-denying toil of the Rev. F. H. Beutel and those who succeeded him. To-day the Christian village of Clarkabad, no longer the only one of its kind, stands forth a magnificent success.

On the 5th of May 1867, an important departure was made when work was begun by the Church Missionary Society in the capital of Lahore. The rules of Mission comity in the Panjab bar the Missions of one Church from undertaking work in a city or district occupied by the agencies of another. The new departure was an evidence of the brotherly concord and true unity between the neighbouring Mission of Amritsar and that of the capital. A number of Indian Christians, professedly connected with the Church of England, but living in total disregard of religion, had gathered in Lahore in connection with various Government offices. Lahore was occupied as a station of the Amritsar Mission by Mr. Clark, at the request of the American Presbyterian missionaries themselves. In accepting this new field, he wrote, "We have to express our deep sense of the great kindness and very cordial welcome which have been shown us by our American brethren, and more especially by one (the Rev. John Newton), who was himself the first missionary in the Panjab, and through whom the first invitation was given, in 1850; to the Church Missionary Society to commence a Mission in this province, and who has now welcomed us to the capital of the Province."

Mr. Singha has given us a picture of Mr. Clark as he went about his work in these years—one that illustrates how he was regarded by Indian Christians. "The all-pervading feature in Mr. Clark's character was that his faith was associated with works. What he preached he himself practised. His sympathy was no matter of spending language. He never passed on a suppliant from his door with a 'Go, be warmed, be fed,' but he ever helped by every means in his power." Well might an Indian gentleman say, "However heavy-hearted a man might be, with whatever trouble, he never came to Mr. Clark without going away with a lightened heart."

Then again, when a rainy season of exceptional severity had rendered the houses of Amritsar dangerous at the most perilous and trying portion of the hot weather, Mr. Singha recalls that Mr. Clark "every day girded up his loins, and, dripping with the pelting rain, went daily to the house of every Christian, consoling, and sympathising, and helping. The doors of his own house were ever open, and his home became the refuge of many a Christian during that deadly rain.

"He heartily desired to see Christians as men of light and leading in the social and religious world of the Panjab. It was a noble gift in him that it gladdened his generous heart to see Christians flourishing. He held it to be impossible for the new wine of

Christian civilisation to be filled into the old bottles. No man could accept the Christian faith without approximating to the higher civilisation.

"On one occasion a native Christian wished to build himself a house according to the former patterns of the land. Before beginning, he consulted Mr. Clark, whose advice was that, both on account of health and of the changes that the future would bring, he should build in Western style. Though he was at that time pressed with the meetings of the Missionary Conference, he made a half-hour in which he himself drew two sets of plans for the new house. It was built according to one of them, and when it was completed he sent a present of fruit trees for the grounds.

"Mr. Clark was intensely gentle and patient, and his loving heart drew all men to him. When he punished it was ever with gentleness. His principle was that, though correction is necessary, we must not thereby slay the man with hunger by withdrawing all means of livelihood, for what is there to which hunger will not drive a man? He was ever ready to help from his own purse those crushed by debt or misfortunes. His sympathy and love extended even to apostates, and he was instant in love to draw them back to righteousness.

"A certain man, after many years of Christian profession, denied the Lord. When he had become a renegade, Mr. Clark wrote him a letter of counsel with this exhortation—'You have never been a Christian yet, but there is yet time; even now, if you come to Christ, He will certainly receive you.'"

Amidst the thronging duties of his over-full daily life, Robert Clark's mind was ever busy in perfecting and evolving fresh plans. The present was to him the germ of the future. Clear and steadfast of purpose, he watched the trend of events, and, moving with the times, was not only prepared for exigencies, but was ready to utilise them in furthering the one aim of his life. We find him anticipating the problems of the education of the children of poorer Christians, the establishment of hostels of various grades for boys at the schools.

In 1868 he pleads for a Medical Missionary, "to commence a new effort of missionary work in accordance with our Lord's own example; a work that He will surely bless, and one that will occupy new ground and gain access to new fields of labour. We earnestly ask that this may be tried in Amritsar. Let only the man be a good, clever doctor, and one who has Missionary work at heart, and I think we shall see great results from his labours in connection with the direct preaching of the Gospel, both in pulpit and bazaar." The request was eloquently endorsed by Sir Donald MacLeod, Lieutenant-Governor of the Panjab, but it was not until 1882 that the Amritsar Medical Mission was established, and then only after the most strenuous efforts on Mr. Clark's part. In the light of events, Mr. Clark's words concerning the value of that Medical Mission have proved prophetic.

The development of zenana work brought its own difficulties. These centred round the question of the seclusion of the harem. Certain purdah or veiled women had become converts, and there followed the question as to what policy should govern the administration of the sacraments to them. Some held that any concession to the purdah would be a toleration in part of the Belial of Muhummudanism that would result in ultimate injury to the Church. Mr. Clark, deprecating an arbitrary interference with the social customs of the country, differentiated between the essentials of the religion of Christ and the Western ideals that have grown up around it. He considered that the work of the Gospel was to bring men to God, and that thereafter the Spirit of God in their hearts would lead them into all truth. The missionary was called on in matters social to declare what he deemed to be the better way, but he was in no wise entitled to enforce as an essential part of the religion of Christ the fruits it had borne in the social fabric of his own or any other nation. His commission was, in the words of his Lord, to teach "all things whatsoever I have commanded you," and that teaching would work out social as well as personal salvation. Thus had Christianity abolished slavery, thus also would it right every wrong. It was clear to Robert Clark that the transition from the great religious systems of India to Christianity must of necessity be accompanied by anomalies that would disappear with the first generation. Within just limits, these anomalies would have to be tolerated; for he was no friend to the mischievous meddlesomeness that tries to right one wrong at the expense of inflicting a greater. In formulating a policy, Mr. Clark's first step in this and kindred subjects was to bring the matter before those whom it primarily concerned; that is, the Christians themselves. The wisdom and justice of the step are obvious, but the course is one that might fitly be more often followed. Thereafter we find him corresponding with Sir William Muir, a close personal friend, then Lieutenant-Governor of the North-West Provinces, than whom there was none better fitted to advise on any matter connected with Islam. He in turn consulted the high authority of Mr. C. B. Thornhill, a civilian whose general experience and interest in native Christians qualified him to speak on the subject. We subjoin Mr. Clark's memorandum of the questions submitted to the representatives of the Native Church, with their replies:—

"(1) May purdah women in any case be baptized privately in their own houses; or should it be always considered indispensable for them to come to the church, to be baptized there in the presence of their own sex?

"*Reply.* The apostles baptized persons in different places according to circumstances, and we think that women whose female relations have been purdah nashins [*i.e.* "sitters behind the veil"] for generations should not have burdens placed upon them that are not distinctly authorised by the Word of God; especially when they are weak in faith, as most persons are when they come to be baptized. They should be urged to come to church, and be baptized before Christian women; but if they cannot or will not come, and there appears to be reason in their action, it is better that they should be baptized in their own houses, rather than remain separated from Christ on account of a matter of detail.

"(2) Should any difference be made in the case of the Muhummudan wives of Christian converts?

"*Reply.* We think not.

"(3) May baptized Christian women who consent to come and sit behind the screen during the Sunday service, but who cannot, or will not, bring themselves to receive the Holy Communion in the midst of a mixed congregation of native Christians, ever receive it in the private place where they sit in church, which is screened off from the male part of the congregation?

"*Reply.* The Lord's Table, the bread and the wine, remain the same. The women are present with the congregation in the church before the Table, and are only separated from the Communion rails by the curtain, behind which they join in public worship of God's house. The spiritual communion with Christ and His Church is not interrupted; and we therefore think that they should not be excluded from the Sacrament, but should be allowed to receive it in their own place."

The authorities consulted went very deeply into the matter from all points, and in the main agreed with the findings of the Christians. We quote a few lines well worthy of thought from Mr. Thornhill's luminous deliverance on the subject.

"I think there can be little doubt that modesty, even perhaps chastity, are held by Muhummudans of the upper classes to be inconsistent with abandonment of the purdah.

"Unless we can gradually bring them to regard the treatment of their women in a different light, the abandonment of the purdah would cause the women to lose their self-respect; and as human nature is prone to rush into extremes, there is just cause to fear that women who throw aside their veil will cast away their modesty with it.

"The danger is far greater than any inconvenience which would result from administering baptism in private, and the Holy Communion behind a screen in the church."

Sir William Muir's contribution towards a solution

of the puzzle was worthy of his reputation. His letter is characterised by his usual research and reasoning. To his mind there could "be no doubt that for a woman brought up in the strictly guarded seclusion of a native family, the habits and feelings connected with the seclusion become a second nature. There supervenes an inability to face the gaze of men, and any attempt in that direction becomes, from lifelong sentiment, inseparably connected with a sense of brazen-facedness, if not immodesty.

"Under these circumstances, we have to look, in our treatment of native women who have lived in seclusion, first to the effect on themselves that would result by insisting on their appearance in public, and also to the effect on the native mind outside.

"In both points of view, I agree with Mr. Thornhill that the result of any such measure would be highly prejudicial, and is to be deprecated.

"The Church should not insist upon it—that is to say, it should not require a public appearance as an essential condition of membership."

On the subject of the administration of baptism, Sir William concurred in the opinions expressed, but he was more doubtful as regarded the observance of the Supper of the Lord. The difficulty lay in the manner of the administration of the elements to the communicant in the Church of England.

"I ought to have said that I think the custom of women remaining seated in their pews, and the elements being carried to them, would in my view be equally objectionable with having a part of the chancel curtained off. I do not know how it would be viewed in the Scots Church, where all receive the bread and wine seated either in their ordinary seats or around a table. It might better accord with that habit. But in the English, I should be fearful that any privilege involving so great a departure from the custom would grow up into prescriptive custom in favour of a certain class."

In conclusion, Sir William writes:—"I earnestly hope that you will be able to have the question determined in such a way that there shall be no compulsory putting aside of the purdah, and that the feelings of the parties concerned and the native community at large may not be alienated and shocked by our forcing women, who have been all their lives shut out from the world, into the world."

The year 1868 brought deep personal sorrow to the home at Amritsar. The tears were scarce dry for the death of Mrs. Clark's father, when Robert Clark's own beloved mother passed away, on the 28th of February.

Strenuous toil had strained Mr. Clark's health. The children had reached an age when it was no longer advisable to keep them in India. The time had come to lay down the burden for a time, and he prepared for his second furlough home. The Christians presented him with an illuminated address and a valuable gold watch. Of the testimonials and presentations he received at various times, none were more highly prized than these. The watch, now in the possession of his son Robert, was the one that, to the delight of the Christian community, he used throughout the rest of his life, no mean link in the chain that bound the hearts of the leader and the people into one. He left Amritsar on the 6th of

January 1869, being sped on his way by the tears and prayers of his loving flock, and the heartiest good wishes of non-Christian friends innumerable.

On furlough, as at his station, Robert Clark was still the missionary. The homeward journey was utilised to fit himself better for service. He visited the Mission at Multan, and thereafter voyaged down the Indus, studying the Missions and cheering the workers in Sindh. He travelled from Karachi by way of Bombay to Egypt; after a break in that country, he continued his journey to Italy, where he made a stay of several months; and, having spent some time in France, he arrived in London on the 29th of May.

Robert Clark's studies while on the Continent were fruitful later in the Panjab. We may fitly conclude this chapter with an excerpt from his journal for Easter Sunday, 28th March, while resident in Rome:—"At St. Peter's at 8 a.m. Some 40,000 or 50,000 people. High Mass performed by Pope at 9. Screens removed from Mosaic pictures. Pillars covered with crimson and gold cloth. Pope carried in procession with peacock feathers and triple crown, denoting temporal and spiritual dominion and the union of the two. Saw them kiss his foot. Seven candles on altar, denoting seven spirits. Stood close to credence table, and saw the chalices washed, and the sacristan drink some of the wine—a precaution against poison. Cup *covered* with diamonds. The dresses of Pope and Cardinals and priests most gorgeous. Worship and adoration of Host. Silver trumpets sounding softly and sweetly from dome. At 11 a.m. square before St. Peter's filled to receive Pope's benediction. Troops present, all bowed down. Trumpets sounded and cannon fired from St. Angelo.

"If ye be risen with Christ, seek those things that are *above*, where Christ sitteth on the right hand of God. Set your affection on things *above*, not on things *on the earth.* Query, How far are the things which I have seen during the week part of heaven above, and how far of *this earth* beneath?

"He that speaketh of himself seeketh his own glory. He that seeketh His glory that sent him, the same is true. These ceremonies seem to stand in the same relation to Christianity that Rome's ruins do to the old Roman Empire. Both the Christianity and the Empire are past; the ceremonies and the ruins alone remain."

CHAPTER XX.

EDUCATING THE CONVERT.

ON arrival in England, Mr. Clark settled at Hampstead, and his house became a centre of attraction for many missionaries and friends of the work. Miss Katherine Hull, who knew him at this time, speaks of him as "the calm, holy, dignified, courteous, and already venerable-looking missionary, full of kindness and thoughtful consideration."

His interest in India never slept. Miss Hull tells us he was especially occupied in maturing plans for a system of higher education for Christian children, and in collecting materials for a commentary on the Scriptures in the vernacular. Events in England that touched the East were his study, and the same correspondent gives us a pleasant glimpse of him at the opening of the Asiatic Lascars' Home in London by Lord Lawrence. "It was pleasant to note the cordial mutual affection of these two eminent Soldiers of the Cross—the distinguished military statesman and the no less distinguished missionary."

Events that were to have an important bearing on Mr. Clark were meanwhile transpiring in the Panjab, and to these we must now turn. The question of a Theological College at Lahore for the training of Indian workers had been mooted by the Rev. T. V. French.

Though the Christians were then only some four hundred in number, Mr. Clark ardently supported the proposal. In his opinion, since the hope of the future "lay in free room for the growth and action of a native ministry," and in developing that ministry to take upon its shoulders the heaviest responsibilities it could bear, the Divinity College could not too soon come into being. We may quote a few extracts from a memorandum of singular force and cogency, in which he urges his views on the authorities of the Church Missionary Society.

He writes in April of 1868:—"I cannot myself believe that the best way of carrying on work is for a number of English missionaries to go out day by day and year by year, for a whole lifetime, into the same bazaars, and preach the same truths, perhaps in the same way, to the same audience, that so often appears to be Gospel-hardened, and whose curiosity has been already so satisfied that they will not even cross over the way to listen to what they have heard a hundred times before. The Gospel must of course be preached in old and new Missions, and there are in all our large cities a number of strangers to whom the Gospel message is probably new; but the question often arises to the mind, whether a small number of English missionaries, sometimes even only a single individual, cannot generally, with a proper staff of native helpers, both bring the Gospel to bear on these, and also superintend the native pastor in his oversight over the native flock. If this is the case, it would be better for the greater part of our preaching missionaries to be away from our large stations, and for each of them to be a centre of missionary work himself, with his native helpers around him, spending both hot weather and cold in the towns and villages, and working in some chosen neighbourhood from some fixed basis of operations, as far as circumstances would allow it, with every due regard to health.

"Whenever the English missionaries are massed too much together, the natives seem to throw all responsibility on them, and to become more or less mechanics. They cannot work freely in an Anglicised community, with too many Europeans around them. The Mission is then a European, not a native one. The Europeans are everything, the native nothing. The Europeans assemble together at their stated meetings and Conferences, and model and arrange everything according to their European notions. The natives see that the Europeans are determined to have everything their own way, and that they are merely servants and agents, and they soon learn to say 'Yes' to everything, and to do what they are told to do, and nothing more. They feel, perhaps, little heart for their work, because it is not so much their own work as the Europeans', and because they are not primarily responsible for it. Some of the better class leave the Mission; and those who remain seem sometimes as uncomfortable and unserviceable in it as a native sepoy does when dressed in an English grenadier's uniform.

"It has often seemed to me that native Christians will hardly go to their own native pastor when they have a number of English missionaries on hand ready to listen to their every want. Inquirers, too, will often go unwillingly to catechists when there are several missionaries at their station, where the inquirers will of course go from one missionary to another, and endeavour to obtain through the kindness of one what they fail in securing from another. The catechist, too, becomes unsettled, if he hardly knows to whom he belongs, and may, any day of his life, be transferred from one missionary to another, whose plans of working are perhaps altogether different. It may become a question whether some of us older missionaries would not perhaps do more good to the station itself were we to leave it, and do also infinitely more good to the neighbourhood around were we to become centres of missionary operations, with full powers to act each one for himself within certain limits, in connection with a sufficient staff of native labourers.

"I think that our native brethren should do everything they can do. Some kinds of work they will do far better than Europeans. They must have free liberty of action, and we must not always consider them to be mere children, but look on them as men, who are not always to be kept under a father's eye, but will gain advantages and become more manly and useful by being sometimes away from their parent's eye, and in a position where they not only may, but sometimes almost must, act for themselves. They must not be always disciples who have everything to learn, and have to keep learning everything over and over again from us; but they must be considered as men who have become teachers in matters that some of them know equally well with ourselves."

In March of 1869, Messrs. French and Knott began the Divinity College at Lahore, "after much advice from prominent men." Land was secured, large buildings were planned, students were enrolled, and all promised well, when there came the sudden stroke of Mr. Knott's death. "The Lord caused him to see the work with his eyes, but he was not permitted to enter in." Mr. French was reduced to sore straits, and disaster threatened the nascent institution. In this emergency, Robert Clark, though on sick leave, promptly resolved to forego his furlough that he might fill the breach at Lahore. The act involved heavy sacrifices that none realised better than Mr. Clark himself. The valedictory meeting for Mr. Clark was held on the 14th of November 1869, and on the 19th he sailed from Southampton in the P. & O. *Massilia* for Bombay. Mrs. Clark remained with the family. She removed from London to her own country of Scotland, and the children received their upbringing in her old homes, first at Fortrose in Ross-shire, and latterly in classic Edinburgh.

The Rev. Maulvie Imaduddin Lahiz gives a graphic account in the columns of the *Masihi* of the moment at which Mr. Clark's decision to return reached the Panjab. Mr. French's need of a colleague had become insistent. In addition to the professorial work, large sums were required; for the fabric of the college had to be erected, and who was there to undertake these vast labours? Friends met in council and deliberated long and anxiously on the situation, but all their thought served only to intensify their perplexity. "Then, said they," to quote the Maulvie Imaduddin, "let us pray to God that from Him may come help and guidance. Even as we finished praying and straightened our backs, there came the rapping of some-one at the door. Mr. French rose, went to the door, and saw a telegraph messenger. The telegram was from the Parent Committee [of the Church Missionary

Society]: 'Trouble not for funds or college buildings; Robert Clark is coming, he will do all.' Then were we all filled with gladness and laughter, and we said, This is the answer of God to our prayer."

Mr. Clark reached his destination on New Year's Day, and some months later was able to report, "The garden is bought and paid for. The foundations of the house are laid, and students' quarters arranged for. We are now writing to all our friends to raise the one thousand pounds that are still required. The college is for all North India, to prepare and send forth native ministers and missionaries to their own people. This is one of the chief wants of India—to make Christianity indigenous, by giving them, with God's help, able pious pastors and evangelists from among their own sons."

The work of the college was carried on in temporary quarters while its own home was being constructed. The part of the building undertaken first was the College Chapel, a step that required no interpretation to the Oriental mind, for it appealed fervently to Christians and non-Christians alike.

Mr. Clark kept touch with Amritsar by periodic visits from Lahore, and it is lovingly noted that, however pressed he was, "he never failed to call on his native friends."

The first month of 1871 found the "School of the Prophets" ready for occupation. It was inaugurated by a special service, at which Robert Clark was the preacher. The Presbyterian missionaries attended in full force, and the happy catholicity of the institution was further evidenced by the noteworthy fact that the agents of the American Presbyterian Missions and those of the Church of Scotland were sent to it for training together with the members of the Missions of the Church of England. The elder generation of the Panjabi clergy of various communions look back to-day to the time when they sat together as brother-students at the feet of Mr. French and Mr. Clark in Lahore.

The spirit of unity and brotherly love that flowed from Mr. Clark is well illustrated by an anecdote narrated by the Rev. Miyan Sadiq (of whom more anon), then a student in the Divinity College. Mr. Clark received a request to open a Mission in the town of Rupar, where no missionary agency was yet at work. Miyan Sadiq, in company with another agent, was sent to inquire and report. On the return journey from Rupar they stayed at Ludhiana, the parent station of the American Presbyterian Mission, and when paying their respects to Mr. Rudolph, the missionary in charge, told him of what they had been doing. "In this connection," continues Miyan Sadiq, "he said, 'Tell Mr. Clark from me, Rupar is near our stations of Ludhiana, Subathu, and Amballa; leave it for us.' I repeated the message to Mr. Clark. He said, 'Mr. Rudolph is one of the chosen of God, we must do as he wishes.' When our report was presented in Committee, all were in favour of commencing work in Rupar; but, merely on the strength of the verbal message I had brought, Mr. Clark would not occupy the town."

The results of Mr. Clark's period of service in Lahore are not summed up by a record of his activities at the Divinity College. Two efforts, amongst the most important in his fruitful life, date from this time. They are concerned with education for Christians, and

Christian literature, and from them both immense results have accrued to the Panjab.

As we have already said, the subject of higher education of Christian girls had been occupying Mr. Clark's mind. The first step in that great matter was taken in a very simple way. Mr. Singha tells us that, when Robert Clark was building the Divinity College in Lahore, "the native Christians had started a girls' school, which then contained just three pupils. Taking advantage of Mr. Clark's presence, the Christians sent an honourable deputation to beg him to take charge of the arrangements of the school. Mr. Clark was not willing to do so in a station of the American Presbyterian Mission without their leave, but when they consented, so wisely did he undertake the work that the result was the establishment of the first High School for Girls, now known as the flourishing "Lady Dufferin School of Lahore." That was but an earnest of other measures to be described at a later period.

The other effort was the production and circulation of Christian literature in English and in the vernaculars of the Panjab. Mr. Clark was himself throughout life an ardent reader and lover of books. Though no man's life was busier, he daily made time to keep himself abreast of what was best and freshest in the literature of the day, and he was in particular a keen student of the special works that dealt with any part of the many-sided problems involved in world-wide missionary enterprise. The immense importance of literature as a missionary agency had long been in his thoughts, and he set to work to arouse interest and enlist friends in this work. His efforts met with a splendid response, for he was endowed to the full with that great gift of the true leader, the power to rally men to a flag. He inspired them with his own enthusiasm and imbued them with his indomitable optimism. His genius never failed to single out the right man for the right place. His labours, in which the Presbyterian missionaries heartily co-operated, now resulted in welding friends of all Churches into a great organisation, "The Panjab Religious Book Society." It is impossible to exaggerate the value of the work done by this Society or the position it holds as a missionary agency. A mere enumeration of the Society's multi-tongued publications would occupy many pages. In connection with it, Mr. Clark promoted the production of books in the vernacular by a judicious system of prizes, and was indefatigable in his efforts to foster the movement he had initiated. To his many onerous duties he for years added the arduous task of Secretary to this Society. He also acted in that capacity for the Panjab Auxiliary of the British and Foreign Bible Society.

But no adequate account of his labours in the cause of Christian literature is possible within the compass of these pages. The record of his activities in India, his efforts at home, and his correspondence with the Bible Society, the Religious Tract Society, the Society for the Promotion of Christian Knowledge, and the other agencies of the kind, would require a volume to itself. Suffice it to say, Robert Clark stands forth as the father of Christian literature in the Panjab. Brilliant fellow-workers collaborated with him. To the zeal and munificence of one, the Rev. F. H. Baring, Christian literature owes the Book Depository situated in a commanding position in Lahore. Branch depositories and the establishment of a network of colportage were further developments. Mr. Clark found an ideal manager for the Central Depository in Mr. Radha Rahman Raha, who was for many years his friend and faithful fellow-worker. Under this able lieutenant the great arsenal of Christian weapons rapidly attained the success that it has ever since uninterruptedly enjoyed.

The beginning of 1872 found affairs so far settled in Lahore that Mr. Clark was able to return to Amritsar. Mr. French had to take furlough, and during his absence Lahore could not entirely dispense with the services of Robert Clark. Despite the many occupations and anxieties of his own station, he for seven months went weekly to the neighbouring city, to give the help of his experience, as well as to teach in the senior department of the College. In no other way could the exigencies of Lahore be met, and so, taking every precaution in his power to avoid a breakdown, he went forward cheerfully. The strain of the extra toil in the hot weather told on his health, but to him missionary work was a campaign, and concentration of the force available at the weakest point was the right principle to follow.

CHAPTER XXI.

VICTORY IN CASHMERE.

THE stage that the struggle with the Maharajah of Cashmere had reached will be fresh in the memory of the reader. In 1871, the waning year brought the battle to a brilliant finish; but alas! the lustre of victory was dimmed by the death of the heroic Elmslie. The war had been prosecuted with unwavering patience in Cashmere and in the Panjab. The story of the dire straits, the toils, trials, and triumphs of the six seasons in which Dr. Elmslie had laboured in Cashmere, is not germane to this narrative. No attempt was made to oust him from the city of Srinagar, in which he took up his abode; but the winter exodus, round which the battle raged, was stringently enforced.

Crowds of grateful patients and friends lined the river banks to bid the doctor farewell as he left the capital of Cashmere in the autumn of 1871. He was exhausted by the efforts made during a severe cholera season, and in no condition to undertake the long rough journey over the lofty mountains to British India; but the Maharajah would allow no respite. Illness came on at once on departure, and his malady increased with the hardships of the journey. "He walked till he could walk no more. His wife gave up her dhooly to him, and then she walked across the

REV. PANDIT NARAIN DASS KHARAK SINGH.

snows, where bears stood and looked at her. When she could not keep up with the dhooly bearers, she was left behind to walk on alone." His illness increased alarmingly, and no doctor was near.

Elmslie reached British territory in a dying condition. Mr. Clark made all speed to him, but when he arrived, it was to find that this true servant of God and loyal member of the Church Missionary Society had just passed away. "Surely God's curse must rest upon this poor oppressed country," said a Cashmeri, when he heard of the tragedy. Mr. Clark writes :—"He died at Gujrat, the scene of that last victory in the second Sikh War which gave over the entire Panjab to our administration. Dr. Elmslie, too, died in the hour of another victory; for at the very moment when he was dying in Gujrat, Cashmere was being thrown open to missionary efforts the whole year round. Now Cashmere is as accessible in this respect to Missions as other parts of India."

There is an overmastering pathos in the death of the hero of Cashmere. Like Nelson, he fell at the moment of victory. During six years he had held the fort and waged the war for the right, only to pass away when yet greater victories of peace seemed emphatically to require him especially of all men. He sojourned, as did Abraham, in the land he had come to possess, and like him he received not the promises, but saw them afar off, and he went hence without even the knowledge of the break of day in the land for which he laid down his life. The wrongs would be righted and the songs of victory sung by others; for him God had reserved some better thing.

For six long years in the Panjab, Robert Clark had

fought the battle of liberty, and now the prize was won. Cashmere, premier amongst the feudatory and tributary states of the Empire, stood with doors wide open that none might shut in the face of the messenger of the Evangel of God;—but the gallant heart was still whose joy would have been to him the crown of rejoicing.

Two days after Dr. Elmslie's death, Mr. Clark received a letter, the last in a long correspondence with the authorities. In this document the Indian Foreign Office granted the Doctor the permission of the suzerain power to remain during the winter in Cashmere. Once again good news had come too late; once again—
"Someone had blundered."

The death of Dr. Elmslie made the continuance of the work in Cashmere the question of the hour. Accordingly, the summer of 1873 found Robert Clark again established in Srinagar. The situation was intensely difficult. The Maharajah, exasperated by defeat, was fruitful in wiles and unremitting in hostility. Delicate handling was required if the victory was not to prove barren.

The bitter humiliation involved in the action of the Indian authorities was not one that the haughty monarch could brook. He had at all costs, in Chinese phrase, "to save his face" before his subjects. Gulab Singh endeavoured, therefore, to retrieve the situation by attempting to put a stop to public preaching. In this and like attempts he was signally routed, and the situation became even more strained than it had been. Matters in Cashmere were truly never in more parlous plight than at this juncture.

While it was impossible to soothe the royal pride by submitting to an infringement of liberty to preach the Gospel, it was clear to Robert Clark that some method must be promptly devised to heal the hurt that rankled in Gulab Singh's mind, and to yield him the honour due to him as sovereign ruler of Cashmere. Accordingly, we find, Mr. Clark sought an audience with the Maharajah on the 25th of September 1875, and at that interview, with consummate statesmanship, craved as a favour from the Cashmeri Court that permission to stay which the suzerain power had granted as a right. The observer unversed in the ways of the East would have deemed the interview fruitless, for the Maharajah gave no sign of assent; but the failure was only apparent; in reality the object was obtained—the point is that he did not say No. As such matters are in the Orient, Gulab Singh would, by an immediate consent, have owned himself worsted, and would have also published his defeat.

The ensuing year, 1874, brought Elmslie's successor —Dr. Theodore Maxwell, a nephew of the famous John Nicholson of Delhi. Robert Clark accompanied Dr. and Mrs. Maxwell to the royal city of Jammu, and when introducing him to the Maharajah he tells us he "watched with interest His Highness' face as he scanned the features of the sister's son of John Nicholson, who had come to be a missionary in Cashmere." Great kindness was shown by the Maharajah, a comfortable house given to the Mission, and a hospital was built at Srinagar. But Dr. Maxwell's health broke down, and he returned to England in the following year.

What had seemed insuperable obstacles in the way of a free course for the Gospel had, however, been surmounted; thereafter the missionary was in nowise harassed by the sovereign of Cashmere.

Lieutenant-Colonel Mackinlay gives us a glimpse of Robert Clark about this time :—"At the end of the year 1871 my wife and I arrived at Amritsar with a garrison of Royal Artillery ; we soon made the acquaintance of the Rev. R. Clark, and rapidly became intimate with him. He was a quiet, dignified man, with good judgment and a sympathetic manner, and he was evidently a power in the Mission, respected and loved by all ; a man with large views, always engaged in varied schemes for the benefit of the good work to which he had devoted his life. When I first saw the Mission House, I remember being struck with the substantial and permanent appearance of the building. He also had a plan on hand to obtain a good sanatorium for the missionaries in a healthy Hill station."

In connection with Dr. Elmslie's death, Colonel Mackinlay observes :—"Here was an occasion for Mr. Clark's love, care, and foresight! We received an invitation to take up our quarters in the Mission House in the city of Amritsar, so that my wife might be there to receive and comfort the young widow on her expected arrival in the course of two or three days, as there were then no wives of missionaries or other missionary ladies at the Station. Accordingly we went there. My wife saw much of Mrs. Elmslie. What was the next step to be taken by the widow? Packing up and returning at once to her friends in Scotland? Not at all. Mr. Clark, with his habit of looking ahead and his appreciation of character, now saw an opportunity to start a work which he had long had at heart—to begin reaching Indian women with the Gospel in a systematic way by lady missionaries, who would visit the zenanas. Consequently, after a little while, he broached the subject to Mrs. Elmslie. How much better that the widow should have the privilege of undertaking this useful and much-needed work, instead of going to Scotland at once with her sorrow!

"Mr. Clark had the faculty of attracting many to himself, and his friends among the military and the civilians in India were numerous. I remember one morning at breakfast he held in his hand a letter which he had just received from the Commissioner, General Reynell Taylor, enclosing a sum of money for the Mission on the anniversary of a remarkable deliverance from death which he had experienced in one of the frontier wars.

"Early in 1873 I was sent to Mian Mir. I not unfrequently met Mr. Clark, but the last distinct remembrance of him was when we met in Cashmere two or three years later, and when he asked me to go and visit the Chief Judge, a Hindu Bengali barrister from India. The Maharajah admired the English system of laws and their administration, but he was too jealous of the English to appoint an Englishman, so he selected a Bengali from India trained in our methods. We duly called on the dignitary—a young man, who received us most courteously, speaking excellent English." Colonel Mackinlay closes his reminiscence of this remarkable visit by observing:—"I mention this incident to illustrate Mr. Clark's faculty of interesting others, such as myself, in the work so dear to his own heart."

CHAPTER XXII.

MEDICAL MISSIONS AND BIBLE COMMENTARIES.

THE first of the Decennial Missionary Conferences of India was held at Allahabad in the year 1873, and it is remarkable for Robert Clark's advocacy of Medical Missions in general. The principle he laid down was that "Medical Missions are amongst the most important means of evangelising India; and the attention of all our Societies should be more distinctly drawn than has hitherto been the case to the opportunities which they afford."

Though these agencies were yet in embryo, Mr. Clark had thought out the basis on which alone they could stand, and the soundness of his conclusions has been justified by the subsequent history of Medical Missions. Honest, painstaking medical work he held to be the first essential in a Medical Mission. Thorough himself in everything, he maintained that in this best of services for God and man, the highest only was the standard worthy of adoption. The amateur who wandered about dispensing pills, plasters, and tracts doubtless had his place. If he were wise enough to know his limitations and sufficiently strong not to overstep the boundary, he could even do useful work amongst the suffering. But Robert Clark claimed the office of Medical Missionary for duly qualified medical men only, and the professional qualifications of these men, he held, should be of the highest. The issues were far too serious to admit of any playing at medical missionary. To expect medical men to undertake their responsible office with inadequate appliances was an insult to reason, and it was a cruel wrong to profess to heal men's bodies for the love of God, while giving them in His name anything less than the very best. He gave short shrift to those who, concerned only with the so-called spiritual side of the work, expected the medical missionary to "get on somehow." Robert Clark did not see in the Mission Hospital, as some would have it, the medical missionary's hindrance or toy: it was his workshop, the field of his richest opportunities and fullest efforts.

The Allahabad Conference marked the beginning of a long drawn campaign on behalf of Medical Missions against a legion of difficulties. Some made merry over the preposterous idea of "converting the heathen with a dose of castor-oil or Epsom salts," while others were doubtful of the propriety of "diverting sacred funds given for the preaching of the Gospel" to such mundane things as the panoply of the surgeon or a full equipment of drugs. It was hard for them to realise that a bolus might, on occasion, be a means of grace equally with a tract published at the charge of a missionary treasury. There were others who frankly confessed they could not "see Medical Missions in the Bible"; and to such Robert Clark's reply was that their copies must differ from his. By voice and pen, he unweariedly continued to teach that Medical Missions were in accord with the example and command of our Lord; that they were the cause of

Humanity as well as the cause of God; and that in neglecting them the Church was passing by a most potent weapon. Friends rallied round him; nothing could withstand his ardent enthusiasm and sound common sense. Little by little the long night gave place to a glorious day, and the splendid Medical Missionary inheritance of the Church in the Panjab to-day is the result of the efforts of Robert Clark.

In the year 1874, Mr. Clark commenced the publication of a series of commentaries on portions of the Scriptures. The project had long occupied his mind. No such books existed in the vernacular, and the effort to supply the lack was a fresh outcome of his mastery of what was essential for the welfare of the Panjab Church.

These commentaries were designed to meet several important conditions in the development and upbuilding of the native Church. They would be helps in the private study of pastors, teachers, and Christian families. Scattered or ill-educated congregations, deprived of regular ministrations, and isolated Christians would find in them a means of grace. They would teach inquirers, but they would also appeal to a far wider field. Exhaustive commentaries on the non-Christian sacred books exist; and these are favourite reading with Rajahs and nobles, with the rank and file as with the leaders of the various faiths. There were many in the land unprepared to have any truck with Christians, or to show leanings to Christianity, who were yet curious for information concerning that faith. Mr. Clark foresaw that, by means of these commentaries, the Gospel would penetrate into the palaces of princes and the strongholds of non-Christian religions. The books would find a welcome in homes, in temples, and in mosques, where the presence of the Christian would be considered defilement.

Robert Clark had realised with true inwardness that the purpose he had in view could not be achieved by books written from the Western standpoint, much less by any mere translations. The remark of an Indian nobleman to the writer in another connection aptly summed up the situation:—"We want the Water of Life, but not in your Western pan." It was essential that the language should be choice, and the work cast in Eastern mould. The instrument was ready to hand in the master mind and unique personality of Maulvie Imaduddin Lahiz; and, as one result of his labours, it is fascinating to observe how the revelation that enshrines our holy faith can appeal to the glowing brain and ardent heart of the Oriental Christian. As we have seen, Mr. Clark had been the Maulvie's spiritual father. The relation of teacher and pupil ripened into loving friendship, that grew but the stronger in the thirty-four years they spent together as fellow-workers at Amritsar.

The material was supplied by Mr. Clark; the Maulvie Sahib cast it into shape; and then, together, they elaborated the book, "built on the foundation, solid, strong, and good, of the Word of God," and, as a native gentleman observes, "without even the smell of the West" about it. But we shall let Dr. Imaduddin tell the story as he gives it in the *Masihi*. Mr. Clark "caused me to write four books in which the major portion of the work was his. It was mine to write, and here and there I interpolated some subject matter, but it was his part to bring the material from the books of the bygone great. He had recourse to about thirty authorities, and certain of the books he did not merely refer to, but read through, ere these four books were written—the Commentary on Matthew, that on John, the Key to the Pentateuch, and the Commentary on the Acts. Our intention was that the Christians who should come into being in this land might by these books know the Lord Christ, and with stalwart faith, being His disciples, should be blessed. During his lifetime our honourable Sahib [Mr. Clark] saw this purpose abundantly fulfilled in many souls."

The other objects Mr. Clark had in mind were equally well served by the books. In one instance a Moslem prince caused the commentaries to be publicly read in full Durbar daily for hours during many months.

The abiding charm of this product of the joint labours of Mr. Clark and Imaduddin rests in the fact that these are the first Eastern commentaries on what, though God's revelation to the world, is yet emphatically *the* Sacred Book of the East.

On the 1st of March 1874, Mr. Clark baptized a notable convert of mature age, Pandit Narain Dass Kharak Singh. He was a ripe Sanskrit scholar, deeply versed in the Vedas, the Hindu philosophies, and the religion of the Sikhs. He had been fashioned in many schools during a romantic, adventurous life. He was, as a convert from amongst Hindus and Sikhs, what Imaduddin had been from amongst Moslems; and, like Imaduddin, he devoted his talents to the service of the Gospel by voice and pen. During the remaining twenty-six years of his life he was a true yoke-fellow with his spiritual father, Robert Clark.

The pressure of the calls made upon him did not prevent Mr. Clark from keeping in touch with the world-wide interests of Missions or from pleading their cause. He sowed beside all waters, and had the joy of seeing the harvest in many quarters. An interesting illustration is found in the life of Dr. Bickersteth, Bishop of Tokio. In 1875, Mr. Clark and his friend Mr. Welland of Calcutta were fellow-speakers at a missionary meeting. Bickersteth was present, and was so profoundly impressed, that in July of that year we find he told his father, the Bishop of Exeter, that he had resolved to organise a missionary band in Cambridge and to lead them for work in India. Amritsar was to be their sphere, in affiliation with the Church Missionary Society, but it was found, on deliberation, that there was reason to fear that the band would not be able to work in harmony with the Evangelical principles and methods of the Church Missionary Society. The Cambridge Mission, in consequence, turned its thoughts to the South Panjab, and eventually, in 1877, settled at Delhi, with the future Bishop of Tokio as its first head.

Mr. Clark was quick to mark men whose abilities seemed to fit them especially for work in the Panjab. Recruits from other parts who came to see or learn were tempted to stay in this enticing field. He had the reputation of attracting "every good missionary" to the Land of the Five Waters. Mr. Welland, then Secretary in Calcutta, protested in 1875 that missionaries lent in the future to Mr. Clark should "be labelled all over—'To be returned.'" The Zenana work under the leadership of Miss Wauton at Amritsar offered many advantages for the training of recruits, but Mr. Welland wrote:—"We don't at all feel disposed to send any of our ladies to the Panjab. That word *training* of yours is a most attractive bait—to me, at least, who knows what it means; but I also know the strong hook that lies beneath. Hearts are 'linked to you with hooks of steel,' and it is easier to go than to return."

The year 1876 witnessed a great forward step in the development of Christianity in the Panjab. Converts in that land are drawn from widely different races and creeds; and distinctions between one and another are sharply demarcated by differences that extend to the most trivial affairs of daily life. The Christians, of necessity, presented the spectacle of a community in which the members differed from one another in diet, dress, custom, and even in the use of the same common tongue. They were, to quote their own phrase, not one sound, solid log, but "sticks picked from every wood and all manner of trees." Robert Clark had long pondered over the means that could be used to fuse the heterogeneous collection of material into a homogeneous mass. The Christians must be welded into a "qaum,"—that is, a clan or people,—even as they had been members of great communities within the pale of their former faiths. But how was it to be done? Robert Clark saw in the visit to India of King Edward, then Prince of Wales, a magnificent opportunity to achieve what he had at heart.

Why should not native Christians, than whom there were no more loyal subjects of the Queen, stand forth as a people amongst the peoples of India to welcome their future sovereign? The step was incumbent on them as a loyal duty, and its performance would make it clear to all that the native Christians of India had become a recognised class in the land. That fact would operate powerfully to promote the consolidation of the community, and it would also materially affect its relation to the Government and the masses of their fellow-countrymen. There was no precedent for the course proposed by Robert Clark, and he was beset by difficulties official and otherwise. But he had fought too many battles to think of retiring from this one, when so much was at stake. Eventually all obstacles were surmounted, and Christians from all Churches in the Panjab assembled at Amritsar to greet the Prince. The intercourse of the Christians from different Missions in the days before the reception was also exceedingly useful in promoting fellowship and fuller knowledge of one another.

Mr. Clark gives us a graphic account of the unique gathering at his house on the evening preceding the royal visit. "There, in one corner of the room, is seated the brother of the reigning Rajah of Kapurthala, who was only baptized a few months ago, the first-fruits of a celebrated Sikh dynasty. There is Imad-ud-din, the learned Maulvie, who is now engaged in writing a commentary on the Bible. There is Rajab Ali, the editor of a native newspaper, conversing with an intelligent Bengali, one of the many converts of Dr. Duff's institution. There is Imam Shah, the native pastor of Peshawar, seated by one of his flock, an Afghan Zemindar, clad in a skin coat, with a scarf thrown loosely over his shoulder. And then, as the eye passes along the side benches, it is arrested by the intelligent countenances of men converted from Sikhism, Mohammedanism, and Hinduism. At the opposite end of the room conspicuously appear five Rajputs. One of them is a Zaildar, or chief, of twenty-two villages. After tea has been served round to all, Professor Ram Chander is called upon to give an address. He is the learned author of 'Problems of Maxima and Minima solved by Algebra,' and therefore speaks, with mathematical exactness, words of sober wisdom. But the address of the evening is that of Mr. Abdullah Athim, an Extra Assistant Commissioner, who exhorts his hearers to distinguish between an outward profession of faith and an inward realisation of spiritual life. He then kneels down, and, in an earnest, simple prayer, supplicates the God of Mercy on behalf of ourselves and our Prince. It was a grand evening, that Sunday evening of 23rd January. 'I wish the Prince would come every year,' said one; 'he did us all good.' 'That can't be; but why should we not meet once a year like this?' said a dear loving native brother. 'It makes us feel that we are a nation—a people.'"

On the 24th of January 1876 the Prince surveyed the expanse of Amritsar from the roof of Mr. Clark's house in the city, and thereafter, in the presence of an assembly of many hundreds of Christians, was graciously pleased to accept a loyal address, enclosed in a silver casket of Cashmere work, together with copies of the Holy Scriptures in the various vernaculars of the Panjab. The presentation was made, on behalf of the Indian Christian community, by H.H. the Kanwar Sir Harnam Singh Ahluwalia, Professor Ram Chander, Director of Public Instruction in Patiala State, and Mr. Abdullah Athim, Extra Assistant Commissioner in the Panjab.

This period of service now drew to a close, and Mr. Clark took furlough in the spring of the year. Mrs. Clark left Scotland to meet him in Egypt, and their respective steamers arrived simultaneously at Port Said.

They visited Palestine and Syria, then coasted along Asia Minor to Constantinople, and amongst other matters Mr. Clark took special note of the state of Muhummudanism in these lands. The homeward journey was continued up the Danube to Vienna, and so across the Continent to London, where they arrived on the 17th of May. A few days later they were united to their children in their home in Edinburgh. The time of rest was brief. The summer was spent at North Berwick; then the Scottish home was broken up; suitable arrangements were made for the family; and Mr. and Mrs. Clark prepared to return to India in the autumn.

These days of furlough were fully occupied, and Mr. Clark was frequently away from home, engaged in furthering his plans for future work. The hour was ripe for an advance in the too neglected field of education of Christian children. Furthermore, experiments made in the development of the native Church now warranted larger measures. The evangelisation of Moslem lands was a subject he was especially anxious to press to the front, and he found time to deliver an address on that topic in his University, on the 16th of October. In masterly fashion Mr. Clark showed how remarkably India influenced other Moslem lands. They borrowed their weapons against Christianity from India, and from that land could they most effectively be assailed. The key to the position, alike for India and the Moslem world, lay in a full use of the fruitful opportunities abundantly present among Muhummudans in the Panjab. Sir William Muir, when asked to indicate the best centre from which to attack Islam, had expressed his opinion that "Amritsar was as good as any,"—"And," Mr. Clark added, "the work can be done in English."

The Valedictory Meeting in London was held on the 13th of November. Two days later, Mr. and Mrs. Clark left for India by way of Genoa. They reached Bombay on the 23rd of December, and, having been present at the great Delhi Durbar on 1st January 1877, when the Queen was proclaimed Empress of India, arrived at Amritsar on the fifth day of that month.

CHAPTER XXIII.

NATIVE CHURCH COUNCIL AND ALEXANDRA SCHOOLS.

THE principles that underlay Robert Clark's efforts towards development of the indigenous Church have already been explained. We have seen that he was no stickler for the Episcopalian form of church government all the world over. God's grace, he believed, does not depend on nationality or forms. He held that it would be time enough for the native Indian Church to deal with ecclesiastical problems, and its Canons and Ordinal, when it had attained sufficient strength to stand alone. It was for Church of England missionaries to stand to their own formularies as long as they had the Indian Church in tutelage, and for that Church to abide by them, but when the native Churches should sail away from the convoy it was their inalienable right to hoist what colours they liked; and he was ever mindful of the fact that the first condition of any independence that was not a sham must lie in financial self-support. The measures he had initiated had been so remarkably successful, that the authorities of the Church Missionary Society felt the time had come when they might promote the formation of a Panjab Native Church Council to forward the development of a self-supporting, self-governing, self-extending Panjabi Church. Robert Clark was appointed Chairman of the body he was instructed to form, and for many years he filled that onerous office. The Council was organised, and its inaugural meeting was held in 1877.

Mr. Singha, himself a member and Vice-Chairman of the Council, writes:—"From the first, Mr. Clark's heart's desire was that all native Christians should unite to form one Hindustani Church. It was clear that he was against ecclesiastical divisions in India, and he strove to unite all sects in the bands of concord into one Church. He sought to effect this purpose by means of Henry Venn's plan of Church Councils. The Rev. John Newton and a number of honourable Presbyterians were present at the first meeting in Amritsar, and, for many years, influential Indian Presbyterians attended the yearly gatherings as members. Mr. Clark's endeavour was to free the Church from foreign money, that it might stand on its own feet and order its own affairs."

The Council was hailed with enthusiasm by native Christians. They gave liberally and worked hard; able men, Europeans and Indian, gathered round Mr. Clark; but, as years went by, the early promise of the Council was not fulfilled. The causes that led to this result are too complex to be dealt with in these pages, and are not such as to tempt the pen to linger: the story is distressful and humiliating. The non-success was, to put it briefly, not due in the main to the Indian Christians. Possibly the plan was premature, but the failure is to be traced to the shortcomings of the foreign workers. Instead of a frank confidence, the Council met with suspicion, jealousy, and opposition in quarters where it should have commanded generous support. Cramping regulations fettered its liberty of action, and the withering blight of a narrow ecclesiasticism stunted its free developments.

Mr. Singha writes :—"Alas! Mr. Clark saw not the fulfilment of his hopes, and in a sense the Church Council realised not the purpose of its being—but, at the very least, this great benefit has accrued: Indian Christians were constantly confronted with the question of self-support, and to some extent it has been hammered into their brain, and if not to-day, yet certainly in time to come, this tree that Mr. Clark planted will yet flourish."

Dr. Imaduddin observes in the columns of the *Masihi* :—"For twenty years Mr. Clark toiled to make the Native Church Council successful. The plan was a revelation of his true love to us Indians, for he saw the great advantages that would accrue to us from it; but we of the land did not fully realise these things, we lost courage, and we have made it evident that God will bring others who will do the work, and in this world will wear the resulting crown of blessedness. By ordering their own affairs in their own land, they will show they have realised the worth and value of the Christian religion. To my mind, in this matter Mr. Clark has gone hence hungry, taking with him the sorrow of the failure of the Church Council in his heart; —yet in its time this work also will be fulfilled."

Mr. Clark himself noted in January 1897, in a document laid before a United Conference of Church Missionary Society's Indian missionaries :—"When our Native Church Council was first established in the Panjab, it appeared to carry everything before it. It elicited the enthusiasm and evoked the sympathy, apparently, of us all. The first Reports are full of it.

If all missionaries had always supported it, it would have worked out a change in the whole country. It was only when two parties were formed in the Church on this question, and Indian Christians ranged themselves, together with European missionaries, on two opposite sides, that trouble arose."

The contrary plan of development, that had for its pivot the amalgamation of Europeans and natives, was opposed by Mr. Clark to the end of his days. It was a retrograde step, it would dwarf the individual Indian, and it would make the native Church a mere appanage of the Church of England; for it is to be remembered that the English Church in India is established by law. The chaplains of the staff are Government officers, the great sees have bishops appointed to them by the Crown as in England, and, however sad the fact may be, the ruling race cannot in general be expected to tolerate an indigenous episcopate. Mr. Clark sought progress, as a consequence, not on the lines of an impossible coalescence, but of a true national development.

"Our missionary policy should always be that we (the Europeans) must decrease, they (the Indians) must increase. In our present state we need more Europeans. We need them for our educational and medical missions, in all our institutions. We need them for our evangelistic work also. As soon as a European has learned the language, let him, if he is an evangelist, at once have his district. With the villages all before us, we shall never be in need of districts for our workers. As soon as an Indian is competent for it, let him have his district also."

Mr. Clark notes in his journal the views of an

eminent Panjabi clergyman. "Wherever the European goes the native is swamped, he has no chance and no heart. The new missionaries who come out now are very poor and weak, only catechists, compared with the older men; they toil less, frequent the natives less, go home quickly, read in their houses, do not get in touch with the people. The leading native Christians will not work with the missionaries, and do not know how to work alone. There is no public spirit, no personal influence for encouragement. Converts are content to be Christians, but do nothing to extend the kingdom of Christ."

His close touch with Indian Christian feeling and his own long experience led Mr. Clark to observe, in the document from which we have already quoted:—"Some of our native friends and fellow-workers are evidently afraid that such amalgamation will retard the great object which both we and they have so much at heart. They fear that it will tend to the domination of Europeans in Church matters. As Europeans living and working in a country which is governed by the English, it is evidently believed that there is some danger in our present circumstances. If this is so, then the more we can keep ourselves in the background, and put the Indians forward, the better it will be for the establishment of an indigenous Christianity in India.

"If the two bodies were amalgamated, the business of the United Council must be carried on by discussion. Without opportunities for discussion there may arise grave disadvantages from the establishment of an amalgamated Mission Council. If there is discussion, the question is whither such discussion may tend? The

Europeans will not, and cannot, agree to a decision, if they conscientiously believe it is wrong on a vital question. In a few years the Indian vote will far outnumber that of the Europeans. Either the Europeans will then dominate the discussions, or there may arise the formation of two opposite parties, the European and the Indian. If an Indian of intellectual and spiritual power and influence should become a leader amongst Indians, whilst at the same time he holds views which in some important points may differ from what we believe to be the plain teaching of our Church Prayer Book, the consequence both to us and to them may be very serious indeed. That this is no imaginary possibility will be understood by all thoughtful men. Whereas, with our present two distinct Houses, the Conference will always be a check (when necessary) on the Native Church Council, and the Native Church Council's opinion will always be an important factor in our Conference proceedings."

In addition to the business of the Church Council, the ever increasing work at Amritsar continued in Mr. Clark's charge. His colleague in the cure of the congregation was the Rev. Miyan Sadiq. Some notes by Mr. Clark illustrate his views concerning the training of a pastor. He first observes that the pastor came of good stock, being the son of the fiscal headman of the town of Narowal. A convert from Islam, he was no novice, having been "received into the Church in February 1859." After "using the office" of a catechist "well" for some thirteen years, he had been unanimously chosen by the members of the Amritsar Native Church to be their pastor. He had been trained in many schools. "He was first an itinerant catechist; subsequently he went to the Lahore Divinity College, where for two years he was trained by Mr. French, and then he was trained by *responsibility*, when he was left alone as the Church's representative in Batala, a city of 24,000 people. During the whole of this time he had been trained, too, in God's own school, to know himself and to know God; and he had been brought straight from his daughter's death-bed, and from hearing her cheerful words of faith and love, to become the shepherd of the souls of the native Christians of Amritsar. Thus the native Church, for the first time in the Panjab, was shepherded by one of themselves, who was baptized and brought up amongst themselves."

To complete the training, Mr. Clark took Miyan Sadiq through Palestine, the first Indian Christian to visit the Holy Land. The step was of value, apart from the illumining effect of the tour, in a manner difficult to realise in the West. The sea is itself a revelation to men who live a thousand miles from its shores. A servant of the writer, after long gazing at the ocean, tasted the water, and then filled a bottle that he might convince his brother-villagers in the far Panjab that he was a true man and no liar when he said it was salt! Only after long conversation did an honoured resident get an acute Hindu merchant of Amritsar city to believe that the holy Lanka, or Ceylon, of Sanskrit literature still existed, nay that he had himself trodden on its soil,—and this in such a city as Amritsar in the year of grace 1887. In like manner, since Miyan Sadiq had actually been to the Holy Land, it was manifest to all that the land was no myth—a first step in some non-Christian minds towards a belief that the events that centred round that land might not be a mere invention of the Europeans.

Another incident in Miyan Sadiq's career illustrates Robert Clark's character. The all-absorbing work of the missionary is apt to contract his horizon; the exigencies of his own field tend to blind him to requirements elsewhere, but it was not so with Mr. Clark. In 1878, when it was clear Miyan Sadiq was wanted elsewhere, he was prompt, at inconvenience to himself, to set him free from the Amritsar charge.

This period of service saw the realisation of Mr. Clark's long cherished plans for the education of Christian children. His scheme for the training of the Christian girls of the upper classes aimed at a sound education in the best environment. The plan formed by Mr. Clark entailed of necessity a very large initial expenditure on buildings and plant, and it met in some quarters with fierce opposition.

We will let Indian Christians tell the tale. "Mr. Clark was not content merely with the spiritual and temporal prosperity of Christians," Mr. Singha observes, "he also did his utmost to promote their intellectual betterment. Although all missionaries are our well-wishers and rejoice in our prosperity, as regards our intellectual improvement their opinions differ. A section consider it unnecessary for native Christians. They think an ordinary standard is ample, anything more spoils us. Mr. Clark was not of this mind. He wished the native Christians to be in the forefront of everything in the land. He projected this school that Christian women should receive the highest education, and despite all opposition would not lower the standard he had set before himself."

Dr. Imaduddin rejoiced in the worthy pile of buildings planned. "Some objected, Wherefore all this tremendous expense and this stately erection? Do you not see Christian girls in such a place will become high-minded? He replied, The time is coming when Christians will be of high estate and dignity, schools worthy of their daughters will be needed, and when their young men want wives, they will look for dignified, refined ladies, and for them I found this school. Boys and girls bred in large surroundings are large-hearted; those brought up in a narrow way are apt to be poor-spirited. This special school is for special cases, for mere ordinary needs there are other schools."

Robert Clark saw a mighty missionary lever in the proposed school. A lady, an ex-pupil of the school, observes:—"Mr. Clark's large thoughts stand out in marked contrast to the pettiness of some other missionaries. As a general rule, missionaries say that the Christians of the land unconnected with Missions do not fulfil their religious obligations. Mr. Clark rejoiced greatly to see Indian Christians filling positions of great responsibility, dignity, and trust, and he held these Christians to be exercising influence over those whom missionaries and their agents cannot reach. In this spirit he observed to an Indian lady in a very high position under Government, 'You are a true missionary.'"

The enormous sums of money required for the erection of the great building entailed much labour, but Robert Clark threw himself heart and soul into the work. Nothing could daunt him. "If there were but one brick left in the Panjab, Robert Clark would have it," was the comment of a friend. He himself said the strain and anxiety added ten years to his life. The noble pile, when completed, was, by permission of the then Princess of Wales, named the Alexandra School. The autograph pictures of herself and our Sovereign, bestowed by Her Majesty on the school that bears her name, are amongst its treasured possessions.

Another outcome of Robert Clark's educational policy was the Middle Class Girls' School that has filled a brilliant place in the Panjab. When the Christian Vernacular Education Society, for reasons which do not concern us here, resolved to close the College that, under Mr. Charles James Rodgers, had done noble missionary work in the Panjab for some thirty-two years, Mr. Clark, through the liberality of a leading Panjab civilian, Mr. H. E. Perkins, later himself a missionary, secured the buildings for the Middle School.

Yet another development is thus narrated by Mr. Singha:—"In 1877, by reason of the evil work of some Christian youths, the Native Church Council decided there was urgent need of a good school for Christian lads. Certain members specially pleaded for this school with Mr. Clark, the Chairman of the Council. He brought the subject before the Rev. F. H. Baring, and the generosity of the latter resulted in the Baring High School for Boys in Batala."

The progress of the Alexandra School, as soon as it was in working order, was such that Mr. Clark was able to write:—"The Alexandra School has sixty-five girls already, and the *church* crowded every Sunday; this is work which will tell fifty or a hundred years hence on the Panjabis and their children, raising up a people to serve the Lord."

At a later date, in February 1884, the most influential of Indian Moslem reformers, Sir Syud Ahmed Khan of Aligarh, an ardent promoter of Western high education amongst Muhummudans, visited the school. Mr. Clark notes:—"He was enthusiastic; he said it was the finest school he had ever seen. He told me he was much opposed by old-school Muhummudans, who object to Western ideas. His college is an experiment; he has three English professors; his pupils pay thirty, fifteen, and eight rupees [each per month]; he has sent up thirty men for the Entrance [Examination]; there are two dining-rooms and two prayer-rooms. Cost £50,000, —the Alexandra £9000. He is a very able, intelligent man, ahead of his times."

Throughout life, Mr. Clark continued to show the greatest interest in the school he had founded. In the *Masihi*, an ex-pupil lovingly recalls that he "knew every girl personally, and all their circumstances, and his interest in them showed no decrease after they had left the Alexandra. Whenever he met any of us, he inquired by name after all such, and gave us news concerning them that may have reached him."

In 1878, when his presence seemed indispensable in the Panjab, Mr. Clark was called to lay down his manifold activities by reason of Mrs. Clark's dangerous illness. At a day's notice, he had to take her to Europe as the one chance for her life. Mr. Clark's work was done with such order and method that the short period of a day sufficed for the arrangement of all his multiplex responsibilities, without hurry, fuss, or confusion. He left on the 3rd of April, and sailed by that week's P. & O. mail steamer *Nepaul.* Great was the astonishment of his children to hear, one mail day, that their parents were actually in Egypt, and on their way to the South of Europe, instead of busy at Amritsar, as the previous letter had told.

In August, parents and children met again at Boulogne. Only a couple of days after the reunion, Mr. Clark was stricken down with pneumonia, and thereafter the cumulative effects of arduous toil and long Indian residence were evidenced in a prolonged failure of health that caused great anxiety. The winter was spent in Algiers, where Mrs. Clark's health again suffered. In the spring, Mr. Clark settled at Streatham Hill; and by the autumn of 1879, though still an invalid, he resolved, on mature thought, to return to India, in the hope, not shared by his doctors, that the land of his adoption would work a cure. Mrs. Clark had to stay in England, and the parting was peculiarly trying. The opening of 1879 found him again at Amritsar. He rapidly regained full health, and was soon busily engaged in new duties, of which we have now to tell.

CHAPTER XXIV.

MISSION SECRETARIAT.

ROBERT CLARK had returned to a new order of things, for certain important ecclesiastical changes became an accomplished fact in 1878. In that year the Panjab was withdrawn from the jurisdiction of the Bishop of Calcutta, and Sindh from that of the Bishop of Bombay, the two countries being united to form the new diocese of Lahore. Robert Clark's name was mentioned in connection with the bishopric, but none rejoiced more heartily than he did when the choice of the Crown, for the first bishop of the new see, fell on the Rev. T. V. French.

What Mr. Clark proved himself to be to his old friend and colleague is shown in a letter written by Dr. French as he was leaving India at the close of his episcopate. Under date 21st December 1887, he writes from Sukkhur :—"At four p.m. this afternoon my resignation takes effect,—and this is probably the last letter I write as Bishop of Lahore : I am glad it should be to you, as you have done so much and co-operated so faithfully to make an episcopate of ten years a possibility to me, and to win for me so many affectionate words of grateful and respectful farewell. I can never forget how much I owe you in this and many other ways, known to me and unknown. God alone can reward you out of His own wealth of grace and goodness!"

One of the first steps Dr. French took after his enthronement was to appoint Robert Clark to be Archdeacon of the diocese. This act roused heart-burnings in the bosom of some of the ecclesiastical establishment of the province; it was also challenged by the Civil Power. The Government of India regards the bishop and staff of chaplains solely as officers entrusted with a portion of its administration, and takes no cognisance whatever of the native Church. The appointment as a Church dignitary of a non-official connected with that body, was therefore held to be an embarrassment.

We learn Mr. Clark's mind on the matter from a letter of that time written to his wife:—"Don't expect to see me Archdeacon yet. The Diocesan Almanac has gazetted me, but Government does not see it yet, and Sir R. Egerton has written to the Bishop about it and to the Secretary of State. I am quite content either way, and of what I see of the Bishop's troubles with refractory chaplains it is clear to me that the office is not to be desired. If this office were His will for me, I should receive it as from Him, and have His wisdom and power and blessing in it; so I believe it is best ordered so, and I am and abide, like old Mr. Newton of Lahore, simply Robert Clark, missionary."

The institution of the bishopric of Lahore entailed certain changes in the organisation of the Church of England Missions in that diocese. Hitherto the Panjab had been a part of the charge of the Church Missionary Society's secretariat in Calcutta, while Sindh had appertained to that of Bombay. A new administration was now formed, and Robert Clark was in 1878 hailed with delight as the first Secretary of the Church Missionary Society's Missions in the Panjab and Sindh.

The work amongst women had gone forward by leaps and bounds. In 1880 it received fresh impetus from the fission of the Indian Female Normal School and Instruction Society into the Zenana Bible and Medical Missionary Society, and the Church of England Zenana Missionary Society. Mr. Clark had been the Secretary of the earlier Society, and he undertook that office for the newly formed Church of England Zenana Missionary Society.

The cure laid upon Robert Clark now embraced the manifold agencies by which the Societies of which he was Secretary worked amongst men and women throughout the Panjab and Sindh. In taking up the new responsibilities, he records in his journal:—"It will be an uprooting to me to leave the City House and carry out elsewhere new ideas and associations, but I feel it is time to give this work to others. I am getting very settled views as to how our Mission work is to be carried on. I suppose by the time my work is finished I shall be beginning to have learned something of how it ought to have been begun; we hardly learn how to live before life is nearly over."

Mr. Clark made Amritsar his headquarters, and from that centre carried on the vast work of guiding the Missions through their encouragements, trials, and needs. Well might he write in 1881:—"Amritsar is becoming more and more the centre and headquarters of the native Christian work, and as Secretary I am more than a bishop in a wider and nobler sphere. French is so worried by his chaplains that he longs to give up and be simply a Gospel preacher: let us be content to leave our circumstances to God's ordering, and ask Him to let us reap in due time where we have sown. I believe already there are fields of work ripening unto the harvest."

It is no matter for wonder, therefore, that when, in 1884, he was invited to accept high missionary office in Bengal, he passed it by. The future of Christianity in India he believed to lie with the Panjabi; the Bengali mind, he considered, was "receptive, not creative; they only reflect philosophy, religion, or infidelity." He further observes:—"About going to Calcutta; I do not see a call, just as a harvest is springing up in the Panjab. If it is a call, we must leave all and go, but we may not try to turn stones into bread, except at God's command, even if we can do so, for any worldly advantage. And though our not doing so seems a loss, He will provide and give all the needful health and means. Let us 'abide in one stay,' trusting Him fully. Again the text comes into my mind, 'Take heed that ye lose not the things that ye have wrought, but that ye receive a full reward.' For thirty-three years I have been sowing in the Panjab, and shall I run away when the harvest is nigh? I have no foundation in Calcutta; please God I will build on my own foundation and have a rich ingathering here."

The prolonged separation from his wife was a heavy trial. He writes to her in 1882:—"It is hard for you and me to be so much parted; but the children need a mother more than a father, and we must commit each other to Him and follow as He leads us. This is for us the way of peace and blessing. If He gives us length of days to live together when the children no longer need you, then we will try and bring forth more fruit in old age, in India, I trust; for here I am 'at home.' I feel very much for you, and I long to have you with me for work and comfort; but you are clearly in your right place with the children now, and we can surely trust Him for the future; He will strengthen our hearts, and may God be with our dear children and bring them one by one to Himself. This is my great wish for them, that they may be safe and happy as children of God, through faith in Jesus Christ."

In the rush of the incessant calls on him, Mr. Clark was ever mindful of his children at home. A long series of letters to them embrace every kind of topic: some are playful, others serious; but, grave or gay, all are full of counsel and encouragement, and are permeated by a close understanding of their lives, born of intense sympathy. He finds time to tell his daughter Sybil of the amusing rascalities of a couple of traders in his verandah, and of the gambols of a troop of monkeys in the woods before his windows. To his son Robert, under circumstances of great trial, he writes:—"Henry has fallen on his feet, and so has Tom, and the day, I trust, will come for you also. . . . Don't listen to anything that is discouraging, but shut your ears to it. He leads us rightly, not wrongly; only go on quietly. Do nothing without God's guidance, sought for and gained by prayer, 'and when thou hast once done, repent not,' says Solomon. Don't look back, look only forward with great hope and expectation, not of yourself but of God's goodness and mercy and love."

In writing to congratulate his son Hamlet on passing his "Little Go," he hopes Cambridge life may be of great benefit to him. "If you receive there as many blessings as I did, it will be so. There is no life like it, when used aright, for young men, in the whole world. No place gives so many privileges; and difficulties are merely things to be overcome; and dangers and temptations may, when met with God's help and prayer, be only occasions and opportunities of making a man a real man, and forming a strong and grand character. I am not anxious about the profession afterwards. God knows what is best for each individual, and He will guide each one severally. The great matter is that, whatever the profession may be, the *life* may be a real one, a real beginning of endless, perfect, strong, manly life, in God's service for ever. As the old poet says—

> 'Vive, precor; sed vive Deo, nam vivere
> Mortis opus; viva est vivere vita Deo.'"

To his son Donald, about to go to Manilla, he writes:—"The longer I live the more I see that life is duty, and to do one's duty is to fear, love, and please God. I hear you stand so well in the esteem of your firm that they propose to send you to Manilla for five years. I would have you go trusting in God. Walk very warily, believe that He can and will keep you even in that far-away and almost heathen land. Don't leave your religion at Port Said or Ceylon, as so many do, but take it on with you. Set up your banner at once on arrival, and show people what you are and mean to be; for God gives us a banner to be displayed because of the truth, and not to be shut up in a bedroom. Set it up at once on board ship, and keep it flying when you first arrive."

It was a glad day for the father when his youngest

son Stuart wrote to tell him of his conversion. "Your letter gave me happiness indeed. God is very good to us—in thus calling one of us after another to Himself. I always felt that if He led me to remain away from you all, as I believe He did, and told me to work for Him in India, whilst you were all at home, it would never be the worse either for Mama, or for me, or for any of you."

Mrs. Clark was not able to rejoin her husband at Amritsar until the year 1889. Meanwhile Mr. Clark had the help and comfort in his home for some years of Mrs. Henry Martyn Clark, and latterly of his daughter Dora, who joined him in India. The house was one that fully taxed a woman's energies, for it was famous for hospitality even in hospitable India, and its doors were ever open alike to friends and strangers. Mr. Clark had always been a lover of hospitality. "His dinner would choke him had he to eat it by himself," said Mr. William Briggs, a colleague and friend since the early days in Peshawar. There was a constant succession of guests, personal and official, Indian and European, among whom were to be found all sorts and conditions of men. There were various types of the "globe-trotter," the explorer, civil and military officers, and missionaries of all Churches.

"The Heydes are with me for a long visit," he writes. "I like to have the house full; to see young people every day, and when my five hours of office work is done to go out and have chats with friends, and to be in the thick of all that is going on; and there is always something to do, or say, for the Master. These Moravians have come from Kyelang;

they have been twenty-one years in Thibet, snowed up for seven months in the year, with all their children at home, never seeing any but chance travellers, and never an Englishwoman. They are so nice and simple. She tells me she was married by lot, and no marriage could be more blest. They are now going to Ladakh, 1200 feet high, where the natives spend the winter in bed, and she, poor old soul, is quite willing and happy to go there. Could you stand such a life? I could not, I fear."

In connection with the visit of Dr. Ullmann, a veteran Presbyterian missionary, he observes :—"These Germans seem to me much more deeply attached to India and the people than our English missionaries; they are more simple-minded, more persevering, possibly they live nearer to God; may we learn of them."

The constant intercourse to which we have referred kept Mr. Clark in close touch with public opinion and the problems of the hour. Keen to mark all that affected the land, he was equally alert to note the bearing of political, social, and religious movements on the missionary problem. Thus, though he had no delight in war, he saw the advance of the everlasting Kingdom in the upheavals of society and the struggles of nations. He realised the advantages that followed in the train of the later Afghan Wars, the "Scientific Frontier," and other measures taken to checkmate the wiles of Russia. The Muscovites, Mr. Clark used to say, had been the best friends of Panjab Missions. Thanks to them, the isolated North-Western Frontier had, as if by magic, been linked to the rest of India. Tens of thousands of workmen had toiled with feverish haste to make splendid roads, strategical railways, and telegraph lines in the shortest time possible. Engineering skill had spanned great rivers, pierced mountains, and triumphed over immense natural difficulties. These things would never have been for many a day but for the Russian menace, and the ways of the armies of Britain were straight paths for the messengers of the Lord. Nor was Robert Clark slow to gather the fruits. His policy was to strengthen the Missions on the Border, to occupy the opening land, and the last link in the great chain of Frontier Missions was forged when Quetta, in Beluchistan, was occupied as a Mission station in 1885.

We have previously noted Mr. Clark's world-wide study of Missions. He was ever on the outlook for hints or plans that might be found helpful in India. For instance, he had keenly followed the developments of the Church Missionary Society's work in East Africa. In his journal for 1882, he notes :—

"Mr. Wigram gave me Hannington's *Life*, which has opened my eyes considerably. If missionary work is wading knee-deep in mud, travelling over waterless plains under a burning sun, shooting lions and rhinos, enduring hunger, dysentery, and fever without doing much appreciable good, then East Africa is a grand sphere for missionary societies. The charm is evidently that of suffering; but if Hannington's life is a sample, very few missionaries indeed will be found 'sufficient for these things.'

"Of course, God's way are unsearchable; but to us in India, in the midst of millions of heathens among whom we can live and work freely, whose languages can be readily acquired, with a fair chance of life and usefulness and health, it seems a misunderstanding of Christ's command to push open closed doors of danger and death while doors of life to millions stand wide open, inviting entrance where harvests are ready and labourers, alas, are few.

"However, the Word must be preached in all the world, and it may perhaps be best to take the worst part first. May God be with those who have to do it; God's times are not ours. Paul was not suffered to go into Macedonia. The doors of Africa will open in His time, and Ethiopia stretch forth her hands."

These African ventures were to influence the Panjab; for, partly as a result of the expansion of Mission work at that time, mainly in Africa, the authorities of the Church Missionary Society resolved on a reduction in some of the older and apparently unproductive stations in other lands. They directed, for example, the closing of Dharamsala, Kangra, and Kotghur, in the Panjab. These places confessedly formed an exceeding difficult field, that had yielded but small results from amongst a bigoted Hindu people, apparently callous to all missionary agencies, but they were the only posts on the line of the Frontier Missions of the Central Himalhyan chain towards Thibet, and Robert Clark, fully alive to their extreme importance, pled for their retention. In masterly fashion he reviewed their past history and present conditions, outlined their prospects, collected the opinion of experts, brought the subject before the Panjab Committees of the Society, and embodied the result of his researches in an exhaustive monograph on the whole subject. We may note in passing that the reviews and monographs on various subjects that Mr. Clark penned from time to time were a most valuable feature of his secretarial labours. Difficult places, he urged, could never be conquered by retreat. That was not the way in which the great Emperor Akbar subjugated the mighty fortress of this very Kangra; after each repulse he massed better troops against it, and brought bigger guns, until the Moghul standard floated over the stubborn citadel. Thus it must be in the war of God, and Robert Clark returned steadfastly to the charge, undeterred by the refusals of the Society.

He writes: "We want more faith: little faith, little blessing; great faith, great blessing. I wonder what the Church Missionary Society really think of me and my ventures of faith; what a trouble I must be to them; why cannot I leave them alone, and do nothing, and go quietly on? I cannot. I seem to set my face as a flint against their retrograde policy, and risk everything, even their approval and good-will. I wonder if they get very angry with my letters? Somehow I can't help it; if I see an important fact to be gained, I cannot give in. They have several times yielded, here they may not. I fancy that I have a sound mind and a right judgment to oppose what I clearly see is not for the good of the work."

In the end, he had the joy of seeing his views accepted by the authorities. The doomed Missions were retained, and shortly after, in 1882, Mr. Clark baptized no less than nineteen persons at Kangra and Dharamsala.

This correspondence may serve to show that the wheels of state did not always run smoothly; but the loyalty of the authorities of the Church Missionary Society at home and of their Secretary abroad to the one great purpose of spreading the Gospel, and their full confidence in one another, brought every difference to a happy conclusion. It is interesting to note that practically in every instance—and there were many such—Robert Clark's views were adopted, and the Society never had reason to regret its decision.

Differences of opinion amongst the staff of missionaries were also inevitable; for, as Eastern wisdom hath it, "There must be clinking where there are many pans." Mr. Clark observes in his journal:—"—— is becoming a leader, much to the disgust of some. As such he lacks tact, and is not conciliatory or courteous to those who differ. Lacordaire says, 'Let me urge great gentleness with the brethren, respect towards the fathers.' . . . I am often in conflict with dear Christian brethren about principles and things to be done, or not to be done; it is difficult to be firm and yet tender of the feelings and wishes of others, and I am still a learner in the meekness and gentleness of Jesus."

The outcome of his quiet tactfulness was an abundant sowing and reaping through others. "I am often surprised how much I can do all over the Panjab in this way. I can sit in my study and direct others in many places and ways. I can tell them to do certain things, and give up doubtful things, and so help and guide God's work."

It is beyond the scope of these pages to discuss the sometimes warmly-debated question whether or not the good ship of the Church Missionary Society has drifted from its old moorings; but it is undeniable that Mr. Clark marked the increase of a narrow ecclesiasticism in the Panjab Mission that filled him with sorrow. He writes in 1884:—"Each day brings its difficulties, so much so that I am exercised as to the advisability of remaining in Amritsar. Glad to go home in December. There is a spirit of restlessness now everywhere; people are dissatisfied with existing institutions, and there is a determination to make changes, contrary to my own feelings and, I believe, those of the Church Missionary Society, respecting some points on Mission work. I have always aimed at introducing Christianity on Church Missionary Society and Scripture lines, those of the Bible and Prayer Book. They now want "Church lines," which each one explains according to his own views. This has worried and perplexed me a good deal, and it is a cross I am taking up in patience and prayer. We want in these days Henry Venn's wise guidance, but murmurs and differences are sometimes God's way of conferring blessings."

The advance in ecclesiasticism marked a spirit divergent from that of the Church Missionary Society, and, in its relation to the native Church, was destructive of true liberty. Mr. Clark pertinently observes:—"If the Church, as in Acts vi., would allow the multitude of the believers to choose men of good report, true men, Christians would be satisfied and Episcopacy be acceptable. Why should the Mission work be thwarted and hindered by the appointment of men who may be unfavourable, why put a topstone on a building not conformable to the building? If Government want Government bishops, let them have them, and let us have Missionary bishops for our work, and let no man be chosen without our sanction and approval. We ought now to make a great positive, not a negative stir. The positive part is that the appointment of the men we need and ought to have will keep out the men we do not want. Let us aim at what we do want, and insist on it, and our work will then prosper.

"The man who is to guide and govern evangelical Missions should surely be an Evangelical, and no Government bishop or archbishop has any right to appoint anyone of different views. Would that the old Gospel way of giving the disciples their proper voice in the election of bishops, which was the custom of the early Church, were revived, and that our action might lead to it. Why should we as missionaries be tied and bound to a State Church which will hardly recognise us, and always ignores our missionary work?"

Any attempt to squeeze the East into the mould of the West was foredoomed to failure, and Mr. Clark held that the Occident would never dominate the Orient in matters religious. The present writer was engaged, together with Mr. Abdullah Athim, in a remarkable controversy with Muhummudans that lasted fifteen days. The Moslem champion, who posed as a prophet, announced that God Himself would decide the controversy between Christianity and Islam by a sign from heaven,—in fifteen months, counting one month for each day that the controversy had lasted, the leaders on the side of the untrue faith would perish.

Mr. Clark notes :—"There is great excitement about the Mullah's prophecy of the death of Athim and of Henry in fifteen months after the great controversy in which they took part. The Easterns we shall never understand. D'Israeli says, 'Ever since the creation, the world has owned the religious supremacy of Asia.' It is only there that God deigned to confer with man, and no other part of the world did He ever visit. We Westerns must be humble. No religion was ever made in Europe, no creed ever founded there; we have never even framed a respectable heresy. The great religions —Judaism, Buddhism, Brahmanism, Mahommedanism, Christianity—all sprang from Asia."

The secretarial work was enormous. One day Mr. Clark's entry in his journal reads:—"My correspondence is heavy. I wrote fourteen letters for this week's English mail, and answered thirty-one letters to-day." The letters written by his own hand were but a fraction of his work. The care of the Missions came on him daily. There were committees, interviews, returns, accounts, and the heavy routine of a busy office. He had a valued colleague in the late Mr. Joseph West, who for fifteen years worked with him as manager of the lay matters that devolved on the Secretary.

Mr. Clark's early business training stood him in good stead. He says:—"The two most valuable years of my life were those spent in Liverpool behind the counter, when I learned to keep clean as well as accurate accounts, and the importance of system and order."

Even more important perhaps than the mere technique of commercial methods was the insight into life which his business training had brought him. He acquired a knowledge of mankind and a breadth of view. His mind became accustomed to deal with large transactions on which much depended, and where decisions had to be promptly and surely made. He had to study the just medium between absolute attention to detail and ability to deal with problems in the mass, qualities which go to make for success in business life. Above all, he was trained in the rare faculty of being able to look at a thing from all sides. He was punctual, to the point, and, by interjecting an occasional word, able to keep discussions from becoming discursive. A few questions put him in possession of the heart of a subject. Matters, however difficult, were resolved into their simpler elements, and were then methodically disposed of, one after the other.

It was a rule with Mr. Clark to keep no one waiting for an interview. "You never know, where Indian visitors are concerned, what sacrifices a man has made to come to you," was his dictum, "nor what may depend on what he has to tell." However busy he might be, the task in hand was laid aside, and the business that had brought the visitor was taken up. A cheery "We will do it now," was his invariable response to any inquiry respecting his convenience, and the concentration he showed in considering the matter in hand was remarkable. For the time being, nothing else existed for him. He reads us his own character in noting:—"Dr. Murdoch is here, active as ever with mind and pen. He is a true man, a man of one idea, and succeeds because he works one thing well. Whatever I have been able to do has been by sticking to one thing and trying to carry it out." "Though himself so hard a worker," comments Mr. Singha, "Mr. Clark was no hard taskmaster, for his principle was, God does not work us beyond our strength. His servants found him most considerate. He required implicit obedience, but left a man free to work as best suited him, and was never concerned to interfere in little things."

The first servant Mr. Clark engaged in India was named Nunda, and only death separated him from his master, after thirty years' service. Nunda filled the place in Mr. Clark's household that Eliezer did in that of Abraham. He was foster-father to the children, and he once accompanied the family to England. An incident will illustrate very early days in the Panjab. On one occasion Nunda had to go to Lahore from Amritsar, and he elected to journey by the railway then just opened. He missed the train, but the driver of a country cart said in all good faith, "Jump in; we will catch it at the next station." They found the train gone; but it was ever to be caught at the next station, and the next; they jogged on through the day, and towards evening, much to Mr. Clark's amusement, actually did catch that train—at rest in Lahore. It was a happy day for Mr. Clark when he had the joy of baptizing this beloved servant after twenty-eight years' service. His Christian life was exemplary, and he was gathered to his people, full of years and honour.

As Secretary, Robert Clark systematically visited all the Missions under his care in discharge of the duties of his office. These tours involved long, fatiguing journeys, but they kept him in close touch with the problems of the various stations, and made him the friend and counsellor of every missionary. In this way he revisited the arena of many an old struggle, to rejoice in the triumphs that crowned the later day.

Always holding the balance without favouritism,

and full himself of plans for the furtherance of the work, Mr. Clark was an enthusiastic helper of like measures that originated with others. It was his fixed policy to let every man have a fair chance, and to give every reasonable plan a trial.

The settlement of lady missionaries amongst village women in the Panjab was an innovation that startled many. Could ladies live and work in the villages? The plan was conceived by the holy genius of Miss Elizabeth Clay, and carried through with unwearied devotion and sacrifice. Mr. Clark ardently furthered Miss Clay in her efforts, and none rejoiced more than he did in the splendid success that crowned her labours.

In 1882 the Government appointed him a Fellow of the University of the Panjab newly constituted. Next year he published his book on the Panjab and Sindh Missions of the Societies of which he was the Secretary. In 1884 a second revised and enlarged edition was called for; and a third, edited by an old Panjab civilian, Mr. Robert Maconachie, was posthumously issued in 1904.

In 1885, Mr. Clark rejoiced to see the valuable literary labours of Maulvie Imaduddin fittingly recognised, when the Archbishop of Canterbury conferred the degree of Doctor of Divinity upon him. He was the first native of North India to be so distinguished, and Mr. Clark characteristically enforced the lesson on the native Church with a terse, "You see one of you can get the best England has to give."

In that year, as the result of a conversation at Mr. Clark's breakfast-table, the writer commenced to publish a monthly newspaper well known in India,

REV. MAULVIE IMADUDDIN LAHIZ, D.D.

and in missionary circles far beyond the borders of India, *The Panjab Mission News*, which he continued to edit for fourteen years. The paper was the direct outcome of Mr. Clark's enterprise. He took the liveliest interest in it to the last day of his life, and was himself a frequent contributor to its columns. It owed much to his resourcefulness and liberality.

On 23rd February 1885, Mr. Clark left the Panjab on furlough, arriving in London by way of the Continent on 3rd June. He sailed again for India on the 17th of October 1887, and took up his work once more in Amritsar on 19th November. In the autumn of 1888 he completed his missionary survey of the Himalhyas by a tour through the country of Kulu, a tract that lies between the Church Missionary Society's frontier station of Kotghur in the Central Himalhya, and the outpost in another direction of the Mission, at Kangra.

In 1891 he again visited the homeland, leaving Amritsar on 19th March, and arriving in England on the 28th of May. He spoke and acted at the time as if it were to be his final farewell to his native country, as indeed it proved to be. Those members of his family who were within call held a reunion in Edinburgh in the summer of that year, and on 22nd October Mr. Clark once more left for India, arriving in Amritsar on 11th November.

Fresh questions had arisen with the influx of masses of converts from among the lower classes. We find Mr. Clark engaged with such problems as the instruction and shepherding of large accessions of new converts, the perils of a mass movement to Christianity, and its control and guidance. Missionaries had been working and praying for converts, but were they ready for such an ingathering, now that it had come? Would it be with them as it was with Rachel, whose cry was that she might have children, and when Benjamin was given, she straightway died? A very important plan elaborated by Mr. Clark in this connection was the formation of reserves, so that missionaries might be reinforced as occasion arose, and that, in the absence of heads of stations on furlough, there might be no break of continuity: successors would be ready to step into their places with a knowledge of the requirements of the station. This proved a great advance on the system of appointing reliefs at random; for, in meeting an exigency as best could be, too often the result was detrimental alike to the work from which a man was taken as well as that of another to which he was sent. Under the then existing régime it was sometimes impossible to send a missionary at all, and the station remained unoccupied. The missionary's absence was Satan's opportunity, and Mr. Clark's observation was that it was always then that apostasies and scandals arose. Under this plan of reserves the Rev. T. Russell Wade became "Secretary in reserve."

The dangers of wholesale accessions to Christianity were not to be apprehended from the ingathering from amongst the outcastes only. Robert Clark's insight into motives and character was never more strikingly shown than in the case of a great Sikh nobleman who came to be baptized. Mr. Clark refused, for he divined that his motives in becoming a Christian were merely political and patriotic. The chieftain had thought that if a nobleman of his lineage and position became a Christian, others would follow suit, and that the best hope for the advancement of the Sikh nation lay in a general acceptance of Christianity. The full strength of the undercurrents that the missionary statesman had thus gauged only became apparent to the rulers of India when, years later, they frustrated Maharajah Dhalip Singh's attempt to return to the Panjab.

Space fails us to enter into many of the matters that occupied Mr. Clark; but we may indicate a few of the more important of those upon which we have not touched. The employment of Christians in Government services, breaches of inter-mission comity, the aggression of the Romanists on Protestant missions in the Panjab, the effect of education in India on legislation, the legal disabilities of Christian converts, the law relating to the baptism of minors and of women,—these were some of the many questions that he dealt with in the closing period of his career. He explains his aim :—"I want to see this work rightly organised, and very widely extended throughout the whole of this great land. That is my wish."

In the busy whirl of the secretarial life, however, his heart yearned for the old Amritsar work. He wrote to his wife :—"It was said of General Gordon that he went and lived in a native serai, *simply that he might be amongst the people*, whom he loved for Christ's sake. I should like to be in my city house again for the same reason, to *be again amongst the people*, and I have many plans in my mind."

CHAPTER XXV.

MISSION SECRETARIAT—*continued.*

ROBERT CLARK had been careful to clarify and crystallise the missionary experiences of his life, and the process had helped to endow him with ripe wisdom for the delicate and difficult tasks of the high office that he now held.

In nothing was Mr. Clark's statesmanship more manifest than in the policy he pursued in his relation to his fellow-workers as the leader of the Panjab Missions. He saw to it that the fullest information was given to every missionary on every point that concerned him. His aim was to keep all together in harmonious action, not so much by controlling as by guiding; and above all he was a perfect master in the rare art of leaving each agent supremely free to exercise the special gift that was in him. It must not be supposed that Mr. Clark undervalued rules and precedents, or "red tape" (that much abused but nevertheless essential appliance), if confusion and disorder were to be avoided. Staunch in his allegiance to law and order, he appraised all these things at their full worth. He regarded himself, however, not as a mere administrator of rules and regulations, but as the general of an army in the thick of battle. Rules, he held, were made for men, not men for rules. Method must not be magnified at the expense of the work it was designed to promote, nor must regulations become the couch of Procrustes. A great secret of his success was that he never shrank from the responsibility of "short and easy" methods, when exigencies had to be faced. He agreed with the policy of a bishop of the Methodist Episcopal Church, who, when a Mission was, by some regulation made in America, hindered from adopting a certain course on which all were agreed, disposed of the difficulty by observing, "The law, my brethren, was not made for good men."

Let an incident illustrate this trait of Mr. Clark's character. It was necessary in the interests of a Zenana Mission to acquire some land in a certain town, but the rancorous opposition of the heathen made the transaction impossible. One day, with startling suddenness, the position changed; for a brief hour it became possible to effect the purchase,—such things do happen in the East,—and if the opportunity went by, in all probability it would never recur. Mr. Clark was not in Amritsar, and the writer, to whom the parties came, had to meet the emergency. A large sum, that had to be refunded by ten o'clock next morning in a neighbouring city, was raised, the bargain struck, and the formalities completed within the hour. Mr. Clark returned home at midnight, and heard the story. There was no talk of committees, references, authority, or sanction. "Quite right," he said, made out the cheque, and laughingly added, as he handed it to the writer, "You had great faith in me." In the small hours a special messenger left Amritsar, and by ten o'clock the cheque was paid in. His words unwittingly hit the mark. His colleagues knew they could turn to him in full assurance of sympathy and help in any emergency. It would be difficult to over-estimate the importance of that certainty, in the conduct of the work. Thus he won love and faithful service.

Mr. Clark was no friend to "systematic action" when that term meant mere love of routine. "Better tyranny than anarchy," urged some in their devotion to method; but the ideals of these "slavish followers of a line," as the East happily styles them, awoke no echo in Robert Clark's breast. The machinery of Missions must be simple, for he saw a speciality in Mission work that made him extremely cautious of over-government, and he was therefore the more careful to leave a wide margin for individualism. On principle, he was non-principled in this matter. The history of Missions, and consideration of the tentative nature of much of the work, convinced him of the folly of tying men down to any one plan. Not the gun, but the man behind the gun, was the vital factor in the war; nor was Robert Clark concerned about the sentinels at the various angles of the fort, if he were sure of the commandant. His dictum was: "Get good men—none other are worth the having—and trust them." It was to him clear that the toilers in the Mission field best see the needs of their respective spheres. The only true policy was to strengthen their hands, further their wishes, meet their views in a spirit of sympathy and not of dogmatism, else there would be dogged submission or open revolt, instead of the blithe, heartsome labour of enthusiastic men.

Mr. Clark expressed his views in these words:—"The efficiency and extension of our work depends, doubtless, far more on the qualities of the missionaries, and on their power of influencing others and setting them to work, than on the number that are sent out. We want men of fire and power, who can organise bands of itinerants, and who will do individually more, in the present state of native society, than the best Committees: we want picked, resolute, talented (as well as pious) men, who can guide the natives in their work, and give them a soul to work."

In missionary enterprise to-day, the thoughtful observer cannot fail to note how much stress is laid on "the work" and on "sacred funds," and, in striking contrast, how little emphasis appears to attach to the worker. This was not Robert Clark's spirit; it was not that funds were less sacred, or the supremacy of God's work less dear, but that he looked at the work through the workers. In their comfort was its stability, in their happiness its prosperity. "Look after the workers," was his dictum, "and you will be doing excellently by the work."

Mr. Clark strongly condemned the incomparably foolish tendency manifest in some organisations, to practise a false economy by effecting savings at the expense of the missionary. That the superb personnel of workers allowed of such an attempt was but the greater reason for its condemnation. As he rejoiced in the gifts and graces of one and another of his colleagues, he never forgot to put such questions as, Is he well housed, comfortable? Does he take care of himself? Has he a good cook? In his efforts to ensure the health of the staff of which he was the leader, Robert Clark had no fear of "luxury" before his eyes. He left that haunting terror to be the monopoly of certain subtle humorists who, amidst the comforts of their peaceful homes, are for ever afraid of the superfluity of luxurious naughtiness into which the missionary abroad may launch forth, on the strength of the pittance he receives as a subsistence allowance. Even a missionary, Mr. Clark held, has his feelings, and he welcomed the little touches in Mission houses that told of comfort and spoke of a home. The men had given their lives to God's work, and if they did not make a home in the land of their exile, where in life were they to make it? And, in proportion as they had a home, they were refreshed and strengthened for their work, and the more permanently attached to it.

In his policy, Mr. Clark showed an extreme disinclination to shift missionaries from one sphere to another. By such transfers, influence was lost and continuity broken; the missionary himself failed to strike root; and, in the event, the wanderings too often became a prelude to retirement from the Mission field.

The right and duty of the supreme authority to deal with its representatives in the field as it might deem advisable in the interests of the work as a whole, admitted, of course, of no question; but Mr. Clark held that plans were only truly furthered when they assured the hearty assent of the individual chiefly concerned. The true policy to follow, therefore, was not one of *sic volo sic jubeo*, but one of such mutual counsel between the authorities and the missionaries as would command not only the obedience but the understanding of the Missionary Society's agents. There is a strong conviction in certain circles that missionaries subject to Committees must unquestioningly receive as the declared will of God their findings on any specific point. With those who could accept the voice of a Committee as the *vox Dei*, or were prepared to consider themselves as officers under the colonelcy of a directing Board, with only the soldier's duty of unreasoning obedience to perform, Mr. Clark had no fault to find. But he could not be oblivious to the fact that all minds are not cast in that mould, nor was it always evident in the light of after events that the decrees of the Committee had veritably been inspired from on high. The analogy of the colonel and his officers could be carried too far, for the factors in the case of the missionary and the soldier are not the same. If a Committee spoke with the voice of God, it was difficult to understand why what was so clear to them had not been made equally explicit to the other party in the transaction. The homely Yorkshire tale will probably in this connection recur to the reader. A certain woman in the West Riding informed a man that it had been revealed to her that he was to wed her. He did not question the revelation, but merely said, "So far I have heard nothing about it: will you mind waiting until I do?"

Not infrequently, also, a recruit volunteers for missionary service in response to an appeal for some special field that comes to him individually as a Divine call. On his arrival, the pressure of local requirements is such that some other sphere is considered desirable for him, and in the recommendations issued it seems implied that the new-comer should at once put aside the call of God to a particular work, in deference to the opinion of the Board. Or, it may be, the same reasoning is applied to those already busy in a work they have made their own. Unable to hear the voice of God in the orders received, they find that obedience only places them in a false position, with resultant friction, difficulty, and unhappiness.

Robert Clark was extremely chary of seeing God's will for others to the exclusion of their own judgment and feelings; even where there was real need of a change of location, his policy sought the truer way. The proposal was not pressed on an agent, the facts were fully laid before the individual best qualified in the opinion of the Committee to fill some special sphere, and he was content to await God's call to that person, or to another for that particular service. Mr. Clark never forgot that "He calleth His own sheep by name, and leadeth them out, and when He putteth forth His own sheep He goeth before them, and the sheep follow Him, for they know His voice." The mere fact that a man had become a missionary showed a certain decision, power, and ruggedness of character, and Robert Clark's directions, accordingly, took the form of suggestions, invitations, and persuasion rather than of commands. The loving tactfulness of his rebukes did not make them the less faithful, but it earned him the gratitude of those who had evoked that rare manifestation of his ministry; for, as the Eastern sage says, "A spoonful of sugar will kill more flies than a barrel of vinegar."

On the subject of the adoption of native dress or habits of life, mooted in the Indian missionary world, this sagacious leader held clear views. He did not judge or oppose those who thereby thought to obtain a closer union with the people of the land, but there were distinct disadvantages in the course, even where practicable, in British India. Mr. Singha notes:—"He used to say, God does not compel us in such matters, nor shall we be required to answer before Him if we cannot live as fakirs or eat native food. . . . We are what we are, and they are what they are; each has gifts that the other has not, and perfection lies not in copying, but in supplementing and complementing each other." The European had a work all his own to do, and, with the true economy of the wise man, Mr. Clark's teaching was:—"Never use the diamond drill for the work that honest iron will do." The ability to be truly one with the people was not a matter of diet or garments, but of heart. The magic that would make missionaries and the men of the land akin lay in the love that ever serveth, and the while "seeketh not her own"; in the sympathy that "changed eyes" with the people of the country, and saw things as they saw them. That was what the man of the West required, to have the key to the heart of the East. An allophylian in some things such a man must always remain, as one born under other skies and the product of another environment; but the people of the Panjab would certainly count him, as their loving phrase beautifully expresses it, not a *begana* (or another's) but *apna* (our very own); for, as the Arabic proverb declares, "The heart hath eyes."

Mr. Clark's attitude towards young missionaries resembled that of Trebonius of Eisnach towards his pupils. The reader will remember how Luther's great schoolmaster invariably met his scholars in the morning with his cap doffed, for he knew not, he said, what distinguished man in embryo stood in their ranks. In like manner, Robert Clark cherished and honoured the young recruits, not only for their work's sake, but because amongst them might be found some of God's distinguished saints and heroes. He was sympathetic in their difficulties, tender in their treatment, wise to guide, and strong to help and bear. The task was not always easy, for youth in the missionary, as in others, has its own distinctive type.

There came the enthusiasts who had yet to learn the wisdom of his apparently paradoxical dictum, "The worker first, the work second, if you would have the work first." Then there were the ardent-hearted, who wanted to wade into deep waters at once, for whom he would point his counsel with the wise remark of a member of the Committee of the Church Missionary Society to a young missionary girding on his armour for the first time, "If you do no particular harm in the first two years, we shall feel you have done excellent work." Like Melanchthon of old, they thought they had but to lift up their voice to put Satan to rout, only to find that "the old Devil was too strong for young Melanchthon."

There were those new brooms, also, that would make a clean sweep of what they found existing. The path of wisdom and victory was abundantly clear to them. Methods were not up to date, the older missionaries were "fossils" or "fogeys"—the writer knows the type right well, for was he not one of them in his salad days as a missionary! Robert Clark was peculiarly gentle to men of this stamp; he fully understood that their intemperate crudities were not the result of sinful pride, but of a deep longing to advance the wheels of the chariot of the King. In the molten lava-torrents that rushed from these volcanic hearts, his prescient eye saw the rich soil on which, in good time, would flourish luxuriant harvests and gladsome vineyards. He would in his own winsome way tell them of Lord

Napier's remark at a crucial council of war, "We are none of us infallible, not even the youngest subaltern here present." He, in meekness, instructed these Hotspurs; listened to them, discussed, advised, moderated, and would gladly learn of them as if he were the veriest tyro in the art of missionary war. He derided no man, discouraged none, quenched no purpose, chilled no enthusiasms, but by patient continuation in well-doing bent energies from destructive paths into those of lasting good.

We may close this chapter by a quotation from a letter of Miss Constance Tuting, of the Church of England Zenana Missionary Society, daughter of Mr. Clark's old friend at Peshawar, as it portrays for us Robert Clark's treatment of new missionaries. "It was my privilege to spend my first days in Amritsar and my first holiday in the hills with Mr. Clark. He and Dora met me on my arrival at Amritsar and took me home with them. It was a kind thought of Mr. Clark's to spare me from loneliness upon first arriving among complete strangers. The next day, Mr. Clark kindly spared time to take me round to introduce me to my fellow-missionaries in Amritsar, and I remember his interest in pointing out to me the strange trees and shrubs and birds which I saw for the first time.

"I spent the month of July with Mr. and Mrs. Clark at Murree. It was an unusually hot year, and the thermometer stood at ninety in the verandah, yet Mr. Clark worked on steadily at his task hour after hour. He would remark occasionally, with kindly commiseration, that he was afraid from the tone of some of the letters from workers in the plains, that it must be very hot there just now. There was never a trace of resentment at their impatience and irritability, and of course he never divulged who the delinquents were, or what was the subject of annoyance.

"Every morning before breakfast he would go for a walk, and allow me to join him, a privilege which I greatly enjoyed and appreciated. His talk would sometimes be of my father and the old days at Peshawur. His far-sighted, statesman-like judgment, sympathetic understanding of all the details and difficulties of our work, and unfailing courtesy and commiseration, were a constant stimulus.

"I shall never forget his joyous, triumphant expression as he passed down the aisle of Lahore Cathedral at the consecration of Bishop Lefroy. It made one realise how his mind was travelling backwards to the days of small things of the Panjab Mission, and contrasting that time with this.

"A little later, in the year he died, he did me the great honour of spending a day with me at Majitha. In spite of the ten miles' drive over that terrible road, he was ready to start out at once to visit the Boys' and Girls' Mission Schools. At the Boys' School a chair was brought for him, but he would not take it until one was brought for me also, an idea that had not occurred to the Oriental mind of the schoolmaster."

CHAPTER XXVI.

RETROSPECT AND REST.

WITH the speeding years, the incessant toil of the Secretariat began to tell on Mr. Clark. There was no diminution of vigour, nor any evidence of failing power in the quantity or quality of his work, but he was conscious of a new note within himself.

The long shadows cast by the westering sun began to deepen on life's pathway. "I have had a hard life," he used to say to the writer, and his thoughts now began to turn towards rest. The feeling grew with the recurrence of passing attacks of indisposition. In 1896 he wrote to Mrs. Clark, whose health had compelled her to take a voyage to Australia:—"Life's work is nearly done now, and we must get ready to depart. I am going through all old letters and papers, and am going to have a great burning. I find plenty to do, and I especially enjoy my study of God's Word. I am reading St. John now in the morning (with a Commentary) after breakfast, and the Psalms in the evening. I am learning daily."

In 1897 he prepared to relinquish the burden he had borne so long, and on the 28th of December the letters from London came to hand in which the Church Missionary Society appointed the Rev. H. G. Grey of the Panjab Mission to succeed him in the Secretariat.

On the next day Mr. Clark notes of the letters :—"They were very kind ones, with the old spirit of the Church Missionary Society in them. Mr. Fox also wrote, and George Hutchinson. . . . I felt a different man when the letters came, and bear no longer the burden and responsibility of the work."

The formalities connected with the transfer of office were completed by the 3rd of January 1898. Mr. Grey, however, desirous of a little time in which to grasp the work and visit the Stations, did not enter into his new duties until the close of March of that year, when Mr. Clark ceased to be Secretary of the Church Missionary Society, after a tenure of twenty-one years. He writes at that time :—"I have made over all Church Missionary Society's work to Grey, and shall now have more leisure, *i.e.*, after a few weeks. I shall then have more time for prayer and thought, and I mean to take again more closely to the study of God's Word. The time cannot now be long, and I want to be nearer to God."

In an early chapter we spoke of a Banyan Tree that Mr. Clark planted when the Amritsar Mission was founded. In the years that had elapsed, the tree had attained noble proportions, and, after the manner of its kind, had sent down shoots which showed all stages of development, from goodly stems to promising suckers that had firmly struck their roots into mother earth. The number of stems curiously enough corresponded to the number of Stations that had directly sprung from the Amritsar Mission, and the genius of Miss Charlotte Tucker (A.L.O.E.) had beautifully emphasised the parable of the Mission Tree. A semi-sanctity attaches to these trees in the East, and the masonry platforms with which they are surrounded are favourite gathering-places of the people. The Mission Tree stood in the writer's compound, and he had the ground suitably prepared. The individual stems were labelled with the names of the Stations they represented, and then, after an appropriate service in the presence of a large assembly, Robert Clark, in the closing days of his office as Secretary, affixed a board with the story of the tree, and his share in it, to the parent stem.

In response to the unanimous wish expressed both in England and in the Panjab, Mr. Clark was content to retain the post of Secretary of the Church of England Zenana Missionary Society. He did not want to be idle, and felt he would "hardly be happy without something," but it was not his intention to hold the office for long; it was better that the Secretariat of both the Societies should be in the one hand. He notes :—"Grey is doing excellently well as Secretary"; and on 6th July 1898 he continues :—"I am a different man to what I was this time last year, and I told Grey that I was ready to make over the whole burden of the Church of England Zenana Missionary Society to him as soon as he was ready to take it. This will, I think, be in September next. I shall then be free. Sleepless nights and constant breathlessness are making me unfit now for responsible work." In the beginning of 1900 he was finally free from this last office that he held.

Concerning the future, he wrote at this period to his wife :—"Both you and I will, I hope, be able to do something yet for God and man. . . . There must now be a change of life, a new page of the book of life is turned over, will there be many more, if any, to turn over?" The death of his sister Susan in 1898, the first break in the family after thirty years, affected him greatly. He was now seventy-three, and he made frequent reference to the fact that he was near the age—seventy-six—at which both his father and mother had died.

He decided against retiring to England. "I am not fit for much now, certainly not for travelling. I should only get ill, and be a burden, whilst doing no good and getting none myself. My heart clings to Mission work and to the workers." There was work he could do in India, and he decided to abide in the land. "As regards the place and the circumstances in which God would have us to spend the remainder of our lives, He must decide. . . . I *believe* the Church Missionary Society will give me a missionary's salary and a house as long as I am in the Mission field and in a Church Missionary Society Station. If I go elsewhere, I suppose I must receive, like other missionaries, a pension. If I live in my own purchased house, I doubt if they will give anything for rent. If in a rented house, I suppose they will give a certain sum per annum."

Eventually, Mr. Clark resolved to live at Amritsar in the winter season, and near Simla in the summer. In this way he would be in touch with the headquarters of the Societies all the year round. The governing bodies would have the benefit of his counsel and presence, and he would be able to pick up many threads of work in the old field. In accordance with this resolve, he left Amritsar towards the end of April, and the 1st of May 1900 found him comfortably settled, with Mrs. Clark and his son Robert, at Bellevue North, amongst the pines and the rhododendrons of beautiful Kasauli, in the Simla range of the Himalhya.

The house well deserved its name, for the prospect from it was extremely lovely. Northward, running east and west, lay the hundreds of miles of the snow-capped Central Himalhya. The nearer ranges of mighty mountains showed field and forest, while homesteads, humble villages, and lordly Simla shimmered in the sun. Southward the eye wandered over hill and dale to the plains of the Panjab, spread like a carpet at the foot of the highlands. Robert Clark revelled in the glorious beauties of nature that met his eyes, turn where he would; but to his spiritual sense the wondrous panorama spoke of a yet deeper joy. He in his own person represented the missionary life of the Panjab in every variety from its earliest inception. As pioneer and founder, as administrator and statesman, he had a master's grip alike of the deepest problems and the simplest details. He stood on Pisgah as he gazed abroad. The eternal snows told of the Frontier system of Missions, of Cashmere and Ladakh, of the confines of Thibet, Afghanistan, and Beluchistan gladdened by the sound of the Gospel. In the teeming plains he could think of the lowing of the kine in the villages of Christians, of the hum of busy schools, the ordered activities of great hospitals, the preachers in town and village, and the soft-voiced teachers in the zenanas, the clang of the printing press, and the steps of the colporteur—of agencies many and varied ever busy in the work of the Lord.

The impenetrable darkness that had once brooded over the land was broken by the blaze of the watch-fires of the army of the Gospel, in a complete and well-riveted chain of investment from the mountains to the sea. The prayers and praises of a goodly people, gathered into the Church of Christ from amongst the kindreds and nations of the Panjab, ascended to heaven. Robert Clark could think of many converts who had crossed the flood and were waiting to greet him on the farther shore, even as he could rejoice over others who were that day fighting the battles of the Lord.

Sunrise had succeeded to dawn in the Panjab, and the growing light was an earnest of the noontide of glory of the Gospel day. He had been the founder of every type of work, had witnessed the seedtime and the growth as well as the mowing of the harvest. "Seest thou a man diligent in business," says the Scripture, "he shall not stand before mean men—he shall stand before kings." So had it been with him. He could look upon a long line of friends and comrades that comprised the governors and great men who had shaped the fortunes of the Panjab. Whatever his hand had turned to had prospered, and he stood, full of years and honour, a king among men, with an unique position in the reverence and affection of his fellows. Like Simeon of old, he too might say, "Lord, now lettest Thou Thy servant depart in peace, for mine eyes have seen Thy salvation."

The veteran missionary statesman was in the seventy-fifth year of his age, and it seemed as if there were yet further service awaiting him. Friends had gathered round him in the brief time he had been in Kasauli; a Bible reading that he started in his house bid fair to become a centre of happy labours; but his work on earth was done. He was to be spared any long waiting, or the encroaching enfeeblements of old age and decay. He awoke one morning in the second week of his residence at Kasauli not feeling in his usual health. There was nothing very definite, but the feeling continued; nevertheless, he dealt with a large correspondence.

Amongst the last letters he wrote was one to his friend Mr. Wade, who, with noble self-sacrifice, had volunteered to meet a special emergency during that hot weather. "It is grand of you to be willing to go to Batala, and it is just like you to go wherever you are the most needed. . . . You will, I am sure, be very careful in Batala, for we shall all of us be somewhat anxious about you." "The letter illustrates," comments Mr. Wade, "Robert Clark's unselfishness and his great care and thought for others, although he was not well himself."

That he was not in his usual health was known in the Panjab, but there was no thought of anything more serious than a passing ailment. On the 14th of May the writer received a letter, probably the last dictated by Mr. Clark, in which it was said, "I know you are very busy, but I should like to see you once again before I go," and by midday of the 15th he was lovingly welcomed in Kasauli. Mr. Clark took the deepest interest in the news of the Mission and of his friends, and entered with his wonted spirit into the discussion of many plans; but it was evident that his condition was extremely grave. With his usual loving kindness, after the first welcome, he would say nothing about himself until the writer had taken some rest, and then Mr. Clark told his symptoms, adding, "Ah, Henry, I suspect we have a much bigger thing than ever before to deal with." There was a period of quiet communion together, and the writer gave him what proved to be his last meal on earth. As the afternoon wore on, restlessness and wandering set in. In his delirium, that great mind was as ever busy with plans for the good of the people he loved, and his prayer for them repeatedly was "that they may know Thy name, Thy great name of Father, Son, and Holy Ghost."

It was a stormy passage into the eternal haven that was granted him. At one in the morning he awoke to consciousness. "What are we all doing here? Why are we not in bed when it is so late?" he said; and then, with the faith and spirit of a little child, he prayed to his Father, "I am very tired; let me sleep, for Jesus Christ's sake." The last words he spoke were those he repeated to himself: "We must, with much tribulation, enter into life." The prayer was heard, and He speedily gave His beloved sleep.

At daybreak, it was evident that Robert Clark was passing. Mrs. Clark sat beside him, whispering into his ear the words of the twenty-third Psalm, and when the valley had been all but traversed, the writer repeated to him, as he lay, apparently unconscious: "My flesh and my heart faileth, but God is the strength of my heart and my portion for ever." A smile seemed to flicker for a moment on the beloved face, then a little later one long-drawn sigh, and at five minutes past seven, on Wednesday the 16th of May 1900, in the early softness of a sweet summer morning, Robert Clark was at rest in his

"Home of fadeless splendour,
Of flowers that know no thorn,
Where they shall dwell as children
Who here as exiles mourn."

As the writer closed those blue eyes, and turned with his brother Robert to the widowed mother, death was for us then and there swallowed up in victory. "Servant of God, well done!" burst from our lips. This man having put his hand to the plough never looked back, and now

> "The shade of time shall never more
> Be seen upon his brow;
> For the former things are passed away,
> 'Tis endless glory now."

Mr. Clark had been the father and friend and helper of all, and it is no mere figure of speech to say that the tidings of his decease stunned the Panjab Church with the sense of an irreparable loss. "My father, my father, the chariots of Israel and the horsemen thereof!" was the cry awakened in hundreds of sorrowing hearts, as the news flashed abroad from Kasauli. He had always said to the Indian Christians, "I belong to you, and amongst you I will be buried." In accordance with his known wishes, it was decided that his grave should be in the Native Christian Cemetery at Amritsar. The funeral was a public one.

The last offices of love to the departed admit of no delay in sultry India. Arrangements therefore were speedily made, and within a few hours the writer was on his way to the plains, while Robert remained in Kasauli with Mrs. Clark. A large number of friends, European and native, met the train on arrival at Amritsar in the early hours of Thursday, and carried the coffin to the writer's house. The funeral took place that evening at six, when the fierce heat of the day had somewhat abated. Short as had been the time available, hundreds upon hundreds of Indian Christians, representatives of thousands more, assembled to lay the beloved leader to rest. Multitudes of non-Christians also evidenced their respect and sorrow. The roads were thronged, and the church was crowded.

Robert Clark had come in 1852, an untried warrior and an unknown man. He was borne to his long home that day, having finished his course, second to none in patience of hope and labours of love, a glory and a rejoicing, a precious possession of the Church of Christ, and a household name in the Panjab. The preliminary portion of the burial service was held in the Mission Church, then to the strains of the Dead March the coffin was carried out, and the huge procession re-formed to go to the cemetery, distant about a mile and a half from the church. It may be mentioned that from the house to the church, and from thence to the grave, the Indian Christians conveyed the remains of their beloved friend.

As the mourners came out of the church, they found that rain was falling—a most remarkable circumstance at that time of year in the plains of the Central Panjab. The downpour ceased almost entirely during the service at the grave, but thereafter soon began again, and continued heavily for some time. The effect of this storm on the minds of Indians, Christians and non-Christians, was deep. The natives believe that "happy is the corpse that the rain rains on." It was no time for rain until the commencement of July, and the downpour could only mean one thing, that he for whom they sorrowed was the especially favoured of Heaven. All looked upon it as a mark of God's approval, and spoke of it again and again as "*Asmani barakat*," or the blessing of Heaven. It should be added that the Bishop of Lahore cancelled an important engagement to take part in the funeral, and that Sir W. Markworth Young, then Lieutenant-Governor of the Panjab, excused himself from a public function held that afternoon in Simla, as a token of his respect for his friend.

Among Mr. Clark's papers was found a memorandum dated as far back as the 21st of June 1896, and docketed "For my tombstone." In accordance with the expression of his desire, his epitaph reads:—

To the memory of
THE REV. ROBERT CLARK, M.A.,
of Trinity College, Cambridge,
Born in HARMSTON, LINCOLNSHIRE,
4th July 1825.
Came to India in 1851,
and died at Kasauli on May 16, 1900.

A MISSIONARY of the CHURCH MISSIONARY SOCIETY in the Panjab for 49 years, during which he was for 22 years first SECRETARY of the CHURCH MISSIONARY SOCIETY, and the CHURCH OF ENGLAND ZENANA MISSIONS IN THE PANJAB AND SINDH.

"I obtained mercy, and the grace of our Lord was exceeding abundant in Christ Jesus."

To this Mrs. Clark added—

"He was among you as one that serveth."

But little remains to be added. Needless to say, Robert Clark was abundantly honoured in death as he had been in life. Even non-Christians mourned "The Angel," as they lovingly called him. The Rev. T.

Russell Wade took the lead in promoting the Robert Clark Memorial Hall in Amritsar; but we may say, as has been said of another — If you would see his monument, look around at the Missions in the Panjab.

INDEX